Pro Microsoft Power BI Administration

Creating a Consistent, Compliant, and Secure Corporate Platform for Business Intelligence

Ásgeir Gunnarsson
Michael Johnson

Apress®

Pro Microsoft Power BI Administration: Creating a Consistent, Compliant, and Secure Corporate Platform for Business Intelligence

Ásgeir Gunnarsson
Hafnarfjordur, Iceland

Michael Johnson
St. Andrews, South Africa

ISBN-13 (pbk): 978-1-4842-6566-6
https://doi.org/10.1007/978-1-4842-6567-3

ISBN-13 (electronic): 978-1-4842-6567-3

Managing Director, Apress Media LLC: Welmoed Spahr
Acquisitions Editor: Jonathan Gennick
Development Editor: Laura Berendson
Coordinating Editor: Jill Balzano

Cover image designed by Freepik (www.freepik.com)

Distributed to the book trade worldwide by Springer Science+Business Media LLC, 1 New York Plaza, Suite 4600, New York, NY 10004. Phone 1-800-SPRINGER, fax (201) 348-4505, e-mail orders-ny@springer-sbm.com, or visit www.springeronline.com. Apress Media, LLC is a California LLC and the sole member (owner) is Springer Science + Business Media Finance Inc (SSBM Finance Inc). SSBM Finance Inc is a **Delaware** corporation.

For information on translations, please e-mail booktranslations@springernature.com; for reprint, paperback, or audio rights, please e-mail bookpermissions@springernature.com.

Apress titles may be purchased in bulk for academic, corporate, or promotional use. eBook versions and licenses are also available for most titles. For more information, reference our Print and eBook Bulk Sales web page at http://www.apress.com/bulk-sales.

Any source code or other supplementary material referenced by the author in this book is available to readers on GitHub via the book's product page, located at www.apress.com/9781484265666. For more detailed information, please visit http://www.apress.com/source-code.

Printed on acid-free paper

To my wife Maria and daughters Ísabella, Freyja and Klara who are always patient with me and give me time and space to participate in the Power BI and SQL Server community as well as take on extra things like writing a book.

To my parents who are gone from this world but during their lifetime instilled in me a work ethic that has brought me to where I am today

AG

To my wife Hayley and children Rachel and Bradley, for their patience, understanding, and support while writing this book.

MJ

Table of Contents

About the Authors

Ásgeir Gunnarsson is a Microsoft Data Platform MVP and owner of North Insights. He works on Business Intelligence solutions using the whole of the Microsoft BI stack. Ásgeir has been working in BI since 2007 both as a consultant and internal employee. Before turning to BI, Ásgeir worked as a technical trainer and currently teaches BI courses at the Continuing Education Department of the University of Iceland. Ásgeir speaks regularly at events both domestic and internationally and is the group leader of the Icelandic PASS Group as well as the Icelandic Power BI user group. Ásgeir is passionate about data and loves solving problems with BI.

Michael Johnson is a Microsoft Most Valued Professional (MVP) for Data Platform and Principal Consultant at Cobalt Analytics. He has experience as a consultant and trainer focusing primarily on the Microsoft Business Intelligence tools stack.

For the last nine years, Michael has run the local PASS chapter in Johannesburg and also runs the PASS Business Analytics Virtual Chapter. Besides organizing events, he enjoys presenting to audiences large and small, both locally and internationally

About the Technical Reviewer

Reid Havens is the founder of Havens Consulting Inc. and is a Microsoft Most Valued Professional (MVP). He has an extensive background in technology and organizational management, and has obtained a Master's Degree in Organizational Development and Business Analytics. He has experience as a consultant working with many Fortune 50, 100, and 500 companies. Additionally, he teaches Business Intelligence, reporting, and data visualization courses at the University of Washington and other universities.

Reid is also an avid content developer. He has authored numerous videos and articles on multiple video platforms and blog sites. In addition to having also developed multiple training curriculums that were delivered to numerous companies around the world. In addition to corporate trainings, Reid has also developed college-level curriculums for the University of Washington and other universities.

Introduction

In the modern business environment, organizations are faced with many challenges when implementing business intelligence tools. In most organizations, IT is not able to keep up with the demand for reports and datasets, so business users are expected to contribute to the development. Power BI is a hybrid self-service and enterprise BI tool. In many organizations, you have both IT and business users, creating Power BI content. These groups are often very different in the way they approach development. This creates many challenges for Power BI administrators and makes it very important to have a good governance policy.

Many organizations operate in many markets across borders, creating a challenge with complying with rules and regulations. Laws such as GDPR or HIIPA put an extra demand on organizations for how they treat data. Having a good process for how you administer Power BI as well as a solid governance strategy for Power BI, you can minimize the impact of external and internal rules and regulations and guide users on how to avoid compliance breaches.

In this book, you will get advice and best practices on administering your Power BI environment, no matter if it's simple or complex. You can read about how you approach administration and in-depth discussion on the most important tasks of the administrator. You will also learn how to set up a successful governance policy and what components it should have. Furthermore, you will learn more details on each component and how it all fits together.

Who is this book for

This book is for IT professionals tasked with maintaining their corporate Power BI environment. For Power administrators, governance responsible and power users who are interested in rolling out Power BI more widely in their organizations.

How is this book organized

This book is divided into two parts. Part I focus on Power BI governance, while Part II focuses on administering the Power BI ecosystem. We believe the book is best read in order; chapters are written such that you are able to read chapter individually. The chapters are:

Part 1

Chapter 01: Introduction to Governance and governance strategies: An overview of governance processes and how organizations can build their Power BI governance framework.

Chapter 02 Licensing: We look at licensing options available in Power BI. How you license Power BI determines the features available to your organization and the associated costs of running Power BI.

Chapter 03 Collaboration: There are many ways for teams to collaborate in Power BI; from small shared workspaces where everyone has permission to consume and create new content through to highly structured and regulated environments where access to content is tightly managed.

Chapter 04 Laws and policy: It is essential to ensure that your Power BI governance policy complies with all laws and regulations, both where your organization resides and where your data is stored and processed.

Chapter 05 Application Lifecycle Management: The key to a well-managed Power BI ecosystem is ensuring that content has been appropriately validated before being consumed by report users. Every organization will have different opinions on how this should happen, and there are many options available in Power BI to achieve this.

Chapter 06 Training: How people create and use report artifacts can be as important as what they consume. Training plays an important role. Report consumers, report writers, and data modelers all have different training requirements.

Chapter 07 Documentation: Documenting both the Power BI environment and individual report artifacts is a vital governance process. This not only ensures that the organization understands what should be in place but also what the intended stats of the ecosystem is.

Part 2

Chapter 08 Roles of the Power BI Administrator: We look at the different roles administrators need to fill in the Power BI ecosystem. In small organizations, these roles may be assigned to a single individual or small team. Larger Organisations will often split these roles amongst multiple groups, creating a separation between the creating, implementation, and monitoring of the Power BI policies.

Chapter 09 Managing the Power BI tenant: The Power BI tenant is the container in which all components of the Power BI ecosystem reside. Ensuring this is correctly set up is an important step that has organizations wide implications.

Chapter 10 Administering Power BI premium capacities: Not every Power BI tenant will include premium capacities. Premium capacities unlock an array of additional functionality aimed at larger organizations, with this functionality comes a greater need to manage the resource to ensure optimal use.

Chapter 11 Workspace management: Workspaces are the primary means of collaboration within an organization. Ensuring that these workspaces are correctly created and administered will allow the organization to maintain control of the Power BI environment.

Chapter 12 Managing User and security: Ensuring users have access to the data they need to perform their job while not having access to sensitive data requires constant attention. This balancing act becomes harder in larger organizations

Chapter 13 Dataflows and Datasets: Ensuring data remains up to date and available is an important administrative task. A balance needs to be found the need to up to date data, and the impact data refreshes can have on their source systems.

Chapter 14 Gateway: The On-premises data gateway is one of the few components in the Power BI ecosystems that is fully managed by the organization. We discuss what the gateway is, when it is needed and how it is set up and maintained.

Chapter 15 Administration tools: There are several tools available for creating and managing artifacts in Power BI. Power BI, Azure, and Office 365 all have their own portals, but there are a number of tools created by Microsoft and third parties that can help you automate many of the development and administrative tasks.

Chapter 16 Monitoring: A core part of governance is ensuring that policies are complied with. The automation of monitoring tasks will aid the organizations in ensuring compliance as well as early detection of issues.

This book was not intended to be a step by step guide to administering Power BI but rather a guide to key principals and concepts of Power BI administration. Where relevant, we have called out the step-by-step guide on the Microsoft site. It is also likely that screenshots of various screens may not look the same when you access them due to the continually updating nature of the Power BI portal.

PART I

Governance

CHAPTER 1

Introduction to Governance and Governance Strategies

Read this chapter to find out more information about

- What a Power BI governance strategy could look like

- What a Power BI governance strategy contains and how to manage it

The Business Dictionary defines governance as "Establishment of policies, and continuous monitoring of their proper implementation, by the members of the governing body of an organization. It includes the mechanisms required to balance the powers of the members (with the associated accountability), and their primary duty of enhancing the prosperity and viability of the organization."[1]

Gartner defines IT governance as "IT governance (ITG) is defined as the processes that ensure the effective and efficient use of IT in enabling an organization to achieve its goals..." and further goes on to define IT supply governance as "IT supply-side governance (ITSG—how IT should do what it does) is concerned with ensuring that the IT organization operates in an effective, efficient and compliant fashion...."[2]

Although business intelligence governance is perhaps not strictly business or IT governance, it shares the characteristics of both. Those responsible need to make sure that Power BI artifacts are secure, correct, and compliant and the developers and users know how to work with it. From the preceding definition, we get that it's about policies/processes, monitoring, people, and being effective which comes with training.

---

[1] www.businessdictionary.com/definition/governance.html

[2] www.gartner.com/en/information-technology/glossary/it-governance

© Ásgeir Gunnarsson and Michael Johnson 2020
Á. Gunnarsson and M. Johnson, *Pro Microsoft Power BI Administration*,
https://doi.org/10.1007/978-1-4842-6567-3_1

Governance is different from organization to organization as they might work in different sectors with different regulations but also with different management styles. Rules and regulations will dictate part of the governance, but a lot of it will depend on the organization and its management. An organization will often want to go a step further than rules and regulations dictate in order to be responsible, establish trust or credibility, enforce management beliefs, or for many other reasons. Due to this, there are often no clear-cut ways to implement governance.

You should not treat this as the only possible way of doing Power BI governance but rather as an inspiration to how you and your organization can implement Power BI governance that fits you and your needs. We are suggesting a strategy that relies on four pillars: people, processes and frameworks, training and support, and monitoring.

The role of governance

Business intelligence governance can roughly be split into two categories, data governance and reporting governance. Data governance is all about governing the data that fuels the business intelligence solutions, and reporting governance is about governing the artifacts created as part of the business intelligence solution.

Sometimes these governance processes are completely separate, but sometimes they are the responsibility of the same team. In this chapter we are going to focus on reporting governance as we are only concerned with Power BI governance as the governance of the data sources is out of scope.

As previously discussed business intelligence governance is about making sure the right people do the right thing within the defined boundaries of the organization. We need to make sure the BI system does not expose data to the wrong people and that the artifacts are stored, shared, and maintained in the right way. Furthermore, we need to make sure that the users, creators, and administrators know how to use, manage, and secure the artifacts.

As Power BI is partly self-service, it is vital that the governance is implemented early and in such a way that it does not impede creators and users unless necessary. Being restrictive in the wrong place can lead to implementation failure and un-governed solutions frequently known as Shadow IT. It´s important to tread carefully to avoid that situation, but at the same time make sure your organization is compliant and secure.

Components of governance

Although governance strategies might differ from organization to organization, there are several components most organizations have. We propose a four-pillar governance strategy. These pillars are People, Processes and Framework, Training and Support, and Monitoring, as illustrated in Figure 1-1.

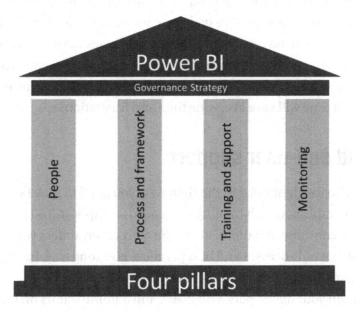

Figure 1-1. *The four pillars of Power BI governance*

People

For your governance strategy you need to make sure the right people are doing the right thing, starting with naming stakeholders and describing their role. Having defined roles and responsibilities will greatly help you and your users to find the right person when needed.

Processes and framework

A major part of a governance strategy are processes and frameworks. Developers, users, administrators, supporters, and others defined in the People pillar need to know how to do their job correctly. Having processes and frameworks will make their job easier and the result more consistent. We highly recommend you make sure all your "people" have processes or frameworks to work from, as it will help them and help you. In some organizations the word processes has a bad reputation as people find them controlling and restrictive. If you are in an organization where processes have a bad reputation, other words for process can be frameworks or best practice documents. This will often make stakeholders more receptive to them. No matter what you call a process, doing things right the first time will save everyone time and frustrations.

Training and end-user support

To help people to do the right thing in the right way, you need to make sure they know how to. This is accomplished with training and end-user support. You cannot expect people to develop, consume, or administer in the correct way unless you help them understand what that is. Processes and best practices go a long way, but training and support makes sure they understood how to do it.

You should train your developers, end users, and administrators on how to use Power BI. The level of training and the medium will differ from group to group, but it´s important that the training is available to those who need it.

Having qualified support personnel who know how to support Power BI is also very important. We have often seen Power BI support reside with general IT support who have not been trained on how to support Power BI. This can be disastrous for your Power BI implementation as the software will likely be blamed if things don´t work and support cannot help. Therefore, it´s vital that your support structure is clear, and your staff is trained to support Power BI.

Monitoring

Monitoring is a big part of governance. Processes, frameworks, and training and support tell people how it should be done, but monitoring will check if it´s done in the way it should be. Besides making sure that things are done correctly, monitoring can also be used to track the progress of your Power BI implementation.

Governance strategy

When deciding how to govern your Power BI environment, there are several things to consider. The first thing to consider is if your organization has a general IT governance strategy that you can tie into. If you have one, it will most likely dictate parts of your Power BI governance strategy. After that you need to consider things such as

- How sensitive is your data?

- How do developers and users work with Power BI?

- How experienced are your developers?

- What kind of security requirements and/or industry standards do you have to adhere to?

- How much audit trail do you need?

Basically, you need to figure out how much control is enough and how do you document and enforce it. It can be hard to find the sweet spot of just enough control, and it can be very different from organization to organization.

One of the key things which will dictate your governance strategy is if your Power BI environment is either a self-service or an enterprise environment. In a pure self-service environment, developers are often less experienced and have little access to developer tools such as source control, automatic deployments, etc. Normally the landscape is simpler, and segregation of duty is little. This means your strategy should be more focused on development best practices, training, and monitoring. In a more enterprise scenario, you will often find fewer but more experienced developers. Here your governance strategy is often more focused on processes, monitoring, and roles and responsibilities. In many organizations you will find that Power BI is used in a hybrid scenario, where you have some development being done by a centrally located IT or center of excellence team, and some being done by business users. In these cases, your strategy needs to encompass both groups. Sometimes you might create a different strategy for each group, but sometimes you create just one that will include everything.

If you consider the aforementioned components of a Power BI governance strategy, your task is to figure out who should be involved, which processes you need, how to train and support your users, and how to monitor what they are doing. You should use any existing IT governance strategies and existing answers to the above questions to figure this out.

Parts of a successful governance strategy

A successful governance strategy will include many parts. In this section we will describe some of the most important parts that make up a successful governance strategy. The setup of a governance strategy will differ from organization to organization, but these parts will almost always be present in some shape or form. We will include why the part is important, what it should include, and in some cases how you can implement it.

Management buy-in

One of the key things to make your governance strategy a success is management buy-in. If you don´t have the backing of both IT and business management, your strategy will most likely fail. You need resources and time to make the strategy work and that is only possible with management backing. It´s hard to enforce processes, best practices, training requirements, and roles and responsibilities without the backing of management.

Clearly defined roles and responsibilities

To be successful with a Power BI implementation in the long run, it´s important to have well-defined roles and responsibilities. This is most likely different from organization to organization, and in some cases the same person might have more than one role. The most common roles are Power BI administrator, Power BI gateway administrator, Data steward, Power BI auditor, and Power BI supporter(s). In this section we will look at each role, its responsibilities, and what type of person should have this role.

Power BI administrator

The Power BI administrator has two main responsibilities: Power BI tenant settings and capacity administration if the organization has Power BI Premium.

Power BI tenant settings, set in the Power BI admin portal, are very important when it comes to governance. The Power BI administrator can change all settings within the Power BI admin portal and therefore has the power to allow for all, allow for certain groups, or limit users' access to certain functionality. A Power BI administrator can also administer Power BI Premium capacities and assign workspaces to those capacities.

More information about the Power BI administrator role can be found in Chapter 8.

Power BI gateway administrator

The Power BI gateway administrator is responsible for ensuring the Power BI On-premises data gateway is running, updated, and has its performance monitored. The administrator also has the encryption keys to the gateway.

The Power BI On-premises data gateway is a central component in the Power BI ecosystem and requires someone to administer it. The person might be part of an infrastructure team as the tasks are mostly about monitoring and updating which is often an integrated part of infrastructure teams.

Data steward

Wikipedia has a definition of data steward which is as follows:

> *"A data steward is a role within an organization responsible for utilizing an organization's data governance processes to ensure fitness of data elements - both the content and metadata. Data stewards have a specialist role that incorporates processes, policies, guidelines and responsibilities for administering organizations' entire data in compliance with policy and/or regulatory obligations. A data steward may share some responsibilities with a data custodian."*
>
> —https://en.wikipedia.org/wiki/Data_steward

As such it's a very important role for the success of your governance strategy, specially if you are using master data in your datasets. Data steward is a role that often exists in organizations with or without Power BI and as such is not specific to Power BI.

Power BI auditor

The Power BI auditor is the one responsible for monitoring the Power BI audit log. The main responsibilities of the role are to make sure the audit data is gathered and stored, and most importantly that Power BI users are acting in accordance with the organization's governance processes. This means reporting on top of the audit data and flagging noncompliance actions. They will often flag parts of the audit log or build reports on top of the audit log to be made available to other people within the organization. The data will often be anonymized when made available to others. The role of Power BI auditor is often in the hands of an internal auditing function, governance team, or security team.

Power BI supporter

For a successful Power BI implementation, there is a great need for someone who can support Power BI developers. The main reason for this is that since Power BI is in part a self-service tool, developers are often business people with different backgrounds that are not necessarily used to developing integrations, data models, or visualizations.

The main responsibilities of the Power BI supporter vary but often are to assist users with Power BI–related problems, assure best practices are followed, champion new functionalities, and generally be the go-to person for the business.

The person(s) selected for this role are often the internal super users or part of the business intelligence function in the organization. The most important thing is that with the role comes allocated time because without it, the quality of the organization's Power BI deliverables might suffer.

What processes do you need?

It will vary from organization to organization which processes and frameworks are needed. There are several processes which most organizations, in our opinion, would want to have. These are

- Development
- Publishing
- Sharing
- Security
- Naming standards
- Support
- Tenant settings

In the coming sections we will go through each document and describe why it´s needed and what it could contain. This is to give an idea for your own processes and should not be taken as the only processes you'd need, or that you are not allowed to create your own version of them.

Development process

A development process most often describes how a report, datasets, or both are developed. They describe where you develop the Power BI content and how you store and version your files.

Developing Power BI content

It is recommended to develop Power BI content in Power BI Desktop rather than in the Power BI Service. The main reasons for developing in Power BI Desktop are the following: The Power BI Service does not have the same capability as Power BI Desktop. You cannot create datasets in the Power BI Service, and you cannot modify existing datasets. Furthermore, you cannot extend datasets with DAX.

At the time of this writing there is almost feature parity on report creation, so it´s possible to create as rich reports in the Power BI Service if using an existing dataset. This is a good option for those who cannot use Power BI Desktop for some reason.

Storing and versioning Power BI content

When you develop in Power BI Desktop, you can store the original file in a secure place and version it. When creating reports in the Power BI Service, you don´t have a source file and cannot store a master copy of it. If someone changes the report or even deletes it, you cannot go back to the original. Another advantage of using Power BI Desktop is that you can put the file into version or source control. This enables you to revert to older versions without storing multiple copies of the report under different names. Many organizations use OneDrive for Business or SharePoint which have built-in version control. Many BI teams have source control systems that they use, but they are often cumbersome for business users that don´t normally use such systems, whereas OneDrive for Business is merely a folder on the computer that stays synced with cloud storage. Working on reports in Power BI Desktop also allows for the developer to have reports as work in progress without interfering with reports in the Power BI Service.

Tip   It's possible to store a Power BI Desktop file on OneDrive for Business and connect to it from the Power BI Service. If you do that, you can update the file, and the results are immediately visible in the Power BI Service without the need to publish from Power BI Desktop.

A development process will describe this in detail, fitting to the needs of the organization. You might end up with two processes, one for your BI team and one for business users as they might use different tools to version content.

Publishing process

The publishing process usually describes how to publish Power BI reports and datasets, and if needed how to set up multiple environments as well as how to promote Power BI content between them.

Before recently the Power BI Service did not have built-in functionality for multiple environments. Now there is a feature called Deployment Pipelines that you can use if you have Power BI Premium. Deployment Pipelines allow the user to take one workspace, either new or existing, and create more workspaces (environment) that are linked to that. The original workspace is the development workspace while the linked workspaces are your other environments. You are limited to three environments at the moment, development, test, and production. You can use all three or only two if you prefer (all three will be created). The Deployment Pipelines also include different properties such as connection strings that you can set for each environment.

If you are using Power BI Pro license, you don´t want to use the Deployment Pipelines, or you need more flexibility that they can give you, you can instead manually create the environments you need. The most common way this can be achieved is through the use of multiple workspaces. You would create one workspace for each environment and move the datasets and reports between them as they go between development stages such as development, test, pre-production, and production.

A publishing process normally describes how this should be achieved and how you go about promoting datasets between environments. This can be done using simple publish in Power BI Desktop or more elaborately using the Power BI REST API. The process will normally reference the naming standards and security processes for the workspace naming and access control.

Sharing Process

Generally speaking, there are four ways of sharing Power BI report or a dashboard with an end user:

- Share the Power BI Desktop file.

- Direct sharing of reports and dashboards.

- Give access to a Power BI workspace where the report and/or dashboard reside.

- Share a Power BI app.

Sharing a Power BI Desktop file is not recommended as the user will have full control over the report which allows them to change whatever they want and access all the data if the data is imported. The user can also make their own copy of the report and change things the original author does not have any control over.

Directly sharing a Power BI report or dashboard is a method that can be used in certain circumstances. However, it's not recommended unless the receivers are few or if you need to share one or few reports/dashboards out of a workspace with many reports/dashboards. The main drawbacks of direct sharing are that it is difficult to keep track of who has access and which reports/dashboards have been shared and which have not.

Giving access to a Power BI workspace can be dangerous as the user can in most cases change or delete the report as well as access all the data in the report. It is possible to add users in a viewer role in the new type of workspaces. I would still argue that only contributors should have admin access to a Power BI workspace and that the viewer role is used for users that don´t need editing rights but will still contribute, such as testers. See next section "Security process" for more details.

The best way to share Power BI reports and dashboards is through Power BI apps. The apps are made to share to a larger audience and include functionalities such as custom navigation and URL links, hosting multiple reports/dashboards at once, and the ability to share the finished report in the app while the report is being developed in the workspace. Microsoft recommends using apps to share Power BI content with end users. Figure 1-2 illustrates the most common way to publish and share Power BI reports in an enterprise environment.

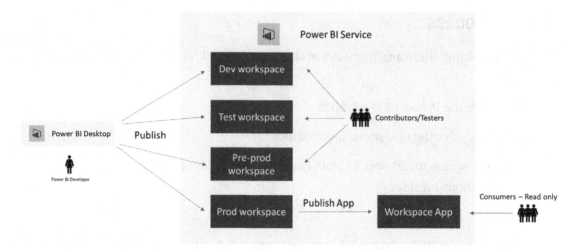

Figure 1-2. *Publishing and sharing in Power BI*

The sharing process describes how to share reports, dashboards and datasets, and links to the security process for more details. It will describe each method, its pros and cons, and when to use it.

Security process

A security process describes how to secure Power BI content. This is usually split into two categories: object level security and data security.

Object level security

There are several types of objects that get created in the Power BI ecosystem and need to be secured. These objects are Power BI Desktop files, workspaces, apps, datasets, Power BI reports, dashboards, dataflow, and Excel files stored in the service. Besides that, it needs to be decided who can publish against certain data sources in the Power BI On-premises data gateway.

It's important not to store Power BI Desktop files where unauthorized people can get access to them. If the dataset uses import mode, then all the data is available to the person who has access to the Power BI Desktop file. The security process will normally point this out and advice on how to store the Power BI Desktop file.

Currently everyone, besides those in the viewer role, who has access to a workspace can see all the data, can change all reports, and download a Power BI Desktop file of all reports in a Power BI workspace. You therefore need to be careful of who get access to Power BI workspaces. The golden rule is that only people that need to contribute to a report or dataset should have access to a workspace. In other words, if you need to WORK on the report or dataset you have access to a WORKspace. A security process will also describe if individuals, Active Directory Security groups, or Active Directory Distribution List should be used to give access to workspaces.

The recommended way of sharing Power BI objects is via a Power BI app (see previous section "Sharing process"). Apps can be considered a read-only version of a workspace and as such will never give the user any modification rights. That said it´s important to give only authorized people access to apps. A security process will normally describe how to give access to apps as well as if individuals, Active Directory Security groups, or Active Directory Distribution List should be used to give access.

Sharing reports/dashboards directly with end users is not recommended in most cases. If you do, you can keep track of who the report/dashboard has been shared with using the Share dialog window. Below figure 1-3 shows the share dialog window for a Power BI report.

A security process will describe how and when you should use direct sharing and how to (manually) monitor who has access.

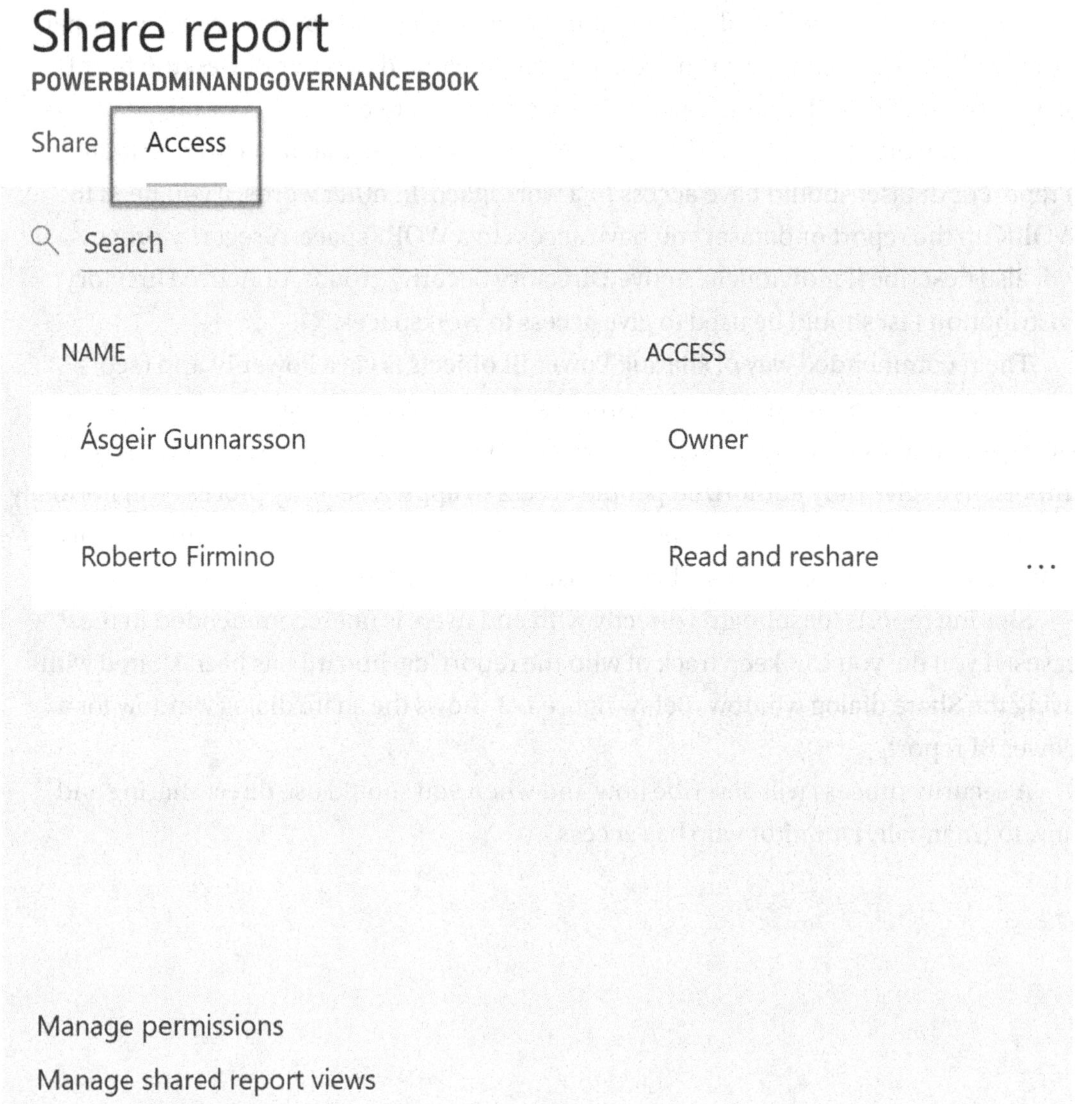

Share report
POWERBIADMINANDGOVERNANCEBOOK

Share	Access

🔍 Search

NAME	ACCESS	
Ásgeir Gunnarsson	Owner	
Roberto Firmino	Read and reshare	...

Manage permissions

Manage shared report views

Figure 1-3. *Share dialog window*

Data security

Sometimes it´s not enough to just control access on an object level. An example of this is when a single report serves the whole organization, but department managers can only see the data for their own departments. If that kind of security should be done using object level security, the author would need to create as many copies of the report as there are departments. Instead it´s more efficient to secure the data instead of the objects. Securing data in that way is known as row-level security or RLS. Power BI allows for row-level security where the report author can apply static or dynamic row-level security, which propagates filters that modifies access to whole tables or specific rows on tables. When to apply data security and how to implement it is often dependent on other security and privacy processes as well as rules and regulations such as GDPR.

Another aspect of data security that is tightly tied to development processes is the best practice to connect to development versions of the source system until the report is ready and has been properly secured. The main reason for this is that development versions of source system don´t usually have real up-to-date data in them, thus preventing sensitive data from getting into the wrong hands. After the author has secured the data and objects as prescribed in the security process, the data source can be switched to other environments ending with the production environment when ready to be released to users.

Deciding how users get added to the Power BI On-premises data gateway is very important. The tendency is to just add all developers to the needed data source in the gateway, but from a governance perspective it´s important to only add users that have been approved. Usually the process is that the data or data source owner needs to approve who can publish against the data source. This is often an excellent opportunity to engage the developer and make sure their reports/dashboards are following best practices and are approved.

A security process will describe how to secure access to objects as well as to data and will often refer to other security and process documents that exist within the organization.

Naming standard process

One of the most undervalued process is the naming standard process. Having this process early in the Power BI implementation will greatly improve the usability of the Power BI environment. Finding workspaces, reports, dashboards, and datasets can be very tricky when you have hundreds of workspaces with no clear naming convention. When each project has development, test, pre-production, and production workspaces (see "Development process"), the number of workspaces can increase fast. Having a clear naming convention describing how to name workspaces as well as how to identify different environment is very important. Another common issue is that the user only sees a certain number of characters in the workspace name. Many users don´t realize this and put the environment name at the end, but when browsing the workspaces in the Power BI Service, you sometimes don´t see the end of the name, and therefore need to hover over the workspace name to see which one is the dev or production workspace. A naming standard process will often be linked to a more general naming standard process within an organization.

Support process

Many organizations neglect to create a proper support organization when implementing Power BI (see "Roles" section). Having a good support process will enable your current support organization or dedicated Power BI support people to more easily assist users when needed. A support process will help non-Power BI supporters to know when to dig in and try to solve a problem and when to refer the problem to the report owner or Power BI support people.

Typically, a support process will describe common scenarios like access requests, permission errors, missing data incidents, wrong data incidents, refresh errors, broken visuals, and change requests to Power BI content and guide the supporter on how to react. Depending on how established your support process is, your support organization might do none, some, or all of the support on Power BI content. If you have a support organization, they will get support requests on Power BI because users are used to getting support there. Therefore, it's important that you integrate your Power BI support into your current support organization even though it's only for them to pass it on to the "real" Power BI supporters.

If your access is generally done via AD security groups or AD distribution lists, a non-Power BI support organization will be able to support Power BI access requests as long as there is a separate support document for each Power BI app. This will greatly reduce the manual work by the Power BI developers or administrators and often reduce the time to get the request resolved.

Your supports should also have a process section on how to handle dataset refresh failures and a way to redirect support requests to the Power BI Application owner or data owner if there is a data issue.

Tenant settings process

There are several settings in the Power BI admin portal that are important when it comes to governance. Publish to web, Sharing outside of organization, Export data, and Internal support page to name a few are all very important for different reasons. It's very important that the organization has a process in place defining how each setting in the Power BI admin portal should be set, who the setting should apply to, and describing why it's important. At the time of this writing the only way to monitor changes to tenant settings is through the Power BI audit log, and it will only include what the setting was changed to. This means that having documentation on what the setting should be is very important.

Training plan

Another part of a successful Power BI governance strategy is a training plan. A training plan defines who should be trained, how they should be trained, and who delivers the training. Often you will have different training strategies for different groups of users. Developers might need several days of in-person training, while short videos available on-demand is a good way to train consumers. Whatever way you decide to do, you should have a clear plan that is available to your users and you follow up on regularly. Having developers and users that don´t know how to use Power BI can severally hinder the implementation and lead to unhappy user.

If you want to have a successful Power BI implementation, then training is very important. You want to train everyone who touches Power BI, but in a different way depending on their role. You want to make sure you get to everyone and deliver the right training based on their needs. In this section we will see examples of what categories of training you can use, the content of each training, and the most effective delivery method. It´s not only governance training that is important. Training users in properly using Power BI and using best practices will allow users to deliver value faster and will make report and dataset developers more compliant.

The most common training categories are Consumer, Report Developer, Report and Dataset Developer, and Administrator. For each category there is a definition of who belongs to it as well as what training content is appropriate and how it should be delivered.

Consumer training

Consumers are normally defined as Power BI users that will only consume reports or dashboards created by others. They will never create or modify any content. This is normally the biggest group of Power BI users and is often overlooked when it comes to training. At the same time this group is the easiest to train.

The content of the consumer training is usually general training around navigating the Power BI Service. How to log in and find content, how to open a report or dashboard, how to use the "toolbar" above a Power BI report/dashboard, and the most common ways to interact with a Power BI report/dashboard such as navigating between pages, using buttons and bookmarks, and using slicers and filters. The appropriate delivery method for the consumer training is often videos or training manuals. Live training is typically not needed and too expensive due to the number of people. The exception from this is if you want to train a subset of consumers on a particular report or dashboard. That is often best done with live classroom training as then training will also involve how to analyze the data from that particular report.

Report developer

A report developer is a person that will create Power BI reports on top of ready-made datasets created by others. They don´t create their own datasets but will use datasets such as Power BI datasets, SQL Server Analysis Services (SSAS) models, or Azure Analysis Services (AAS) models.

The training for this group of people will often contain topics such as Visualization, Storytelling, and Publishing and Sharing.

The report developer training is best done in a live classroom training, but can be done via online webinars if required. It´s also possible to create an on-demand video course, but commonly the users will get the fastest start and biggest benefit from an in-person live classroom training.

Report and dataset developers

Report and dataset developers are the most advanced group of users that will both create their own datasets and reports.

The training for this group of users will often contain all the topics from the report developer course plus data topics such as getting and transforming data, data modeling, calculated measures, security, and refreshing data.

The report and dataset developer training is best done in a live classroom training. It´s also possible to create an on-demand video course, but commonly the users will get the fastest start and biggest benefit from an in-person live classroom training. There is usually a need for a person in the room to help people out, as the deep dive portions of the training can often be quite challenging.

Administrators

Administrators are the users who have the Power BI administrator role in Microsoft 365.

The training for this group of users will often contain topics such as the role of the administrator, navigating the Power BI administration portal, security, user management, and managing data.

As there are normally very few administrators, the training is best done in a live classroom training. The training is very specific, and as the administrator is a very important role in the governance of the Power BI platform, it´s important to make sure the person has taken the training on board.

Making the governance strategy available to users and management

Having a governance strategy, processes, and other important material is of no use if the intended audience does not know them or is aware they exist. One of the main challenges is how to get these documents to the relevant stakeholders. This section describes considerations, tools, and techniques you can use to better your chances of reaching your audience.

Storing the documents in the right place

Storing the documents in the right place is paramount to adoption. Making sure documents are easily discoverable and that everyone who needs it has access to them is key. That location can be different from organization to organization. Check what other system owners in your organization are doing, and see if you can use the same location. If you are storing the documents in a location that has not been used in this way before, make sure your users know about it and can find it through your intranet or other place where they are most likely to search.

Automate the delivery of documents based on roles and actions

In many organizations it´s not easy to know who is developing Power BI content as they might be spread around the business. How do you make sure they know the governance strategy and have the processes they need? In these situations, you might consider automating the delivery of documents to users based on their roles and actions. Power BI has REST APIs which you can use to see who is creating content. You can also use the Office 365 REST API to see who has Power BI license. By leveraging this information, you could, as an example, send the development process to a user when they create their first object or send links to training material when a user gets a Power BI Pro license. This can be automated so that you can make sure that if a new user starts developing or consuming Power BI content, they get sent the relevant material and are aware where to find other documentation. This will save you from having to know who these users are to make them aware of the documents and it will make all users aware of the governance strategy and it´s components.

If you have management buy-in, get them to help you promote the strategy and get permission to automatically deliver documents to relevant people.

Enforcing the governance strategy

Having a governance strategy is important but without enforcement it´s not very useful. You need to make sure that people know the strategy, know all the relevant components and if they are following the strategy. This chapter describes tools and methods you can use to help you enforce the strategy by having the right backing, making documents available, and monitoring if the strategy is being followed.

RACI for governance

A RACI describes who is Responsible, who is Accountable, who needs to be Consulted, and who needs to be Informed. RACI is one of the best tools at your disposal for governance enforcement. It´s very hard to enforce any strategy if there is nobody responsible or accountable. The accountable is preferably the owner of Power BI within the organization or BI in general. Having the right person accountable will give you the chance to enforce the strategy with their backing.

Monitoring for governance

As mentioned earlier in the chapter, one of the major components of governance strategy is monitoring. You need to set up monitoring to be able to see if users are doing things correctly and adhering to the standards you have set in the governance strategy.

You should use the Power BI audit log to monitor what people are doing. This will help you answer questions such as who is creating, modifying, and deleting objects. It will tell you who is viewing objects which will in turn tell you that they have access. There is a lot of information in the audit log which is useful from a governance perspective but also information for other purposes such as monitoring implementation progress. Currently you can access the audit log in two places. The Office 365 Security and Compliance Center stores the audit logs for 90 days by default. You need to be an Office 365 administrator, in the auditor role, or in a custom role that gives you access to be able to see the audit logs in the Office 365 Security and Compliance Center. You can either manually look at the audit log, export it manually, or use the Office 365 REST API to export it. Note that to get access to the Power BI audit logs in the Office 365 Security and Compliance Center, you need to have access to all the Office 365 logs. It´s also possible to get the Power BI audit log via the Power BI REST API. To do that you need to be a Power BI administrator. The Power BI REST API will only expose the Power BI audit log, so there is no need to have access to other Office 365 audit logs. The logs are stored for 30 days. As the logs are only stored for a certain number of days, it´s very important to export them and store them outside of Office 365. This allows you to get a longer history than 30/90 days, and you can also combine the data with other data such as data about users and organizational structures.

The Power BI REST API will give you information about the objects being created. This will allow you to monitor things such as what is being created, object naming, and ownership. The REST API will give you a snapshot of how things are at any given time. If you need to have a history of how things are developing over time, you need to store the data outside of the Power BI tenant. The information you get can also be useful for monitoring the Power BI implementation and allow you to build a catalog of objects to be shared within your organization.

Combining the data from the audit log with data about Power BI artifacts and user information, as illustrated in Figure 1-4, you can do a comprehensive reporting on your Power BI environment and implementation effort.

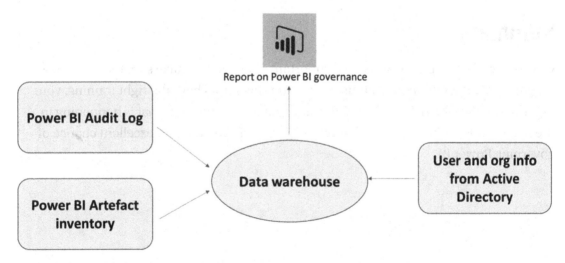

Figure 1-4. Monitoring architecture for Power BI

Monitoring the Power BI On-premises Data Gateway

The Power BI On-premises data gateway is a Windows service running on an on-premise server. The gateway needs to be monitored as other Windows services. The main things to monitor are the service uptime and server performance. Normally monitoring is in the hands of an infrastructure team (if one exists).

Automating monitoring

Effective monitoring is automated. Collecting the information daily (or at whatever frequency that makes sense in your organization) should be automated, as it is very time consuming to do manually. Data can be stored in a database, and the whole history is at your disposal when you need it. The collection of the data can be automated using PowerShell or with your favorite tool that can read data from REST APIs. When you have the data, you then need to make sure it´s available to the right people either through visualizations or alerts. Creating alert rules to automatically let the relevant person (this is where the RACI comes in good hand) know of governance breaches can be complicated but is normally worth the while. If you don´t do that, you need to manually monitor the data and react to breaches.

Summary

Governance of data platforms is very important. You need to make sure that you have the right processes in place, your users and administrators have the right training, your organization has the right roles defined, and you are monitoring what is happening in the platform. By doing these fundamental things well, you have an excellent chance of governing Power BI.

Call to action

- Good governance strategy has four pillars, people, processes and frameworks, training and support, and monitoring.

- Processes and frameworks help your users to do things right the first time.

- Training is important for all types of users to help them be effective and compliant.

- Defined roles help your organization to allocate resources to Power BI and make it easier for users to find help.

- Monitoring is the key to make sure your users are compliant and gives great opportunity to document your implementation.

CHAPTER 2

Power BI Licensing

Read this chapter if you would like to find out more information about

- What types of licensing are there in Power BI

- What each type of license includes

- When to buy Power BI Premium

Licensing is always a hot topic when it comes to software, and Power BI is no different. This chapter will focus on understanding and allocating Power BI licenses. Even though Power BI administrators cannot typically purchase Power BI licenses and only partially allocate them, it's important that they understand the licensing structure and how to obtain and allocate them.

Types of licenses in Power BI

There are two ways to license Power BI. An organization can either buy and allocate personal licenses or they can buy and allocate capacity. Note that if you buy capacity, you will still need to buy personal licenses for creators of Power BI content. The following sections will explain each type of license.

It's important to note that when we talk about Power BI licenses, we are only talking about publishing, sharing, and collaborating. Authoring in Power BI Desktop does not require a license as it is a free download and can be used without signing in.

27

© Ásgeir Gunnarsson and Michael Johnson 2020
Á. Gunnarsson and M. Johnson, *Pro Microsoft Power BI Administration*,
https://doi.org/10.1007/978-1-4842-6567-3_2

Personal license

A personal license comes in two variations, Power BI Free or Power BI Pro.

A Power BI Free license will allow you to publish your reports to the Power BI Service and consume those reports. With the free license you are not allowed to share your reports, dashboards, or datasets, and you cannot consume what others have shared with you. In summary, the free license is a personal license where you can only consume your own work through your personal workspace, also known as My Workspace.

A Power BI Pro license allows you to do everything you can with the free license plus share content with other users and consume other users' content. You can create, share, and consume what others have shared with you. The only limits are the limits posed on you by the capacity you work on (see section "Benefits of Power BI Premium").

Figure 2-1 illustrates the different capabilities between Power BI Pro and Power BI Free.

Per-user license type comparison

Here is a list of features supported by per-user license type.

	Free	Pro
Connect to 70+ data sources	✓	✓
Publish to Web	✓	✓
Export to PowerPoint, Excel, CSV	✓	✓
Enterprise distribution		
Apps	✗	✓
Email subscriptions	✗	✓
Embed APIs and controls	✗	✓
Collaboration		
Peer-to-peer sharing	✗	✓
App workspaces	✗	✓
Analyze in Excel, analyze in Power BI Desktop	✗	✓

Figure 2-1. *Power BI Pro vs. Power BI Free*

It's worth noting that if you don't have a dedicated capacity (see next section on "Capacity license" for more information about dedicated capacity), all users including consumers need to have a Power BI Pro license to collaborate.

The free license is readily available in Office 365 and can be allocated to users in the Office 365 admin center at no cost. Power BI Pro is included in the Office 365 Enterprise E5 or can be purchased and allocated in the Office 365 admin center. To be able to purchase a Power BI Pro license, the person needs to be a member of the Global administrator or Billing administrator roles. To assign licenses in the Office 365 admin center, you need to be a member of one of the following roles: Global administrator, Billing administrator, License administrator, or User management. Power BI Pro licenses can also be assigned through the Azure portal. Assigning licenses can be automated with PowerShell. As of January 14, 2020, users in an active commercial Office 365 tenants can purchase Power BI Pro license themselves without the involvement of Office 365 administrators. To be able to do that, the users' account needs to be in an active Azure Active Directory, and they need to have a credit card to pay for the license. If this is unwanted in your organization, the Office 365 admins can turn this capability off via PowerShell. The Office 365 admins also have the capability to monitor who has bought self-service licenses. It's important to note that self-service bought licenses might have a different (most often worse) price than organization-wide licenses. This makes monitoring even more important as you might buy organization-wide licenses to replace self-service bought licenses to save money. The main benefit of self-service bought licenses is that the license cost is paid by the users or their departments instead of being centrally managed. This means that departments or individuals with budget can quickly buy Power BI Pro without the need to wait for a centralized decision or budget.

As each Power BI Pro license costs money, it's important to monitor the usage. If a user is not using Power BI, you can re-assign their license to another user or simply deactivate the license to save money. With monitoring you can also see who has signed up for trial licenses and plan for purchasing licenses for them before the trial ends. All users in an organization can sign up for a 60-day Power BI Pro trial if the Office 365 admin has not actively disabled that option.

If you remove a person's Power BI Pro license, there is still a 30-day grace period for individually bought licenses and a 90-day grace period for volume license purchase. This means that the users' data and objects are only available to the admins in that period and after that they are deleted. If you assign a Power BI license to the user again within the grace period, the data and artifacts are still there for them to continue using.

Capacity license (Power BI Premium)

Instead of licensing each user as described in the above section, the organization can also purchase a capacity. A capacity is basically hardware resources that are allocated to tasks. So instead of buying a license for individuals to use, you buy dedicated compute resources to host and execute Power BI workloads. When you only use Power BI Pro licenses, your content is on a shared capacity. This means that the performance of your reports, dataset refreshes, etc. can be impacted by users in other organizations. When you buy Power BI Premium (license capacity), the resources are dedicated to you instead.

Benefits of Power BI Premium

Besides the obvious benefits of having dedicated hardware resources, buying Power BI Premium comes with other benefits such as

- Consumers of reports don't need to have a Power BI Pro license

- Paginated reports

- Increased maximum dataset size

- Increased storage capacity

- AI-powered data modeling

- Higher number of scheduled refreshes per day

- Ability to have data in different regions

- Ability to run Power BI Report server on-premise

An up-to-date comparison of Power BI Pro and Power BI Premium can be found at `https://powerbi.microsoft.com/en-us/pricing/#powerbi-comparison-table`.

Size matters

Dedicated capacity comes in two flavors: EM/A SKUs and P SKUs. EM SKUs are meant for embedding purposes, and P SKUs are meant for embedding and enterprise purposes. A SKUs are meant for testing purposes or to get access to Power BI Premium features while still using Power BI Pro license for all consumers. A SKUs also support app owns data scenario which is beyond the scope of this book. To get access to all the Power BI Premium features with an A SKU, you need to buy at least A4.

When you license dedicated capacity, you are renting hardware. This hardware has specifications that you need to be aware of. Each capacity has backend v-cores and frontend v-cores as well as RAM. Backend v-cores do all the core Power BI functionality such as query processing and model refresh, while frontend v-cores handle functionalities such as web services, scheduling, and access rights management (`https://docs.microsoft.com/en-us/power-bi/service-premium-what-is`). Figure 2-2 shows different SKUs and their resources distribution.

Capacity Nodes	Total v-cores	Backend v-cores	RAM (GB)	Frontend v-cores	DirectQuery/Live Connection (per sec)	Model Refresh Parallelism
EM1/A1	1	0.5	3	0.5	3.75	1
EM2/A2	2	1	5	1	7.5	2
EM3/A3	4	2	10	2	15	3
P1/A4	8	4	25	4	30	6
P2/A5	16	8	50	8	60	12
P3/A6	32	16	100	16	120	24

Figure 2-2. *Power BI capacity sizes*

Buying capacity

From a licensing perspective, capacity purchases are more complicated than personal licenses. First of all, you need to figure out how much capacity you need. You can use the Power BI Premium calculator to help you figure out how much capacity you need (`https://powerbi.microsoft.com/en-us/calculator/`). If your needs surpass the specifications of one type of capacity node, then you need to figure out what combination of capacities you will buy to obtain the desired capacity. This means deciding if you want to buy one large or two smaller capacities. There is no right answer as it all depends on your workload. You might also want to separate content on different capacities. As an example you might decide that reports for upper management need to perform well all the time and therefore should have their own capacity; or you might have a requirement that data needs to reside in different regions so each region needs its own capacity. As you can see, it's very important to map out the needs before you buy any dedicated capacity.

When you have bought a dedicated capacity, you, as a Power BI administrator, can assign workspaces to the capacity. This implies not all your content is necessarily in the dedicated capacity and nothing is put in it automatically. See more about assigning workspaces to capacities and using shared and dedicated capacity together in Chapter 10.

It's very important to note that even though you have dedicated capacity, your content creators still need to have Power BI Pro license. The big difference is that your consumers only need to have a Power BI Free license. When a content is stored on a dedicated capacity, a user with Power BI Free license can consume the content via Power BI app, via direct sharing, via embedding, or via read permissions in the workspace. For any content authoring or editing, the user needs a Power BI Pro license. This includes having access to a workspace via any role other than the viewer role.

Power BI Premium (P SKUs) can be purchased in the Office 365 admin center. To be able to purchase Power BI Premium license, the user needs to be a member of the Global administrator or Billing administrator roles. EM and A SKUs can be bought in the Azure portal, and you need to be at least a capacity admin to make the purchase. EM and A SKUs are billed by the hour while P SKUs are billed monthly or annually.

When to buy Premium

When do you buy Power BI Pro only and when do you buy Power BI Premium? The answer to this question is not straightforward. However, there are guidelines you can follow. If you have more than 500 consumers (who are not creators), Power BI Premium becomes more cost-effective, as 500 consumers cost as much in licenses as a P1 SKU. If you need any of the features that come with dedicated capacity, you might consider buying dedicated capacity even though you have fewer users. This could be features such as Paginated reports, more than 8 scheduled refreshes per day or the need to keep data in separate regions. The important thing to note is that, as Power BI is based on a subscription model, it's fairly easy to move between subscription types, but take notice of the resignation notice on your subscription before buying them.

Summary

There are two basic types of licenses for Power BI. One is a personal license model which can either be paid, Power BI Pro, or free, Power BI Free. The second type is capacity licensing, Power BI Premium. They come with different price points and different functionalities. The administrators do not usually buy or allocate licenses, but it's important for them to understand it, so they can better administer and govern the Power BI platform.

Personal licenses are simple and easy to administer, while capacity licensing is more complicated as you need to figure out how much capacity you need and administer that capacity well.

Call to action

- You can choose between two types of licenses for Power BI – personal licenses or capacity license.

- Creators of content always need a Power BI Pro license even though the organization has capacity license(s).

- More functionality comes with capacity license.

- Can be difficult to determine when to buy personal licenses and when to buy capacity.

CHAPTER 3

Collaboration

Read this chapter if you would like to find out more information about

- What is collaboration and sharing
- How to collaborate and share in Power BI
- Best practices for collaboration and sharing

One of the main advantages of reporting and analysis is the ability to share and collaborate on the results. When reports, analysis, or data are shared, it increases the value of it as many will benefit from the work of few. There is a risk though when sharing and collaborating on reports, analysis, and data. If not done correctly the data can get into the wrong hands or get exposed to those who shouldn't see it. This is especially important if you have personally identifiable information (PII). This chapter will discuss the ways to collaborate and share in Power BI as well as best practices from a governance perspective. We will also talk about monitoring and reaction if breaches occur.

What is collaborating and sharing?

Collaborating and sharing can mean many things depending on the situation and context. Collaborating and sharing in the context of Power BI is the act of interacting with others on Power BI artifacts. This interaction can be sharing Power BI objects with others, commenting and collaborating about Power BI reports, or building Power BI objects in a collaboration with others. These artifacts include dashboards, reports, Excel workbooks, datasets, dataflows, and machine learning models. The interaction can be two-way, such as discussions on a report in the Power BI website or it can be one-way such as sharing a dashboard with someone. You can collaborate as an end user, meaning you don't have permission to change the artifact, or you can collaborate as a contributor where you have permission to change artifacts. Usually collaboration and sharing means that

© Ásgeir Gunnarsson and Michael Johnson 2020
Á. Gunnarsson and M. Johnson, *Pro Microsoft Power BI Administration*,
https://doi.org/10.1007/978-1-4842-6567-3_3

people will get access to data and analysis someone else has created. From a governance perspective, sharing data, analysis, and insights is often a question of authorized access. Discussion on collaboration and sharing is therefore tightly connected to discussion on security (discussed in Chapter 13) and laws and policies (discussed in Chapter 4). Another governance angle on collaboration and sharing is that the receiver of data, analysis, and insights needs to know the context and constraints of them to be able to interpret the results. This is where training comes in as a factor in collaboration and sharing from a governance perspective.

Sharing

Sharing is the act of giving someone access to a dashboard, report, or dataset. This can be a person or a group of people, either inside or outside of your organization (see Chapter 13 on security). Sharing can grant permissions to view, or it can be to alter or build upon. It's not always obvious what type of access you are giving, so it's very important to have a clear strategy on how sharing should be done as a part of your governance work. Power BI offers different ways to share artifacts. In this section we will discuss the different ways of sharing and what their advantages and disadvantages are from a governance standpoint.

Types of sharing

In this section we will discuss sharing dashboards, reports, and datasets. There are four primary ways to share reports and datasets and three to share dashboards. These are

- Sharing the BI Desktop (PBIX) file (not for dashboards)
- Direct sharing
- Granting access to workspace
- Granting access to app

Each of these methods has its pros and cons from a usability perspective, but here we will focus on the pros and cons from a governance perspective.

Sharing PBIX file

One of the easiest ways to share a Power BI dataset or report is to share the PBIX file. When you author datasets and reports in Power BI Desktop, it's stored as a file in the PBIX file format. This file can be shared with other people, either by giving them access to the file storage or sending them the file. While this is easy and doesn't require a Power BI license (Power BI Desktop is a free product as described in Chapter 2), it does have some governance issues. If you use import mode when getting data into Power BI Desktop and you share a PBIX file with someone, they get full access to all the data stored in the file. They also have full access to the data model and can make any changes to the file, though if they do not have access to the data source they cannot edit or refresh the queries. They can either overwrite your file if they have write access to the file storage or save their own copy if not. Having access to the data and being able to change the report can be a potential security risk and risks the integrity of the analysis. Another potential security issue is if you have applied row-level security (see Chapter 13) as it is only enabled in the Power BI Service, since Power BI Desktop is a development environment with full access and control of the file for authors.

It is therefore not recommended to share PBIX files with someone unless you need them to collaborate on the creation or maintenance of the report or dataset. Safely storing PBIX files and not sending them in email or other file exchange programs is recommended to minimize risk of exposing data to unauthorized users.

Direct sharing

A dashboard, report, and dataset can be shared directly with people, distribution groups, and security groups. For dashboards and reports there are share buttons in many places, but for datasets you need to go into Manage permissions to find the sharing options.

When you directly share dashboards and reports, you have the option to allow the users to do the following:

- Allow users to share your dashboard/report.

- Allow recipients to build new content using the underlying datasets.

- Send an email notification to recipients.

All these options are pre-checked checkboxes. It's very important to think carefully before using direct sharing and if you do which of the preceding options you want to use. The first thing you need to think about is if direct sharing is the right way to accomplish what you are trying to do. When you do direct sharing, it can be hard to keep track on which dashboards or reports have been shared and with whom they have been shared. The next thing to consider is the sharing options. Do you want those who you share with to have the ability to share with others? You can quickly loose track and control of who the dashboards or reports are shared with. The only way to find out is to open the share dialog and look at the Access tab or access the Power BI Activity log. The next thing to consider is if the users you are sharing with should be allowed to create new content using the underlying dataset. If you keep that checked, users will have full access to the dataset unless you have row-level security, in which case they only see what they are allowed to see. Nevertheless, they will potentially have access to bigger parts of the dataset than intended.

When you directly share datasets, you have the option to allow the users to do the following:

- Allow recipients to reshare the artifact.

- Allow recipients to build new content from the underlying datasets.

Both these options are pre-checked checkboxes. When you share datasets with other users, you are giving them full access to all the data in the dataset unless row-level security is applied, in which case they only see what they are allowed to see. If you leave the Allow recipients to reshare the artifact checked, you allow them to reshare the dataset to whom they want. This can be undesirable as you can quickly loose track and control of who has access to the dataset. The only way to check who has access is in the Manage permissions dialog or in the Power BI Activity log. If you leave the "Allow recipients to build new content from the underlying datasets" checked, you allow them to build new reports and dashboards based on the dataset. You have no control over what they create, and they have full access to the dataset if there is no row-level security applied. Another big drawback on allowing creation of new content from the dataset when sharing dashboards, reports, or datasets is that you need to be careful with all future changes to the dataset as there might be dashboards and reports that you don't know about but depend on it. Figure 3-1 illustrates direct sharing.

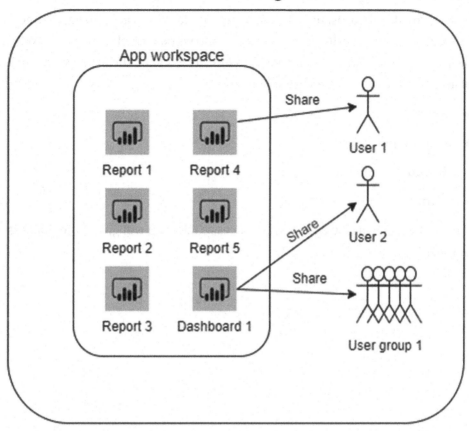

Figure 3-1. *Direct sharing*

Directly sharing a Power BI report or dashboard is a method that should only be used in certain circumstances. It's not recommended unless the receivers are few or if you need to share one or few reports/dashboards out of a workspace with many reports/ dashboards. Direct sharing is not recommended from My Workspace as the user who owns that workspace is the only person who can access it. If that person leaves the company or is for some reason not able to log in, there is no way to maintain dashboards, reports, and datasets in the workspace. The main drawbacks of direct sharing are that it is difficult to keep track of who has access to them and which reports/dashboards have been shared or not. Directly sharing datasets is only recommended if you need to allow users to create new reports and dashboards from an existing datasets but you cannot for some reason give the user access to the workspace the dataset is in.

Giving access to a workspace

One way to share dashboards, reports, datasets, and dataflows is by giving people, distribution groups, or security groups access to the workspace they reside in. When you give access to a workspace, you give the same access to all the artifacts within it. The types of access you can give to a workspace are

- Viewer

- Contributor

- Member

- Admin

In Figure 3-2, you can see exactly what access each level will give. Note that this list is as of June 2020.

Capability	Admin	Member	Contributor	Viewer
Update and delete the workspace.	X			
Add/remove people, including other admins.	X			
Add members or others with lower permissions.	X	X		
Publish and update an app.	X	X		
Share an item or share an app.1	X	X		
Allow others to reshare items.1	X	X		
Feature apps on colleagues' Home	X	X		
Feature dashboards and reports on colleagues' Home	X	X	X	
Create, edit, and delete content in the workspace.	X	X	X	
Publish reports to the workspace, delete content.	X	X	X	
Create a report in another workspace based on a dataset in this workspace.1	X	X	X	
Copy a report.2	X	X	X	
View and interact with an item.3	X	X	X	X
Read data stored in workspace dataflows	X	X	X	X

Figure 3-2. *Types of access in a workspace*

As Figure 3-2 shows, the viewer permission allows the users to view and interact with artifacts within the workspace as well as read data stored in a dataflow in the workspace. The contributor permission allows the same as viewer plus create, edit, and delete all artifacts in the workspace except workspace apps. The member permission allows the same as contributor plus the ability to give access to others (except admin access) and publish and update workspace apps. The admin permission gives you full control over all artifacts in the workspace as well as the workspace itself. The main takeaway here is that all permission levels above viewer allow the user to change and delete most objects in the workspace.

As mentioned earlier the same permission level is applied to every artifact in the workspace. This is a very important information, especially if you give anything more than viewer permission. Figure 3-3 illustrates giving access to a workspace.

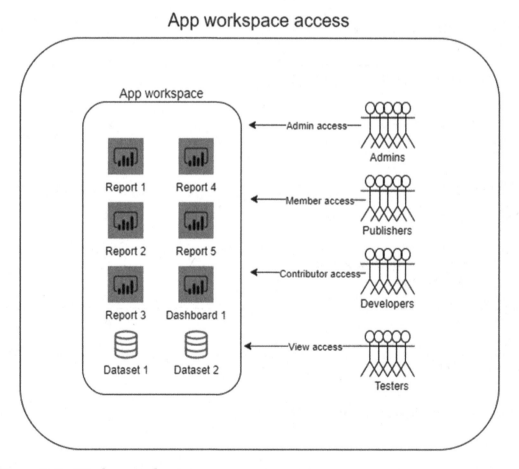

Figure 3-3. *Workspace sharing*

Giving access to workspaces for sharing artifacts is best suited for users that need to contribute to the content. Although you can use viewer permission for consumers, it's recommended to use apps for that as it simplifies maintenance of access.

Apps

Power BI artifacts can be shared with people, distribution groups, or security groups via apps. Apps can be described as a read-only version of a workspace. You can however decide if you include individual reports and dashboards in a workspace in the app. Apps also include some enhancements to how users consume content such as custom navigation and custom support URL. When you share an app, you get the following options:

- Allow all users to connect to the app's underlying datasets using Build permission.

  - Allow users to make a copy of the reports in this app.

- Allow users to share the app and the app's underlying datasets using the share permission.

The options mentioned are checkmark options with the first two pre-checked. When you share content using apps, you need to consider if you want your users to be able to create new content based on the datasets. This will give them full access to the data in the dataset unless row-level security has been applied. If you allow the user to create new content based on the datasets, you can then allow them to create a copy of the reports in the app. Without the first option, the second option is not available as creating a copy of the reports in the app is creating new content. If you check the last option to allow user to share the dataset, you will need to monitor who has access. This is done on the Manage permission tab of the datasets area in the workspace the dataset is residing or in the Power BI Activity log. All these options make it harder for you to know who has access and what content is relying on the datasets. Make sure that these risks are acceptable before you decide if they should be checked or not. Figure 3-4 illustrates sharing via app.

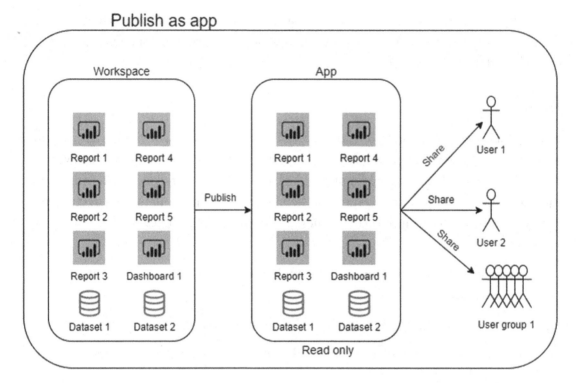

Figure 3-4. *App sharing*

Apps are the way Microsoft recommends sharing dashboards, reports, and datasets to users in Power BI. Apps allow you to share "packaged" content including multiple dashboards, reports, and datasets with custom navigation, custom website links, and embedded video. The users will always only get view access to the content, although you can give them permission to build their own content using the datasets and reports in the app. Another functionality of apps is that they contain a cached version of the report so that the report in the workspace can be modified without affecting the cached report. Note that the dataset will always be updated in the app if you update it in the workspace.

How should I share content?

When answering the question "how should I share content?" the answer is often, it depends. For larger audience using apps is the best way as it gives you one place per workspace where sharing is done, and you can add custom navigation and support URLs. For smaller audiences or when you need to share part of a workspace to someone, direct sharing might be justifiable, but it should be used sparingly due to the lack of insight into what is shared to whom. Giving access to workspaces to share content is best used for contributors rather than consumers, although the viewer permission allows you to consume content without the option to change.

To simplify your governance strategy, it might be a good idea to stick to one option and say that all content is shared to consumers via apps. This will remove any doubt on what the correct way to share content is, which can be very useful if you have many content developers with different amount of experience. In Figure 3-2 you see how a typical publish and sharing process might look like. Notice that consumers only have access to the app.

You can embed Power BI reports or apps via secure embedding or via specific SharePoint embedding. We believe that kind of sharing will follow the exact same principles as sharing through the Power BI Service. The only difference is that the content is accessed from a different place.

Collaboration

Collaboration differs from sharing in that it's usually two-way in nature. Two or more people work together to develop content. In the context of Power BI, this task can be analysis of data in a ready-made report, it can be building datasets, report, reports or dashboards together, or it can be management of Power BI tenants and content. In this section we will focus on analysis and content creation. Management of Power BI tenants and content is discussed in Part 2 of this book.

Types of collaboration

In general terms there are two types of collaboration in Power BI. Collaboration as an end user and collaboration as a contributor. End users have view-only permissions and most often collaborate on reports made by others. Contributors most often have write permissions and collaborate on by creating or modifying content. We will discuss each type separately in the coming sections.

End-user collaboration

End-user collaboration is when two or more people work together to create insights from existing reports. In Power BI that is done via the Comments feature. Comments allow users to comment on a report or dashboard and the context is kept. The user can also tag other people within the organization in the comment. This way users can collaborate on getting insights. Power BI reports can also be embedded into other software that allows for direct collaboration. It's not in the scope of this book to discuss all those options.

Contributor collaboration

Contributors can collaborate on creation and modification of Power BI content by sharing artifacts. As discussed in the sharing section of this chapter, there are several ways to share artifacts. Generally speaking, developers which need to collaborate on a set of Power BI artifacts will place them in a workspace and make sure all the relevant developers have at least member access to it. If developers have the appropriate permissions, they can create or modify artifacts. For contributors such as testers that don't need write access, you would add them as viewers in the relevant workspace. It's worth noting that there is no true multi-developer capability in Power BI that allows multiple people to develop the same artifact at the same time, as you often can in software development. It's possible to work on the dataset at the same time as the report is developed if the report is developed on top of a shared Power BI dataset, but otherwise it's one developer at a time per artifact.

Developers of datasets can use dataset certification to communicate to report developers that a dataset is of certain quality. Dataset certification has two levels:

- Promoted dataset

- Certified dataset

The meaning of promoted and certified datasets is different from organization to organization. It does not come with any functionality except it moves the dataset higher in the lists of datasets in the workspace. Each organization needs to describe when to use which level of certification. By default, every dataset owner can promote their dataset. To give users the ability to apply the certified label to datasets, you need to add them to a group that has the appropriate permissions. It is recommended to have a limited number of people who can add the certify label and be very consistent in what it means for the dataset. Many organizations only certify datasets that are created and maintained by a central business intelligence team and have gone through rigorous testing to verify that the data is correct, but there is nothing to prevent your organization to create your own process for certified datasets.

Collaboration strategy

As a part of your governance strategy, you should have a collaboration strategy. Often it will consist of processes that describe what the preferred way of collaboration is. It can be one process, or it might be split into smaller processes. The main areas to include in the process are

- Sharing options
- Preferred sharing method
- Reference to security process
- Reference to naming standards
- Reference to training material

Sharing options

This section of your process would describe the different ways you can share content in Power BI. It would list the pros and cons of each method as well as the risks it presents. The section would also describe how well each sharing method aligns to the organization's governance strategy.

Preferred sharing method

This section of your process would describe what the preferred sharing method is. There might be more than one preferred method or there might be only one. If there is more than one method, you should describe when each of them should be used. Example of when only one method is preferred could be

All sharing of dashboards, reports, and datasets to end users should happen via apps.
Example of multiple methods could be

As a general rule, all sharing of dashboards, reports, and datasets to end users should happen via apps.

Exception: When sharing a single report out of many in a workspace, you can use direct sharing. This prevents you from having to create a new workspace and putting in it a duplicate copy of the report. If you directly share the report, you are responsible for making sure only appropriate users have access.

Reference to security process

A collaboration process is tightly connected to the security process. A lot of information will be duplicated between them as both describe how to securely handle Power BI artifacts. The collaboration process is rooted in governance, so it does not necessarily detail the security aspects of sharing and collaborating. In your collaboration process it's important to link to the security process to easily enable the readers to get to it and get more in-depth information on the security aspect of sharing and collaborating if they need it.

Reference to naming standards

Although a lot of naming is done during development, it's possible to name apps when you share them with users. Having consistent naming of objects in Power BI will help a great deal with administration and governance. There might be a specific naming standard for Power BI, or there might be a more general naming standard in the organization that is used for Power BI. No matter which, you should link to it from your collaboration process so that your users have easy access to it.

Reference to training material

Even though your collaboration process describes the methods available and which method to use in which situation, it will most likely not describe how to implement them. If you have training material or run regular training sessions, you should link to the training material and/or signup to training sessions. Lots of governance issues come from users who implement things in the wrong way, so clear training material and well-trained developers will go a long way in preventing governance risks.

Monitoring collaboration compliance

Monitoring collaboration compliance is not straightforward. Most of it will be manual. In Power BI there is no way to automatically extract who has access to an artifact. Through the activity log you extract who has accessed the artifact but not who has access. Even though you can extract who has accessed the artifact, it does not tell you if they should have access. If you have information about who should have access to an artifact stored somewhere, it can be compared to those who have accessed the same artifact. If you don't have it stored anywhere (like most organizations), you will need to do manual audits to verify if there is a breach. For more information on monitoring, please refer to Chapter 16.

Preventive measures

The right training of Power BI developers and consumers can help you a great deal as people who know how to work with Power BI and know the governance strategy well are less likely to cause unintentional breaches.

Another way to prevent breaches is to have tight access control in Power BI development. Make sure there is a separation between development, test, and production workspaces (see Chapter 5) with only few people having access to the production workspace. It's a tight balance between fast development time and tight governance control so you have to make sure you are not impeding developers too much. If you have many business developers, you might find that too tight of control will feel like you are hindering their productivity. If you have many business intelligence developers, they will most often be used to tight environment control and will not be as challenged by it.

Summary

Sharing and collaboration has many forms. In Power BI the main ways of sharing content are via apps, workspaces, or direct sharing. The recommended way is via apps. There are security risks when sharing Power BI content as, if not done correctly, it can leave data in the hands of unauthorized people.

Collaboration in Power BI is most often around content development, but it's also possible to comment on reports and dashboards. Using multiple environments (workspaces) can help keep control in collaborative development.

Call to action

- Sharing is best done via apps.

- When sharing apps, you need to be careful with the extra options on build permission and resharing that are pre-checked.

- Collaborating on Power BI development is best done with multiple environments (workspaces).

- It's possible to comment on Power BI reports and dashboards.

CHAPTER 4

Laws and Policies

Read this chapter if you would like to find out more information about

- How internal and external laws and policies impact your governance strategy

- Different international laws and regulations that impact many industries

- What Power BI offers to help you govern your environment for compliance to internal and external laws and policies

It's not just your own organizational policies that influence your governance strategies. Sometimes your organization is in an environment where laws and policies are created by a third party and dictate how you must govern your BI platform. These laws and third-party policies might be region, industry, or data specific. In this chapter we explain what you need to be aware of when dealing with external requirements, how you should incorporate them into your governance strategy, and what the Power BI platform offers to help you to meet some of these requirements.

Impact of external laws and policies

When you operate in an environment where you are required to follow laws and third-party policies that impact your governance strategy, it increases the complexity of the governance strategy and how you monitor and enforce it. There can be a wide variety of laws and third-party policies that you are required to follow. They might even conflict with each other or your internal policies which increases the complexity even further.

When it comes to BI platforms, the laws and third-party policies typically impact how you need to handle data. They dictate how you should protect the data and make sure the data does not fall into the hands of unauthorized people. This means you need to pay special attention to how you store data, how you transfer data, and how you display data.

The number of laws and third-party policies can be vast depending on which industry you are in, in which region you operate or reside in, as well as what type of data you handle. Some organizations operate in multiple regions or industries making this even more complex. In this chapter we will not cover all of the laws and third-party policies, but instead try to cover the biggest and most widespread laws and third-party policies and use them to show how your governance strategy is impacted and how the Power BI platform is capable of minimizing the impact.

Major data and privacy laws

Data and privacy laws are centered around the disclosure or misuse of sensitive information about private individuals or legal entities. Normally they focus on private individuals although that is not always the case.

Most countries and regions in the world have adopted comprehensive data protection laws with one major exception being the United States. Most of these laws are built in such a way that you are required to follow them if you do business in these regions even though you are based outside of them. The most notable of such laws is the General Data Protection Regulation (GDPR) which is part of the laws on the European Economic Area (EEA) which has the European Union (EU) and European Free Trade Association (EFTA) as its members.

Several industries have their own laws or policies with regard to data protection. These are normally industries which deal with highly sensitive personal data. One of the most known laws is the Health Insurance Portability and Accountability Act of 1996 (HIPAA). Another well-known standard is the Payment Card Industry Data Security Standards (PCI DSS). What makes it different is that it's not law but a standard developed by the major credit card companies and maintained and enforced by the Payment Card Industry Security Standards Council (PCI SSC).

Besides major laws and third-party policies, some organizations elect to be certified by certification standards such as the ISO standard. When you do that, your organization must live up to the standards and will be monitored regularly by an independent auditor. These standards, if your organization has elected to be certified, will also impact your governance strategy.

We will discuss each of the aforementioned laws or standards and see how they impact your governance strategy. Even though your organization is impacted by other laws or standards, we hope that the discussion is general enough so that you can apply the principles to your governance strategy.

General Data Protection Regulation (GDPR)

GDPR was created by the EU in 2016 and came into full effect in May 2018. The GDPR laws have been adopted by all EU and EFTA member states. The GDPR replaced the retired Data Protection Directive.

The main aim of the GDPR laws is to give private individuals control over their personal data. The GDPR applies to any organization that processes personal identifiable information (PII) about a person inside the EEA no matter where the organization is located. The GDPR dictates that an organization must have appropriate technical and organizational measures to fulfill the data protection principles. When designing systems that handle PII data, the organization must design it with privacy in mind. The main principles of GDPR are consent, contract, public task, vital interest, and legal requirement:

- The person has given consent to you collecting the data.

- You are collecting it to fulfill a contract between yourself and the person.

- You are collecting the data out of public interest or legitimate interest of an official data controller or third party.

- You are collecting the data because of vital interest of the person or other person(s).

- You are collecting the data to fulfill legal obligations.

When you collect PII data, you must clearly disclose to the user that you are collecting it, it's a lawful collection, what the purpose is, how long you will store the data, and if you are sharing it with anyone. The subject of the PII data has the right to ask for a copy of the data (the copy has to be in a common format). They also have the right to have the data erased as long as you don't have a conflicting legal requirement to keep the data longer.

If you have a data breach, you must disclose it within 72 hours. If you have a breach and you were not following the law, you can be fined up to 20 million Euros or up to 4% of your global turnover, whichever is the highest.

Health Insurance Portability and Accountability Act of 1996 (HIPAA)

HIPAA is a law in the United States from 1996. Its focus is on protecting PII data, stored by healthcare organization, from fraud and theft. The HIPAA has five titles. Title 2 is the one focused on the PII data and therefore the only one we will discuss in this chapter. In it are set policies and procedures for maintaining privacy and security of PII data. There are five rules in title 2:

- Privacy Rule

- Transaction and Code Sets Rule

- Security Rule

- Unique Identifiers Rule

- Enforcement Rule

The Privacy Rule, which came into effect in 2003, deals with any parts of an individual medical record or payment history and covers all those storing protected health information (PHI) as well as their associated businesses. It stipulates that the data can only be disclosed to others to facilitate treatment, payment, or healthcare operations as well as law enforcement authorities without written consent. The individual can request to have their data, and the provider needs to comply within 30 days. If the data is incorrect, the individual can have it corrected. If the individual feels there has been a breach, they can complain to the Department of Health and Human Services Office for Civil Rights (OCR).

The Transaction and Code Sets Rule is a standard on how electronic communication of PHI data is done. It is not relevant for business intelligence platforms, so it won't be covered in any detail here.

While the Privacy Rule deals with PHI data in both electronic and analog form, the Security Rule is specific to Electronic Protected Health Information (EPHI). In it there are set three types of compliance safeguards: administrative, physical, and technical. For each of these safeguards, there are required and addressable implementation specifications. The required specification must be adopted while the addressable specifications are more flexible.

CHAPTER 4   LAWS AND POLICIES

- Administrative safeguards are policies and procedures that demonstrate how the organization will comply with the Security Rule.

- Physical safeguards are how you physically prevent unauthorized access to PHI data.

- Technical safeguards are how you control access to IT systems as well as protecting data at rest and in transit.

The Unique Identifiers Rule explains how to identify individuals in a transactional system and is not relevant for business intelligence platforms. It will not be covered in any more detail.

The Enforcement Rule says how the HIPAA will be enforced and the punishment for breaches. If in breach of HIPAA an organization can be fined or forced to take corrective actions. Like with many of these privacy laws and policies, the biggest damage to a breaching organization is often reputable damage.

Payment Card Industry Data Security Standard (PCI DSS)

The PCI DSS is a set of standards developed by major credit card companies in 2004. In 2006 the Payment Card Industry Security Standards Council (PCI SSC) was formed to maintain and enforce the standard. The aim of PCI DSS is to ensure that merchants who accept credit cards meet minimum levels of security for storing, processing, and transmitting cardholder data.

The PIC DSS has 12 security standards split into 6 groups:

- Build and Maintain a Secure Network and Systems

    1. Install and maintain a firewall configuration to protect cardholder data

    2. Do not use vendor-supplied defaults for system passwords and other security parameters

- Protect Cardholder Data

1. Protect stored cardholder data

2. Encrypt transmission of cardholder data across open, public networks

- Maintain a Vulnerability Management Program

    1. Protect all systems against malware and regularly update antivirus software or programs

    2. Develop and maintain secure systems and applications

- Implement Strong Access Control Measures

    1. Restrict access to cardholder data by business need to know

    2. Identify and authenticate access to system components

    3. Restrict physical access to cardholder data

- Regularly Monitor and Test Networks

    1. Track and monitor all access to network resources and cardholder data

    2. Regularly test security systems and processes

- Maintain an Information Security Policy

    1. Maintain a policy that addresses information security for all personnel

Each requirement must have a declaration, testing processes, and guidance.

There are broadly speaking four compliance levels in the PCI DSS which depend on how many transactions an organization handles and individual credit card brand requirements. The fewer the transactions the simpler the requirements.

Impact on governance strategy

If you are required to follow a data protection law of any kind, you need to make sure that your governance strategy covers them. Most of the compliance work for an organization will be outside of the business intelligence platform, but some of it will be included. Most of the time you will be required to document that Power BI does not violate any of the laws or third-party policies you are required to fulfill. This is usually done via monitoring which will be covered in Chapter 16. The governance strategy is where you set the rules for users of the platform, and it's then used to compare against monitoring to ensure compliance.

As you can read in the earlier sections, these laws are mainly focused on protecting PII data. Some of them apply to an industry while many of them apply to a geographical region. We can therefore conclude that the impact of them on your Power BI governance strategy is the following:

- How to identify PII data

- How to protect PII data in the Power BI platform

    - How to protect PII data where it's stored

    - How to protect PII data while it's being used

- How to make sure data stays in the right region

To ensure your governance strategy covers the laws and third-party policies you are required to follow, a five-step approach can be used:

1. Identify laws and third-party policies you need to follow.

2. Identify specific requirements.

3. Identify overlap and conflicts between different requirements (including internal requirements).

4. Identify which requirements are covered by the platform directly.

5. Incorporate remaining requirements into governance strategy.

In step three, if you identify conflicts, they will need to be resolved. This can be tricky, but a good rule is that the most restrictive should always be chosen. This ensures over compliance which is usually preferred over under compliance. If the conflict dictates that to comply with one you need to breach another, it's advisable to seek legal advice before implementing.

Options in Power BI

Power BI offers several things to help you comply with various laws and policies. The Power BI platform is built on Azure and Microsoft 365 and can take advantage of many features in those platforms that help protect data. In this section we will discuss the most prominent features and how they can help protect your data.

Microsoft Information Protection sensitivity labels

Sensitivity labels are labels that can be applied to artifacts which the Power BI Services then treats differently. Power BI uses labels from the Microsoft 365 Security and Compliance Center. Because Power BI uses the labels from Microsoft 365, the users will see the same labels in Power BI as they see in the Office tools.

In Power BI it is possible to add a sensitivity label to dashboards, reports, datasets, and dataflows. You can create customized labels for your organization in the Microsoft 365 Security and Compliance Center. This could be labels such as Personal, Public, General, Confidential, or Highly Confidential. When you create the labels, you can define what type of protection the label has. It can be things such as encryption, can only be viewed by logged in users, cannot be printed, or many other settings.

For more information about Microsoft Information Protection sensitivity labels in Power BI, please look at the following Microsoft site `https://docs.microsoft.com/en-us/azure/information-protection/what-is-information-protection`.

The important thing here is to create labels that have clear meaning and your users understand. When you apply a label to an artifact in the Power BI platform, the protection settings on them are carried to other software when the user exports data. This applies to Excel, PowerPoint, and PDF. Note that it does not apply when users export data as CSV.

In addition to sensitivity labels, you can also use Microsoft Cloud App Security to set conditional access policies as well as anomaly detection policies for Power BI artifacts.

Both Microsoft Information Protection and Microsoft Cloud App Security come with an extra licensing cost. If in doubt, ask your Microsoft licensing reseller for prices.

Multi-geo tenants

If you are using Power BI Premium, you can decide in which region your premium capacity is. This can allow you to comply with laws that compel you to keep data in a certain region or that restrict you from moving data to certain regions. When you choose a region for your Power BI Premium tenant, Microsoft guarantees that your data is stored in that region alone.

Supported geographies at the time of the writing are

- United States

- Canada

- United Kingdom

- Brazil

- Europe

- Japan

- India

- Asia Pacific

- Australia

- Africa

Each geography can include more than one region. It's worth noting that there are some artifacts that are not moved to the region but instead stay in the home region of the Power BI tenant. These are

- Push datasets

- Excel workbooks

- Dashboard/report metadata: for example, tile names, tile queries

- Service buses for gateway queries or scheduled refresh jobs

- Permissions

- Dataset credential

- Dataflows

If you are legally required to keep all data in a region, you must evaluate if these restrictions will allow you to follow the law.

See more about home tenant and Power BI Premium in Chapters 9 and 10.

Encryption

Encrypting data is one of the best ways of protecting it. When data is encrypted, an unauthorized party cannot read the data even if they can get a hold of it.

Power BI supports encryption on multiple levels. Data can have two states; it's either at rest (stored somewhere) or it's in process. In short data at rest or data in transit is encrypted in Power BI, while data in use can be unencrypted in memory.

All metadata about the Power BI subscription, including artifacts, is encrypted in an Azure SQL Database. All data that is stored in Azure Blob storage is encrypted as well.

Data at rest is encrypted in Power BI. How it's encrypted and where the encryption keys are stored depend on the storage type.

Power BI uses HTTPS, TCP/IP, and TLS for data in process to ensure its encrypted and that the data maintains its integrity. When data is actively being used by a user, Power BI Service creates an in-memory Analysis Services database for the dataset. Data is stored unencrypted in the Analysis Services database to allow the user to access it. When the user is done, the database is evicted from memory and does not exist anymore.

Another feature of Power BI Premium when it comes to encryption is the Bring Your Own Key (BYOK). If you have a legal requirement to encrypt data using your own encryption keys instead of Microsoft's, you can use your own encryption key to encrypt data at rest.

For more information about encryption in Power BI, please look at the Data Storage and Movement section at the following Microsoft site `https://docs.microsoft.com/en-us/power-bi/whitepaper-powerbi-security`.

Power BI compliance offerings

Because Power BI is a part of the Microsoft 365 and Azure platforms, it inherits a lot of security and compliance certifications from those platforms. Power BI has ISO 9001 quality management system standard and ISO/IEC 27001 Information Security Management Standards certifications among many others. If Power BI is certified in any of those certifications that you are certified in, it can help you stay compliant.

For more information about Power BI compliance offering, please look at the following Microsoft site `https://docs.microsoft.com/en-us/ microsoft-365/compliance/offering-home?view=o365-worldwide`.

Summary

There are many laws and third-party policies that might impact your organization. If they do, you need to make sure you are compliant to them. Power BI offers many features that can help you stay compliant. We suggest a five-step approach to ensure your governance strategy, plus the Power BI platform, covers these laws and third-party policies.

Call to action

- Identify which laws, regulations, and policies you need to adhere to when using Power BI.

- Resolve conflicts between laws, regulations, and policies by choosing the most restrictive requirement or seek legal advice before implementing less than the most restrictive requirement.

- Make use of Power BI offering such as Microsoft Information Protection sensitivity labels and multi-geo tenants to help you stay compliant.

- See if the compliance and security certifications that the Power BI platform has can alleviate some compliance requirements.

CHAPTER 5

Application Lifecycle Management

Read this chapter if you would like to find out more information about

- What is Application Lifecycle Management in the context of Power BI

- What tools does Power BI offer for Application Lifecycle Management

- Automation of the Application Lifecycle Management

Building business intelligence dashboards, reports, and datasets involves many steps. Sometimes the process is structured and sometimes it's less structured. Most of the time it follows a basic pattern of requirement gathering, designing, building, testing, and deploying. This is what is called an application lifecycle. The management of this process is called Application Lifecycle Management (ALM). The details of the process differ from organization to organization and even sometimes from project to project, but overall the process is similar. For some organizations, the objective is to automate as many processes as possible; for others manual process is fine. In this chapter we will look at defining what application lifecycle for Power BI is, what Power BI offers to support the application lifecycle, and how you can automate parts of it.

ALM for Power BI

Like any other business intelligence system, you need to follow the traditional ALM process when developing for Power BI. The ALM process is a part of governance, and it helps maintain consistent quality and security of the Power BI artifacts.

Below we describe the different parts of an ALM process and why it's important. We also separate those parts which you can impact with Power BI.

© Ásgeir Gunnarsson and Michael Johnson 2020
Á. Gunnarsson and M. Johnson, *Pro Microsoft Power BI Administration*,
https://doi.org/10.1007/978-1-4842-6567-3_5

ALM process

To develop impactful Power BI reports and datasets, you need to do the following tasks:

Gather requirements

Power BI is a hybrid self-service/enterprise tool. Some reports or datasets are created to answer ad-hoc questions, while others are reports that support regular business processes. For ad-hoc reports you might not have formal requirement, but even though you are doing small projects, there is always some form of requirement gathering even though it might only happen in the developer's mind.

Requirement gathering is normally not a technical process but rather a communicative process. For this reason we will not include requirement gathering in the ALM discussion for Power BI.

Design

After gathering requirements, you will normally design your report or data model. For smaller reports and data models, the design might happen at the same time as you build them, but often you will design them first. If you do formal design, it's normally not done in Power BI but in other tools such as PowerPoint or on paper. For this reason, we will not include the design in the ALM discussion for Power BI.

Build

Building reports and datasets is what most people associate with Power BI development. Reports and datasets can be built using Power BI Desktop or the Power BI Service. Additionally, tables of data can be created using Power BI dataflows in the Power BI Service. There are several best practices and considerations when developing Power BI reports and datasets, including the choice of development tool, storage location, and source control. For these reasons, building reports and datasets are included in our discussion of ALM for Power BI.

Test

When a report or dataset has been built, it's important to test that the results are accurate before it's released to end users. For smaller projects testing might be done only by the developer during the build, but in other instances, testing might be a formal process. The actual testing is not a technical process, but where you store reports and datasets while testing impacts deployment which is covered in the next section. For this reason, testing is included in our discussion of ALM for Power BI.

Deploy

When a report or dataset has been built, you need to publish it in a place where the end user can consume it. This process is called deployment. It takes the report or dataset and moves it from the development environment to the next environment defined in your process. You might have only one environment, in which case there is no deployment, but you might have multiple environments, in which case you have multiple steps in your deployment.

The credibility of a report or a dataset is defined by the end users, so making sure they don't get the report before it's completed and tested for accuracy and design is very important. Deployment is therefore a major component of ALM for Power BI.

Focus

Even though an ALM process includes many parts, we will only be focusing on the technical parts where you can use Power BI. It does not mean that other parts such as requirement gathering or design are not important. It doesn't mean the parts we leave out shouldn't be a part of your ALM process; it just means that they will be similar no matter what tool you have and are therefore not specific to Power BI.

This chapter will focus on the build, test, and deployment processes.

ALM strategies and architectures in Power BI

When Power BI first started, Microsoft envisioned it primarily as a self-service tool. It wasn't until later that Microsoft realized that Power BI had become a popular enterprise tool as well. When they realized that, they needed to start adding enterprise features. While the rate of new features in Power BI is phenomenal, many ALM-specific features are still missing.

ALM strategy is tightly coupled with Power BI architecture as each affects the other. If you decide on a multi-environment architecture, then your ALM strategy must adhere to that. Likewise, if you decide on a multi-environment ALM strategy, your architecture decisions must adhere to that.

Enterprises and IT developers, in particular, are used to and are often required to follow a certain process when they develop business intelligence solutions. These processes include integration to source control systems, testing systems, having multiple environments, and automated deployments.

There is no one-size-fits-all ALM strategy that will work for all organizations. Besides that, your ALM strategy might have different options for different scenarios. You might have one option for IT-driven enterprise reports and datasets and another for self-service reports and datasets, or you might have several options that fit many different scenarios.

Below you will find the different options for build on one hand, and test and deploy on the other. We group test and deployment together as they are tightly coupled.

Build

When considering building Power BI artifacts from an ALM perspective, there are few things to consider:

- What tool to develop in
- Where to store the PBIX files
- Source/version control

Development tool

Power BI has three development tools:

- Power BI Desktop
- Power BI Report Builder
- Power BI Service

Besides those three you can in some instances use third-party tools to develop Power BI datasets as discussed in the following section.

For some artifacts, you can only use one of the tools, but for others you can use multiple options. When you can use more than one, you need to make a decision if you want to allow users to use their tool of choice, or if you want to require them to use one over the other. Your ALM strategy will most often include a section where you name those preferences. Your choices will be influenced by storage and source/version control requirements.

Power BI artifacts you can develop in either Power BI Desktop or Power BI Service:

- Datasets
- Reports

Besides the Power BI Desktop and the Power BI Service, datasets can also be developed using other tools such as SQL Server Data Tools (SSDT), or Tabular Editor if you have Power BI Premium and have enabled the XMLA endpoints.

Power BI Paginated reports can only be built in Power BI Report Builder and other artifacts such as dashboards, and machine learning models can only be developed in the Power BI Service and are therefore not discussed here.

Power BI Desktop has a richer development experience than the Power BI Service and gives you greater control over where you store the artifacts and is an easier option to manage source/version control. Power BI Desktop also has a larger number of source systems to which it can connect.

The Power BI Service offers the option to develop reports and simple datasets in the browser, thereby eliminating the need to install a software (besides a browser) on the user's computer.

If you have Power BI Premium and have XMLA endpoints enabled, SSDT and Tabular Editor offer great flexibility and built-in support for things like source control and scripting. Both these tools are relatively advanced and will mostly be used by IT developers or advanced dataset authors.

Note   If you use SSDT or Tabular Editor to edit a dataset residing in the Power BI Service, you will not be able to use Power BI Desktop to work with that dataset again.

The authors recommend you require your users to use Power BI Desktop over the Power BI Service to develop reports and datasets. The desktop application provides a richer development experience, easier options for source/version control, as well as the option to store the PBIX file in a secure location, making it a better option for most organizations. One exception to this is when you have Power BI Premium, XMLA endpoints enabled, and the technical experience to know how to use advanced tools such as SSDT and/or Tabular Editor. In this case we recommend using them to develop the dataset. Only when you are unable to install Power BI Desktop on users' computers and cannot use external tools such as SSDT and Tabular Editor should you consider using the Power BI Service as a primary development tool for reports and simple datasets.

Where to store the PBIX files

When developing in Power BI Desktop, you have two options to get data. You can either use import mode, which does store the data within the PBIX file, or you can use direct/ live query which does not store any data in the Power BI Desktop file (PBIX). For many reasons not detailed here, many developers use import mode when developing Power BI datasets. If a person has access to the storage location of a PBIX file that has been developed using import mode, they can open the file in Power BI Desktop and get an unrestricted look at all the data. They cannot refresh the data unless they have access to the data source, but the previously imported data is accessible. For this reason, your ALM strategy should require developers to store PBIX files securely. Another reason to specify where users should store PBIX files could be that you require them to use source/ version control (see next section), and to be able to do that they need to store the PBIX file in a particular storage location.

Note   If a user has access (other than Read) to the workspace, the Power BI report has been published to they can download a copy of the PBIX.

Source/version control

At the present time, there is no built-in source/version control in Power BI Desktop or the Power BI Service. External tools such as SSDT and Tabular Editor do offer source control integration, and storage locations such as OneDrive for Business offer automatic version control.

Since the majority of users use Power BI Desktop to develop Power BI reports and datasets, using source/version control is not easy. Power BI Desktop does not have any integration with source/version control tools. If you want to enforce the use of source/ version control, it has to be done using some manual work. The user can manually add the PBIX file to source control after saving it in Power BI Desktop, or you can set your source control system to watch over certain folders where the files are saved. If you require that your developers add comments (recommended) when files are added to source control, you will need them to manually add the PBIX to the source control system if they use Power BI Desktop to develop.

If the developer uses SSDT or Tabular Editor to develop Power BI datasets, they can check in their dataset into their source control system when done developing and add comments directly from the user interface of the development tool. Since SSDT and Tabular Editor can only work with datasets, a report will always be developed in Power BI Desktop or in the Power BI Service. If you require reports to be in source control, they need to be developed in Power BI Desktop and stored manually in source control or developed in the Power BI Service and downloaded as PBIX before being put into source control manually.

If you only require version control, many storage systems, including OneDrive for Business, have automatic version control. The user only needs to save the PBIX in the storage system, and it's automatically versioned. Some of these storage systems allow for comments, but they need to be added after the file is added to source control or while manually uploading the PBIX to the storage system.

One vital thing to consider when putting PBIX files into source/version control is that if the developer uses import mode, the data is included in the file. This gives two concerns. The first is a security concern. If a user has access to the storage system or to the source control system, they can open the file and see the data. The second concern is storage space. If there is a large amount of data in a PBIX file, it can easily grow to 10s or 100s of MB or even to GB. When you put those files in source/version control, a new version of the file is created each time. This is due to the fact the file format is binary, and the source/version control system is not capable of figuring out changes to the metadata and only save those between versions. If you save a 500 MB file multiple times (it's good to save often, right?), you will take 500 MB of space each time.

Note   From the March 2020 version of Power BI Desktop, a new metadata format of the Power BI Desktop file has been introduced in preview. This new metadata format makes it easier for tools to separate metadata from data. This feature should make it easier to only commit changes into source/version control systems.

At the moment, the easiest solution to the problem with using a lot of space is to save the PBIX files as template files (PBIT). When you save a file in Power BI Desktop as PBIT, Power BI Desktop will remove the data and thereby shrink the size of the PBIT file to metadata only. This will bring the size of the file down to a few KB or MB at most. This is an extra step that the developer needs to perform each time they save the file to source/version control.

As with other parts for the ALM process, you might have different strategies for source/version control depending on several factors: how important is the report/dataset, how many users does it reach, how experienced is the developer, what tools does the developer know and have access to, etc. You might, as an example, require IT developers to use source control with commenting, while you require business users to use version control only.

Testing and deployment

As mentioned earlier in this chapter, testing and deployment is all about environments. Environments in BI development are containers that are separated for the purpose of developing, testing, and consuming. In enterprise IT managed BI solutions, there are usually at least three environments: development, test, and production. Sometimes there are additional environments such as pre-production, but there are almost always the previously mentioned three. Many enterprise IT teams are required to have multiple environments. They are often also required to use development data sources for the development environment, test data sources for the test environment, and production data sources for the production environment. This makes the move from one environment to another more complex. Another consideration is that developers are often only allowed to access the development environment, so they are unable to manually deploy to the other environments. Power BI doesn't have any formal concept of environments. Workspaces are normally used as environments in Power BI, and in the newly introduced Deployment Pipelines, workspaces are chained to environments.

The deployment part of the ALM process is about how many environments you should use and how you move content from one environment to the other.

Testing and deployment will be handled together in this book. We do this because testing is in itself not a technical process that has anything specific to do with Power BI but where you test does. If you decide that formal testing is required before reports and datasets are seen by end users, it will affect how complex your deployment process is. Using only one environment (workspace) is not applicable if you require formal testing, so you will have to have at least two.

In Power BI, there are two ways to deploy a report or a dataset. You either deploy using the development tool, or you use the Power BI REST API. Using the development tool is always a manual process, but using the Power BI REST API can be automated.

Recently Power BI introduced Deployment Pipelines meant to make it easier for users to manage deployment. When this is written, there are only manual deployments using the GUI in Power BI Deployment Pipelines.

In the following sections, we have described the two most used deployment strategies that are used with Power BI. One is simpler and often used by business developers, while the other is more complex and often used by more advanced business developers and IT developers. There are other options, but these represent two approaches that are most commonly used by the two typical Power BI development groups: business users and IT developers.

Simple deployment model

Not everyone needs a complex ALM setup to work with Power BI. Some reports and datasets are used by a small number of people or change very infrequently, and are not required to go through rigorous testing. In these cases, a simple deployment model might be enough. The most common simple deployment model is where you have one workspace and one workspace app. In these instances, the development environment is Power BI Desktop, the test environment is the workspace, and the production environment is the workspace app. The author develops using Power BI Desktop, then publishes to a workspace in the Power BI Service, and then publishes the workspace app when the report/dataset is ready for the end user. Figure 5-1 shows the simple deployment model with one workspace and a workspace app on top of that.

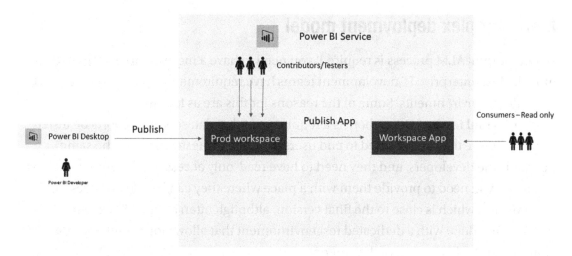

Figure 5-1. *Simple deployment process*

This type of deployment model has several pros and cons.

Pros:

- Simple and easy to setup.

- Easy to manage how content goes from one environment to another.

- Possible to separate access to environments.

Cons:

- All manual process.

- Changing connection from a development data source to test and/ or production has to be done in Power BI Desktop, requiring another deployment, or using parameters in the Power BI Service.

- Although changes to reports and dashboards are not available in the workspace app until it is (re-)published, changes to datasets are available immediately, which can cause reports and dashboards to brake or become visible to end users untested.

This simple deployment method is best suited to situations where the development is entirely in the hands of business users, or there is little need for formal testing, and the data source doesn't have multiple environments. It's important from a governance and administration perspective to make sure that users know the limitations of this approach, so they don't accidentally expose data to end users that is untested or wrong.

More complex deployment model

When a formal ALM process is required, you need to have a more complex deployment model. Most enterprise IT development teams have requirements that dictate the need for multiple environments. Some of the reasons for this are as follows:

For formal testing. Often there is a requirement that datasets and reports be tested formally before they are released to end users. Usually, the testers are not the same people as the developers, and they need to have read-only access to the content. In these instances, you need to provide them with a place where they can have read access and test a version which is close to the final version, although often built with test data. This is most often done with a dedicated test environment that allows for granular access control and stable versions of the content.

Switching between data source environments. Many enterprise systems have multiple environments. When a Power BI report or dataset is developed against these systems, the developer might not have access to the systems production environment. This is both for security and performance reasons. In these instances, the developer will develop against the development environment of the source system. When the report or dataset is ready for testing, the dataset needs to be handed over to the test environment and the data source changed to point to the test system. The same goes for when the dataset is deployed to production. How you change the connection string manually or automatically depending on your deployment strategy.

Separation of duties. In some instances, you don't want the same person to do the development and be responsible for releasing a report or dataset to production. Some of the reasons for this are

- The developer doesn't have access to production data

- The report or dataset being deployed to production is only a part of a larger deployment, and thereby the deployment needs to be in the hands of someone with the oversight of the whole

Whatever the reason is, you can accomplish this by using multiple environments and giving the correct access to each environment for those who need it. For more information on users and security, see Chapter 12. Figure 5-2 shows how a more complex deployment process might look like.

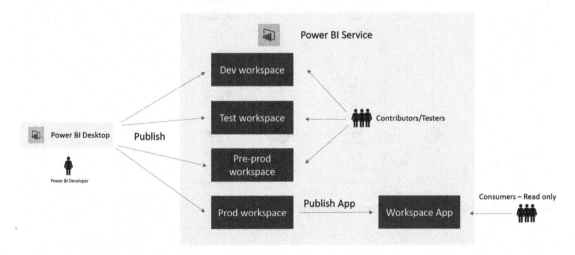

Figure 5-2. *Advanced deployment process*

If you decide you need a more complex deployment model, you can go down two different paths: manual or automatic. What path you choose will depend on things such as level of expertise, tooling available, and cost-benefit.

Manual deployment

Manual deployments in a setup with multiple environments can be done in two ways: using the development tool to deploy the report or dataset or using the Deployment Pipelines in Power BI.

Manually using development tool. Using the development tool to deploy from one environment to another is a simple setup. Each user who is responsible for a deployment opens the PBIX file or dataset model from the chosen storage location and deploys it to the desired environment. The pros of this method are that it's simple when the setup is done and can be done in all versions of Power BI. The cons are that each user needs to know what the destination workspace is called and make sure they publish to the right one. They also need to have development tools installed on an available machine, and you can only deploy one report and/or dataset at a time. Figure 5-3 shows how a manual deployment process might look like.

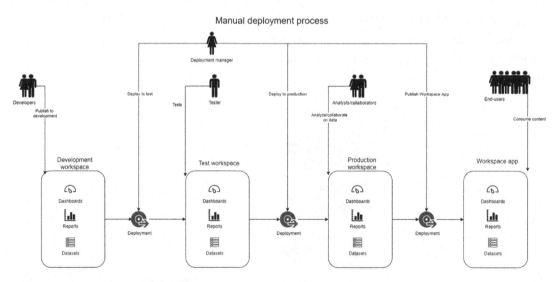

Figure 5-3. *Manual deployment process*

Manual using Deployment Pipelines. If you have Power BI Premium, you can use Deployment Pipelines to manage the deployment between environments. Deployment Pipelines are (at the moment of this writing) three different workspaces where you can migrate content between them. The nice thing about the Deployment Pipelines is that it's a wizard-like experience where you can pick and choose which items you want to move between the environments. At the moment it is only possible to have three environments, development, test, and production. You need to manually create the one environment, but you can use the wizard to create the other one or two environments depending on your needs. You can set up parameters and rules to manage values that change from one environment to another such as the connection string. The pros about this method is that you can do partial or full deployment of all content in one go. Since it's wizard driven, it's very easy to use. Another big benefit is that only the workspace admins and members can use the Deployment Pipeline making it easier to control the process. The cons are that it's Power BI Premium only; if you don't have Premium, you don't have this option. Another drawback is that it's only available through the user interface which makes it manual only. In Figure 5-4 the Deployment Pipeline can be seen.

Figure 5-4. *Power BI Deployment Pipeline*

Automatic deployment

Automatic deployments can be done using the Power BI REST API. In some cases, and this is especially important for mission critical reports and datasets, you want to automate as much of the ALM process as possible. One of the reasons you might favor automating your deployment process is that you have a very established DevOps/ CI process that includes automated deployments. You might also do this as a way of optimizing and/or securing the process from manual errors. Whatever the reason, you can automate the deployment process for Power BI workspace content. Figure 5-5 shows how an automated deployment process might look like.

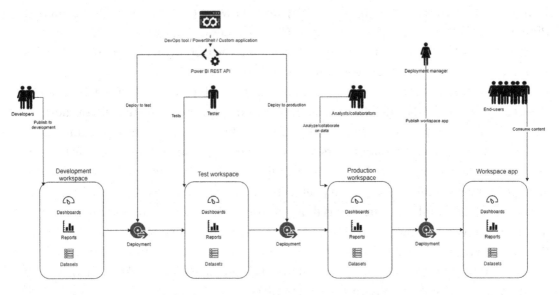

Figure 5-5. *Automated deployment process*

Automatic deployments with a custom developed process. If you want to do automated deployments, you will have to program it yourself. If you have Power BI Premium, are using the XMLA endpoints to manage your datasets, and have an established SQL Server Analysis Services deployment process, then you might be able to add Power BI datasets to that. Otherwise you need to create your own scripts. The scripts you create can either use the PowerShell modules Microsoft has created for the Power BI REST API, or you can build your own encapsulation of the REST API endpoints. Once you have developed your scripts, you need to add them to some type of automation tool that can handle running them on demand or automatically based on some rules.

Creating automated deployments for Power BI requires technical knowledge and effort. Before deciding to go down the automated route, you should create a cost/benefit analysis to see if the development effort is worth it. When doing the cost/benefit analysis, you should consider the following:

- Time

    - Saved developer time

    - Faster deployments

- Accuracy

- Possible human errors during deployment

- Deployed on the wrong time

- Not right artifacts included

There might be other things to consider, but the point is that it's not just the actual developer time you should consider when deciding whether or not to develop automated deployments.

Summary

There are two parts of the ALM process that can be impacted by Power BI, build and deployment. For build you want to include a process for file storage and use of source/version control.

For deployment you need to consider several things. For small projects or when you don't need formal testing, using one workspace is enough. Then Power BI Desktop is the development environment, the workspace is the test environment, and the app is the production environment. If you need formal testing or if requirements dictate that you use multiple environments (workspaces), you have to use a more complex deployment process. This process can be manual, or it can be automated using the Power BI REST API. It is important to consider if automating is worth the cost of developing it, but when doing so consider many different factors besides development cost such as quality and speed.

Call for action

- During Power BI development, ALM processes are sometimes used as a formal process.

- Then building Power BI artifacts, you should consider safe storage and source/version control.

- Power BI doesn't have a concept of environments, but workspaces can be treated as such.

- In smaller deployments you might consider using Power BI Desktop as a development environment, workspace as test environment, and app as production environment.

- When doing bigger, more critical deployments, you will most often have different workspaces as different environments and deploy artifacts between them.

- When deploying Power BI artifacts, you can do it manually or automated.

- Power BI has a feature called Power BI Deployment Pipelines you can use to deploy from one environment (workspace) to another.

- Automated deployment is done via the Power BI REST API.

- When deciding on whether to use automation or not, consider cost, potential for errors, and time savings.

CHAPTER 6

Training

Training is one of the key components of a governance strategy. This is no different for Power BI governance. If users know what the governance strategy includes and they know how to use the tool correctly, the chances of an unintentional governance breach are far less. This chapter discusses what the training requirements are for Power BI, who to train in Power BI, how to best organize training, and ways to discover what training is needed.

Training requirements

If you want to have a successful Power BI implementation, training is very important. You want to train everyone who touches Power BI but in a different way depending on how they use the product. You want to make sure you get to everyone and deliver the right training based on their needs. Training users to properly use Power BI and apply best practices will deliver value faster and will help report and dataset developers adhere to governance standards. To make it easier to define training requirements, it's a good idea to create different categories of training.

Training categories

As with most types of software, how you use Power BI will dictate what training requirements there are. Some users will use all of Power BI as content creators, some will use parts of it as content creators, while others will only consume content created by others. Superusers might create and consume, and a person might go from one type of user to another over time. It's important to define training categories that fit how people use Power BI. The most common training categories are

Á. Gunnarsson and M. Johnson, *Pro Microsoft Power BI Administration*,
https://doi.org/10.1007/978-1-4842-6567-3_6

- Consumer

- Report developer

- Report and dataset developer

- Administrators

For each category, there is a definition of who belongs to it as well as what training is required. In the following section, we will describe each category and what training is needed.

Consumer training

Consumers are normally defined as Power BI users that will only consume reports or dashboards created by others. They will never create or modify their own content. This is normally the biggest group of Power BI users and is often overlooked when it comes to training. This is the easiest group to train.

The content of the consumer training is usually general training in navigating Power BI. How to log in and find content, how to open a report or dashboard, how to use the "toolbar" above a Power BI report/dashboard, and the most common ways to interact with a Power BI report/dashboard such as navigating between pages, using buttons and bookmarks, and using slicers and filters.

Report developer

A report developer is a person that will create Power BI reports on top of ready-made datasets created by others. They don't create their own datasets but will use datasets such as Power BI datasets or SQL Server Analysis Services models.

The training for this group of people is mostly about the presentation of data. It will often contain topics such as visualization, storytelling, and publishing and sharing.

A typical training course for report developers will consist of the following topics:

- Introduction to Power BI

  - Components of Power BI

- Data visualization

  - Introduction to visualization best practices

  - Visualizing data in Power BI

  - Native and custom visuals in Power BI Desktop

- Storytelling
  - Bookmarks and selection pane
  - Report page tooltips
  - Designing for mobile devices
- Power BI Service
  - Introducing workspaces
  - Sharing options in the Power BI Service
  - Dashboards vs. reports
- Introduction to the Power BI development process
  - Where is the document
  - Content of the document
- Governance
  - Where is the documentation
  - How do I make sure I'm compliant
  - Best practices and common sense

Report and dataset developers

Report and dataset developers are the most technical and challenging group of users that will create both datasets and reports.

The training for this group of users will often contain all the topics from the report developer course plus data topics such as getting and transforming data, data modeling, security, refreshing data, and DAX.

- Introduction to Power BI
  - Components of Power BI
- Getting and cleaning data
  - Connecting to data
  - Direct/Live query vs. import

- Query editor
- Transformation(s)
- Data modeling
  - Why is data modeling important?
  - Relationships in Power BI
  - Attribute properties and formatting
  - Date table
- DAX
  - Introduction to DAX
  - Calculated columns vs. measures
- Data visualization
  - Introduction to visualization best practices
  - Visualizing data in Power BI
  - Native and custom visuals in Power BI Desktop
- Storytelling
  - Bookmarks and selection pane
  - Report page tooltips
  - Designing for mobile devices
- Power BI Service
  - Introducing workspaces
  - Sharing options in the Power BI Service
  - Dashboards vs. reports
  - Row-level security
  - Scheduled refresh vs. other types of connections
  - Data Gateway's role in the service
- Introduction to the Power BI development process

- Where is the document
- Content of the document
- Governance
  - Where is the documentation
  - How do I make sure I'm compliant
  - Best practices and common sense

Administrators

A Power BI adminitrator is a person who has the Power BI administrator role in Microsoft 365. Normally there are not many Power BI administrators compared to the other groups of users. They also have different kinds of responsibilities than content creators and consumers. However, the same applies to the administrators as other groups of users that a trained administrator is more effective and less likely to breach governance than not trained one.

The training for these individuals will contain training in the Power BI admin portal, security, data administration, and workspace and app administration. There might be a specific gateway administrator, but if not the Power BI administrator should be trained in administrating the gateway. If the organization has Power BI Premium, they will also be trained in capacity administration.

Note   Power BI is updated nearly every month, and is therefore evolving fast. These topics represent what we find essential knowledge of Power BI functionality and theory that a Power BI Developer/Administrator should know. If there are functionalities in Power BI at the time when you read this which you find essential, then they might have been added to the product after this book is written.

It's worth noting that the preceding training requirements are only focused on the tool and the governance strategy. Developers and consumers might need additional training specific to the type of business, culture, and region the organization operates in. These topics can be essential to the successful implementation of reports and analysis but are not specific to Power BI and therefore not covered here.

Training delivery

Deciding on the type of delivery for Power BI training can be difficult. Ideally, everyone gets one-on-one training from an expert for as long as they need and have unlimited access to material and trainers. This is, of course, unrealistic. Normally the decision comes down to balancing quality and cost. You want to spend your effort where it gives the most value and automates as much as possible.

You can roughly divide training delivery methods into the following five categories:

- In-person
  - Tutoring/mentoring
  - Instructor-led classes
- Online
  - Instructor-led classes
  - Self-paced guided learning
  - Self-paced open training

Generally speaking, the cost of in-person training is greater than online training, but the outcome will often be better. Of course, people learn in different ways, and some might get more out of a self-paced guided learning compared to instructor-led classes. As the cost of in-person training is normally greater but with better results, you might want to focus in-person training on employees needing the most complex training. Another approach would be to figure out where self-paced online training makes sense and have in-person training for the rest.

Tip   It's worth mentioning that Microsoft offers online self-paced guided learning that organizations can use free of charge. You find it here: `https://docs.microsoft.com/en-us/power-bi/guided-learning/`.

Suggested delivery method

People react differently to training, and each organization has different budgets and other considerations. This makes deciding on a delivery method hard, and there might even be more than one delivery method for each training category. The next section presents our suggestion on the best delivery method for each training category. It's not the only way this can be done; it's just the most effective way to delivering training in our opinion.

Consumers

The appropriate delivery method for consumer training is videos or training manuals. Self-paced open training or guided learning is sufficient and often more appropriate for this type of users as they might want to learn about specific functionality instead of everything at once. In-person training is not needed and normally too expensive, due to the number of people. The exception from this is if you want to train a subset of consumers on a specific report or dashboard. That is often best done with live classroom training as it can also include analyzing relevant data.

Report developers

The report developer training is best done in instructor-led classroom training, but can also be done via instructor-led online training if that better fits the budget of the organization. It's also possible to use self-paced guided learning by creating an on-demand video course, but it's the authors' opinion that the users will get the fastest start and biggest benefit from an in-person classroom training.

Report and dataset developers

This group of people are the most advanced users and are key in successful implementation. Like with the report developer training, the report and dataset developer training is best done in instructor-led classroom training. Still, it can be done via instructor-led online training if that better fits the budget of the organization. It's also possible to use self-paced guided learning by creating an on-demand video course, but it's the authors' opinion that the users will get the fastest start and biggest benefit from an in-person classroom training.

Who to train and how to prioritize

One of the things the authors have seen with many organizations is that they struggle to know who to train and how to prioritize when to train them. Normally the training budget is not endless, and you want to focus training on those who need it and when they need it. If you train a user as a report and dataset developer and they don't use the acquired skills for few months, the chances are they will need to be, at least partially, retrained. This section will give an idea of how you can identify and prioritize who to train.

Who to train

As mentioned previously, you want to focus a limited training budget on those who need it. In many organizations, a vast number of people use Power BI. Those who manage Power BI don't necessarily know everyone using Power BI, so they have difficulty offering training to the right people. Generally speaking, you want to train those who use Power BI in any shape or form, and in some cases you might want to train them before they start using the product. In other words, you want to train everyone who has a license and uses the product.

Information about who is using Power BI can be extracted from the Power BI Activity log (see Chapter 16). Information about who has Power BI Pro licenses needed for development can be extracted from the Microsoft 365 API. You need to store the information about the licenses gathered from the Microsoft 365 API as you want to be able to target new licenses only. There is no need to offer training to the same users over and over.

We suggest the following:

- For everyone who has gotten a Power BI license (Pro or Free), you send them an invitation to go through the consumer training, which is in the form of online videos or training manuals so that the users can do it in their own time.

- When you can see in the Power BI Activity log that a person creates a report or a dataset for the first time, you point them to the governance documentation, and if you are offering regular training, you point them to where they can sign up for it.

Depending on how you offer training, much of this can be automated. Getting data about creators and licenses can be automated using familiar data integration tools. Querying the data and sending emails with the location of governance and training material as well as signups for training courses can also be automated with workflow tools such as Azure Logic Apps or Microsoft Power Automate.

Summary

Training plays a key role in a successful Power BI implementation and a well-governed platform. Trained users deliver greater value and are less likely to breach governance. The best way is to design different types of training for different types of users and use an appropriate delivery method based on requirements and budget. Discovering who needs to be trained and offering training can be partly automated, but the main thing is that you train all users for their role.

Call to action

- Train all users of Power BI.
- Tailor the training based on user type.
- Tailor the delivery method based on the type of training balancing budget and requirements.

CHAPTER 7

Documentation

Many people in IT feel that documentation is a necessary evil. As a result, it's often done late, at the wrong level, and not maintained properly. This makes many people wonder, why bother? Well-done documentation can be very valuable to many stakeholders, and it's not just the author who will benefit from good documentation. In this chapter, we will discuss why you should document your Power BI solutions, what types of documentation you should consider, and how to store the documents. We will also provide a list of appropriate documents as well as examples of some of them.

Why document Power BI solutions

Documentation comes in many shapes, and there are many reasons why things are documented. In our mind, the main reasons for documenting a Power BI solution are

- Compliance
- Support requirements
- Overview documents

Compliance

Sometimes the purpose of a document is to show that a solution is compliant with internal and external governance requirements. In these cases, the correctness, maintenance, and storage of the documents are often critical. Some compliance requirements dictate what you need to document in addition to how and how long you should store the documents. Sometimes the requirements won't dictate this, but even so if your solution gets audited, it's very important that the documents are clear, concise, and readily available.

© Ásgeir Gunnarsson and Michael Johnson 2020
Á. Gunnarsson and M. Johnson, *Pro Microsoft Power BI Administration*,
https://doi.org/10.1007/978-1-4842-6567-3_7

Support requirements

Supporting a solution can be hard. If you were not involved in the development, it can take a great deal of time to familiarize yourself with the solution enough to be able to service a support request. Supporting a well-documented solution with up-to-date documentation is much easier than supporting a poorly documented one. This is equally valid for developed solutions, solution architecture, and administrative setup of the tenant. The documents need to be readily available and at an appropriate level so that the support person has the best possible opportunity to solve support requests fast.

Overview documents

Sometimes the purpose of documentation is to give stakeholders an overview of the solution. This can be to secure funding, document progress, or any other reason where you need to provide stakeholders an overview of the solution. These documents might be architectural documents, or they might be solution development documentation. The documents are often project-based but are good to have when someone new needs to familiarize themselves with the solution without going too deep.

Types of documents

Generally speaking, there are three kinds of documentation you might consider for a Power BI solution:

- Administration documentation and processes

- Governance documentation and processes

- Content documentation

As the focus of this book is on administration and governance, we will focus on the first two groups, administration documentation and processes as well as governance documentation and processes. Although content documentation is very important and will document how the solution is built and therefore if it's compliant, it's not considered administration or governance documents. In the following section we try to categorize the two groups we cover in this chapter and define what documents fall under them. Please note that this definition is not exhaustive, and there might be other types of documents you would want to add to the categories.

Administration documentation and processes

In the administration documentation and process category, you will find documents that describe the following:

- The overall setup of the tenant

- Documentation of the tenant-level setting

- Maintenance process documents

- Capacity administration processes

The documents in this category are aimed at tenant-level administrators, and in some cases, capacity administrators. They either describe how the tenant is set up or how administrators should work with tenant-level settings or capacity administration.

Governance documentation and processes

In the governance documentation and processes, you will find documents that describe the following:

- What internal or external standards and regulations Power BI needs to follow

- How content should be developed

- How content is distributed to end users

- What security requirements Power BI solutions need to adhere to

- What training requirements are toward content creators and consumers

The documents in this category are aimed at all users of Power BI, but most of the documents are aimed at administrators and content creators. Most of the documents describe how you should create content or administer Power BI.

Storing documentation

In some cases, your governance strategy will dictate how to store certain documents; in others it won't. Having a strategy for how you store different kinds of documents will greatly improve the accessibility of your documents as both document creators and users will know where to find them. If you have a document management system, you should consider placing the documents there, especially if your users are familiar with it and know how to use it to find documents. If you don't have a document management system or you are unable to use it for Power BI documents, you will need to find an alternative storage option. When you consider what storage is best suited for these documents, you should consider the following:

- Who has access

- How is access controlled (are you able to control access yourself or do you need help)

- Can you link to the storage using a relative path

- Are you able to categorize the documents

- How easy is it to discover the documents

Who has access

When choosing a storage option for governance and administration documents, it's important that users can access it. All too often, we see organizations choose a place where not all of the intended users have access, and it's difficult to add new users. This is typically some IT document storage. To help you in finding the right place, you should map who needs access to every type of document, and based on that, find a storage solution these users can access.

How is access controlled

When choosing a storage solution for governance and administration documents, it's important to consider how access is controlled. You want to have a clear process for adding or removing users and who can edit the documents. If you choose a highly governed storage where the process of adding people is very strict, you need to make sure if your intended target group can get access at all and that the process is not a hindrance for adoption. Most of the administration and governance documents for Power BI don't need highly governed storage as you would ideally get them in front of every user of Power BI. Of course, some documents are only relevant to some users, but there is rarely anything that needs to be hidden from users. With this in mind you might want to find storage where access control is easy or even in some cases non-existent. This is not to say that anyone should be able to edit the documents, but read access should be as open as possible. In general, it's better to focus on categorization and ease of use than security. If you have governance or administration documents that include sensitive information, then in these cases, security is important.

Can you link to the storage using a relative path

One of the most certain things in life is change. Having the ability to use relative paths to your storage allows you to change the location of the storage or even switch storage completely without too many interruptions for the end users. A relative path is a path or a URL which behind the scenes is mapped to the real location of the document. In contrast a fixed path points to the exact place where the documents are stored. If you change the underlying storage location, the relative path can be re-pointed to the new storage location without the users having to change anything or even knowing the change took place. If you have fixed paths and need to change, you will need to communicate the change well so that users are still able to access the documents after the change.

Are you able to categorize the documents

Some storage systems and even some document management systems don't allow for categorization or only allow for limited categorization. Before finding the right storage, try to draw up how you would like to categorize the documents. You can survey actual end users to get to know how they normally navigate documentation content to help you design the right way to categorize the documents. The main thing is that you want to make sure that users can quickly and easily find the correct documents.

How easy is it to discover the documents

If users don't know where the documents are or if they cannot find the correct documents, then the effectiveness of the documentation effort is reduced. Therefore, you should consider how users discover and find the right document. If users are used to finding documents in a certain place in your organization, you should make sure that the administration and governance documents for Power BI are discoverable in the same place. It doesn't mean that the documents need to be stored in the same place, just that users can find them the same way as with other documents. When the users have discovered the location of the documents, you need to make it easy for them to find the correct document. One of the things that help them find the right documents is the categorizations mentioned earlier, but when you choose your storage, you should make sure that users can search for documents in as easy manner as possible. Before you invest to much in search, you should consider how many documents you have. If you have very few, search becomes less important; however if you have many documents, it's more important. Here it is important to think ahead and try to envision how many documents you will have when the implementation is done.

What to document

This section describes different documents that we feel are relevant when it comes to Power BI administration and governance documentation. This is not an exhaustive list, rather examples of documents that we have found useful. Your requirements might mean that you need more or less documents or that you will combine or split up documents in this list.

Administration documentation and processes

These are the documents we often see in the administration documentation and processes category:

- Tenant setting documentation
- Changing tenant-level settings process
- Adding new administrators process
- Administrating Power BI Premium process

The following section will go through them one by one and suggest what content they should cover.

Tenant setting documentation

The tenant setting documentation includes documentation on all settings found in the Power BI admin portal. Some settings, such as publish to web or external sharing, are very important from a governance perspective, but all of them impact the tenant usage. As you cannot automate the import of these settings, you will need to write the settings down manually and maintain that document. The Power BI Activity log can show you if a setting was changed, but it will only show you what it was changed to, not what it was changed from. For this reason, having all the settings documented is very important. If a setting is changed by a mistake or malicious intent, you need to know what to change it back to.

Most of the tenant-level settings have two components. The first being if the setting is on or off and the second is for which users does it apply. We recommend that both components are documented. In Figure 7-1 Power BI tenant settings documentation, you can see an example of how such a document could look.

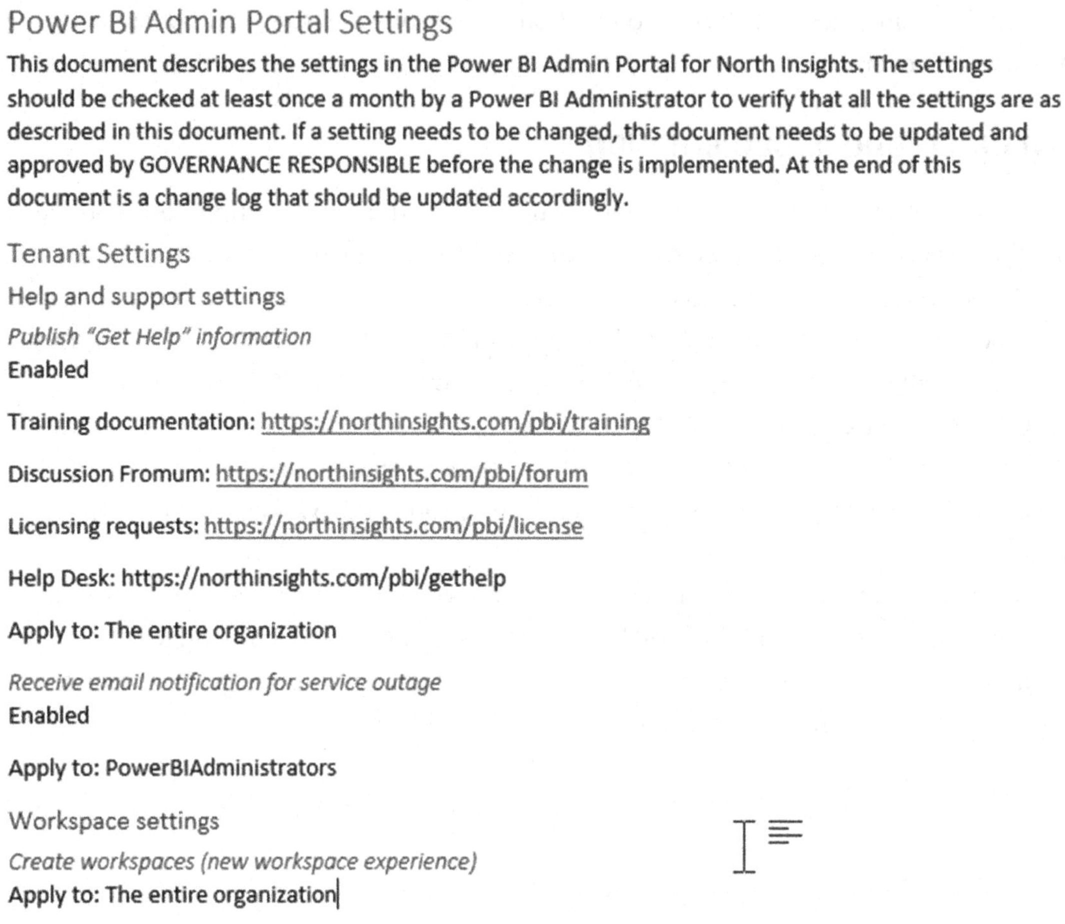

Power BI Admin Portal Settings

This document describes the settings in the Power BI Admin Portal for North Insights. The settings should be checked at least once a month by a Power BI Administrator to verify that all the settings are as described in this document. If a setting needs to be changed, this document needs to be updated and approved by GOVERNANCE RESPONSIBLE before the change is implemented. At the end of this document is a change log that should be updated accordingly.

Tenant Settings

Help and support settings

Publish "Get Help" information
Enabled

Training documentation: https://northinsights.com/pbi/training

Discussion Fromum: https://northinsights.com/pbi/forum

Licensing requests: https://northinsights.com/pbi/license

Help Desk: https://northinsights.com/pbi/gethelp

Apply to: The entire organization

Receive email notification for service outage
Enabled

Apply to: PowerBIAdministrators

Workspace settings

Create workspaces (new workspace experience)
Apply to: The entire organization

Figure 7-1. *Power BI tenant settings documentation*

Changing tenant-level settings process

The changing tenant-level settings process describes how you go about changing tenant-level settings. It will describe who can do it, who gives permission for it, and whom to inform. It will also describe how you do the actual change. This process is normally not very big but can be very handy for newer administrators. It also makes sure that the user follows the right governance procedure when changing tenant-level settings. It's important that the administrator is careful when changing these settings as they impact every user in the tenant.

Adding new administrator process

Adding new Power BI administrators is not done in Power BI but in Microsoft 365. A Power BI administrator cannot add other Power BI administrators. The process of adding a new Power BI administrator might, therefore, not be more than a description of how to request new administrators. In some instances, it will just be a description of how to add a person to the Power BI administrator role in Microsoft 365, in which case it's a process shared with Microsoft 365 administrators who are the ones that can add the role to users.

Administrating Power BI Premium

If you have Power BI Premium, there are additional administration tasks associated with that. The administrating Power BI Premium process describes the administration of Power BI Premium capacities. The document will detail how to assign and monitor capacities as well as how to request more capacity.

Governance documentation and processes

These are the documents we often see in the governance documentation and processes category:

- Governance strategy documentation

- Standards and regulation documentation (these might be several documents)

- Development process

- Publishing and sharing process

- Security process

- Naming standard process

- Support process

- Training requirements

- Roles and responsibilities

- Monitoring strategy and requirements

- Reporting breaches process

The following section will go through them one by one and suggest what content they should cover.

Governance strategy documentation

The governance strategy documentation covers the overall governance strategy. It will often have references to all the other governance documents or be placed in a document management system so that it is clear that this document is not the detailed document for each section. It will often include a RACI (document describing who is Responsible, Accountable, Consulted, and Informed) or other documentation of who is responsible for the strategy as well.

Standards and regulation documentation

The standards and regulation documentation might be one or more documents describing what internal standards and regulations Power BI solutions need to adhere to. There might be one document for each standard or regulation, or there might be one document with a section for each. These documents will often refer to other documents residing outside of the Power BI governance documentation repository. This is because the actual documentation of the standard or regulation is normally not contained in the Power BI governance documentation, as the standards and regulations will most often impact all data and information systems.

Development process

Power BI content can be developed in different places; if you don't have a process describing how it should be developed, developers will do it in unstructured ways and potentially store the source files in ways that compromise the data.

The development process document will describe how Power BI content developers should go about developing Power BI solutions. It will typically describe where (e.g., in Power BI Desktop and/or Tabular Editor) you develop the content and where and how you store the development files, including usage of version/source control.

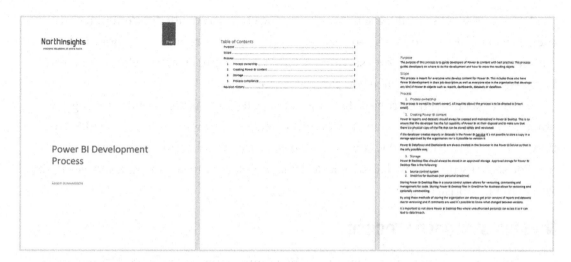

Figure 7-2. *Example of a development process*

Publishing and sharing process

The publishing and sharing process will typically describe how to set up multiple environments in Power BI, how to promote content from one environment to another, and how to share content to content consumers. For organizations with Power BI Premium, Deployment Pipelines can simplify and make publishing and sharing easier. No matter if you have Power BI Premium or not, it's not a trivial topic, and having a process that helps users setting publishing and sharing up and how to get content from one environment to another is a very important part of Power BI development. This process will describe different approaches and when to use which approach. Not all developers will use the same approach as it might depend on the content's complexity, importance, and number of users, how many environments to use, as well as how to promote content from one environment to another. Sharing Power BI content is where most governance breaches happen. If users are unsure on how to share, they might share content too broadly or with the wrong consumers by accident. This process will describe different approaches to sharing content and when to use which approach. Not all developers will use the same approach as it might depend on the content's security requirements, data sensitivity, and the type of consumers what sharing approach to use.

Security process

A security process describes how to secure Power BI content. This is usually split into two categories: object-level security and data security.

For object-level security, the process describes how to secure different objects such as Power BI Desktop files, workspaces, apps, datasets, reports, dashboards, and dataflows. It will often have one section for each type of object, although it might also have one section for each place you can secure the object.

For data security, the process describes how data is secured beyond securing the object. This will most often involve how and when to use row-level security (RLS) in Power BI as well as how and when to use the security model of the data sources.

The security process will also include a section on how to secure data sources in the Power BI Enterprise Gateway.

Naming standard process

One of the most undervalued processes is the naming standard process. Having this process early in the Power BI implementation will greatly improve the usability of the Power BI environment. Finding workspaces, reports, dashboards, and datasets can be very tricky when you have hundreds of workspaces with no clear naming convention. Often this process will reference a corporate IT naming standard (if one exists). In general, this process will describe how names are constructed for different objects. This includes how to name workspaces for different environments.

Support process

The support process will describe common scenarios like access requests, no data incidents, wrong data incidents, and change requests to Power BI content and guide the supporter on how to react. Depending on how established your support process is, your support organization might do none, some, or all of the support on Power BI content. If you have a support organization, they will get support requests on Power BI because users are used to getting support there. Therefore, it's important that you integrate your Power BI support into your current support organization even though it's only for them to pass it on to the "real" Power BI supporters. The support process will also have a section to show the support team how to identify an owner of a Power BI object so they know who to contact for expert help. The process will also contain the location of solution documentation for Power BI content. The main purpose of this process is to shorten the time to resolve support requests and prevent IT support organizations from neglecting Power BI support requests as they often don't have the expertise (as the authors have frequently seen).

Training requirements

Training is one of the best ways to prevent governance breaches. A trained developer or consumer is less likely to accidentally breach the governance policy. Many organizations don't allow users to publish content until they have received training in the tools as well as the governance strategy, to prevent accidental breaches. The same goes for consumers of solutions with sensitive data. However, your approach to this is having a training strategy that lists the training requirements for users can greatly help your governance effort. The training requirements document will describe what training or type of training a user needs to have to perform a certain task. It will also describe how the user can access or request the training.

Roles and responsibilities

To have a successful Power BI implementation, it's important to have well-defined roles and responsibilities. This is most likely different from organization to organization, and in some cases the same person might have more than one role. The most common roles are Power BI administrator, Power BI Gateway administrator, Power BI auditor, and Power BI supporter(s). This document will describe the roles and their responsibilities. The purpose is twofold. One is to make it clear and obvious what the roles require, who occupies them, and how and when users can contact them. The second purpose is to make it clear that the people occupying those roles have a definition of them and can justify the time it takes to perform the role.

Monitoring strategy and requirements

The monitoring strategy and requirements document will describe the purpose of the monitoring, what has to be monitored, and how the data is processed and stored. The purpose of these documents is not necessary to describe how Power BI is monitored, but more to describe the overall strategy and requirements for the monitoring. It will often reference data processing policies and the standards and regulations process if there are sensitive data in the monitoring output. Most of the time, it will include a section on auditing type of monitoring and sometimes inventory type of monitoring depending on the needs of your organization.

Automation method for delivering documentation to the end user

One of the main hindrances for governance implementation is the difficulty in making the users aware of the documents. One of the ways you can use is to automate as much of it as you can. You can consider automating the delivery of documents for the following:

User consumes Power BI content for the first time: You can compare the Power BI Activity log entries with historical activity log data to see if a user consumes Power BI content for the first time. If you see in the Power BI Activity log that a user consumes Power BI content for the first time, you can automatically send them a link to the governance documentation and point out specific processes for consumers. You can also point them to training content (internal or external) relevant to consumers of Power BI content.

User creates Power BI content for the first time: You can compare the Power BI Activity log entries with historical activity log data to see if a user creates Power BI content for the first time. If you see in the Power BI Activity log that a user creates Power BI content for the first time, you can automatically send them a link to the governance documentation and point out specific processes for content creators, including the development process, publish and sharing process, and the security process. You can also point them to training content (internal or external) relevant to content creators.

Summary

Administration and governance documentation are a very important part of ensuring compliance of Power BI implementations and solutions. You need to consider what type of documents to create, how, and where to store them, and what they should include. This chapter has guidance on these questions and example of the content for different documents we feel are important.

Call to action

- Document Power BI to ensure compliance and to help administrators and supporters.

- Administration and governance documents are both describing best practices and how to's as well as processes around different ways of working with Power BI in a compliant way.

- Make sure you store the administration and governance documents in a place where users find them easily, you can catalog them well, and the users can search the documents.

- Make sure that all users that need access to the administration and governance documents (most often all users that touch Power BI) can get access to the document storage.

- Consider automating the delivery of the governance documents to users when they start using Power BI.

PART II

Administration

CHAPTER 8

Introduction to Power BI Administration

Read this chapter if you would like to find out more information about

- Different administration roles in the Power BI ecosystem

- Tasks typically undertaken by the Power BI administrator

Power BI administration, like the administration of any IT system, focuses foremost on ensuring that the system conforms to all legal, governance, and operational requirements set by the organization. In addition to this, the administrator needs to ensure that the system runs efficiently. As we discussed in Chapter 1, there is no single correct approach on how to administer a Power BI environment. Every organization has different policies and will implement these policies differently; policies and implementation may even differ within business units. The Power BI administration role is also multi-faceted, and it is unlikely that a single individual or team would be responsible for all administrative tasks. An example of this is the separation of individuals roles. Individuals responsible for creating workspaces should be different from those who monitor compliance with the policy.

In addition to ensuring that the Power BI ecosystem is compliant with laws and governance policies, Power BI administrators are also responsible for monitoring the usage and distribution of Power BI reports, workspaces, apps, as well as user activities. Administrators would be expected to make recommendations on the smooth and efficient operation of the environment.

© Ásgeir Gunnarsson and Michael Johnson 2020
Á. Gunnarsson and M. Johnson, *Pro Microsoft Power BI Administration*,
https://doi.org/10.1007/978-1-4842-6567-3_8

Roles of the Power BI administrator

Power BI administration consists of the implementation of processes and procedures to implement the Power BI governance policies such as those set out in Part 1 of this book. The role of the administrator broadly consists of two key functions:

- Administration of Power BI artifacts

- Monitoring

The next two sections delve deeper into areas of focus under these roles.

Administration of Power BI artifacts

Administration of the various Power BI artifacts is the first of the two primary administration tasks. In this section, we highlight some of the critical objects for which the administrator is responsible.

- Tenant administration

- Capacity administration

- Users administration

- Workspace and app administration

- Data administration

- Gateway administration

- Security administration

In many organizations, the deployment of Power BI artifacts such as reports, dashboards, and datasets is part of the development pipeline. We discuss the development pipeline in greater detail in Chapter 5.

Tenant administration

A tenant is a container within Office 365 that holds collections of subscriptions (the services that collectively make up Office 365 product), users, domains, and other objects used by an organization. Power BI is only one of many subscriptions hosted within the tenant; other subscriptions include Exchange for communication and SharePoint for collaboration.

Note   There is no cost associated with a tenant, and expenses are only incurred for subscriptions and user licenses.

As the top-level object, the tenant is where the majority of the organization-wide setting are configured. Access to these settings is restricted to the *global-administrator* or *Power BI administrator* roles. Settings set at this level are enforced across the entire tenant, so ensuring that these comply with the governance policy is imperative. Examples of tenant-level settings include "Publish to web" and "Export data."

See Chapter 9 for more on managing the Power BI tenant.

Capacity administration

Capacities in Power BI are dedicated compute that can be purchased through either the Office 365 portal (Premium) or Azure (Power BI embedded). Because these additional capacities are provisioned at an additional expense and are not managed by Microsoft in the same way that the Shared capacity is, it is important that these capacities are correctly configured and well utilized. As Power BI Free users are only able to access shared content that is in one of these capacities, it is tempting to move all workspaces to this capacity. This could be a mistake, as not all workspaces need to be assigned to the dedicated capacity. As each workspace takes up valuable resources, it may be more appropriate to assign as many workspaces as possible to the shared capacity.

The key decisions to make here are the location of these capacities and who can assign workspaces to these capacities.

It is also important that these capacities are correctly monitored. An oversubscribed tenant will be slow and frustrating for users to use. Similarly, an overprovisioned capacity is a waste of resources that could better be spent elsewhere.

See Chapter 10 for more on managing Power BI Premium capacities.

User administration

While the act of provisioning user accounts does not typically lie within the Power BI administration role, assigning users appropriate licenses and granting them access may. There may also be a need for external users to access these Power BI reports and may require the Power BI administrator to facilitate.

Typical users administrative tasks include

- Creation of new users

- Assignment of appropriate licenses to users

- Identify training requirements

- Reclaiming licenses from inactive users

- Granting users (usually developers) appropriate permission to workspaces and gateways

Some tasks, such as creating a new user, and assigning licenses, are not done in the Power BI portal but the Office 365 portal. Other settings, such as granting permission to a workspace, are done using the Power BI portal. Chapter 12 will look more closely at the management of users in the Power BI ecosystem.

Workspaces and apps administration

The administration of a workspace is not always done by a member of the administration team but is often delegated to the report development team or a business unit.

Critical decisions for the workspace include

- Workspace names that make business sense.

- Assigning a workspace to a dedicated capacity.

- You are assigning other users to contributors or consumer roles.

- Creation of apps.

Poor administration of workspaces may result in users having unauthorized access to report artifacts. With this access, users could access sensitive information or modify or delete report artifacts.

Chapter 11 discusses the administration of workspaces in more detail.

Data administration

While the creation and validation of datasets or dataflows are not an administration function, there are still several administrative processes involved.

- Ensuring appropriate refresh schedules are created

- Ensuring data refreshed do not create performance problems for their source

- Certification of datasets and dataflows

- Tagging datasets that contain sensitive data

An important administrative function is ensuring that only data that is required to meet the needs of the business are stored and that only appropriate users have access to that data. This is particularly important for personally identifiable information (PII).

See Chapter 13 for more on administering datasets and dataflows in Power BI.

Gateways administration

The On-premises data Gateway used by Power BI and other services such as Power Automate and Power Apps provides a link between the Power BI Service and any on-premises data sources. As the gateways play an increasing role in the organization, ensuring that these gateways are correctly configured is very important. Gateways support the creation of clusters providing a mission-critical, Highly Available solution. Ensuring that the gateways are up-to-date is also vital to ensure that the gateways can support the latest features.

See Chapter 14 for more on administering Power BI gateways.

Security administration

Security in Power BI is managed by Azure Active Directory (AAD). AAD supports a single sign-on experience for users as they move through the different subscription services in the Office 365 stack. Often organizations have additional security requirements such as requiring Two-Factor Authentication or limiting access to Power BI to certain devices or locations. Many of these requirements are configured through the Azure Active Directory.

Additionally, there may be a requirement for the service to be secured using a key owned by the organization; this, too, can be achieved using the Bring Your Own Key (BYOK) feature.

See Chapter 12 for more on security administration.

We have looked at the seven areas of administration. Next, we look at the second role of the Power BI administrator, which is monitoring.

Monitoring

Monitoring is the process of collecting metrics about the operations of an IT environment to ensure that everything is functioning as expected to support the applications and services.[1] These metrics are collected from a variety of sources, including telemetry from within Power BI and Office 365. These metrics can be supplemented with measures from the gateways and user feedback.

Usage monitoring

Monitoring the use of reports by users is another key task that should be performed by the Power BI administrator. Accurate monitoring of user activity enables the administrator to determine if users

- Have been assigned an appropriate license

- Are accessing reports that they should not have access to

- Are not using the licenses that have been assigned to them

Observations such as these may result in the need for greater awareness and training or the possibility of reclaiming assigned licenses to be assigned elsewhere.

Similarly, monitoring report usage is important to identify unused reports. Unused reports result in clutter as well as unnecessary report refreshes, this in turn can result in a negative impact on the source systems and costs associated with moving large volumes of data over the Internet.

Compliance monitoring

Chapter 1 discussed the need for Power BI governance as part of a broader governance policy within your organization. Ensuring that this policy is adhered to is another essential function performed by the Power BI administrator.

The tasks required for compliance monitoring vary but may include

- Are users receiving adequate training before they access the system?

- Do users have appropriate permissions to access the data they need to perform their jobs?

---

[1]https://searchitoperations.techtarget.com/definition/IT-monitoring

- Are reports being made publically available via "Publish to web" when they contain sensitive data?

- Do workspaces and reports conform to specified naming conventions?

Stakeholder feedback

Understanding how users use the system is essential, but usage monitoring alone does not provide you as the administrator with enough information to determine how successful a Power BI implementation is. Often additional sources of information are required to form a more holistic picture. Other valuable sources of data include

- **Call center logs**: By monitoring the types of calls made to a call center, issues within the platform or lack of user training is identified.

- **User surveys**: Occasional surveys or focus groups are used to understand how users use the Power BI environment and gauge their overall satisfaction with the organization's Power BI implementation.

While often subjective, user feedback can be an early smoke test to detect problems.

Summary

Building an effective and efficient Power BI administration function within your organization is an essential component of a successful Power BI deployment. This Power BI administration function consists of multiple roles that may all be assigned to a single individual, team or can be divided among various teams, ensuring a clear separation of duties.

Call to action

- Clearly define administrative roles guided by organizational Power BI governance policy.

- Establish working relationships with functions such as Azure Active Directory administrators and Global administrators.

- Creations of RACI matrix ensuring a clear understanding of who is Responsible, Accountable, Consulted, or Informed regarding the different areas of administration of the system.

CHAPTER 9

Managing the Tenant

Read this chapter if you would like to find out more information about

- How to set up or take over a tenant

- Understanding the different tenant settings

- Tenant level roles

A tenant is a logical container that sits within the Office 365 data center and contains the users, subscriptions, and licenses used by an organization. Power BI is one of many subscriptions that reside inside the tenant. Therefore, many settings required to manage Power BI exist at the tenant level. Most of these settings are available within the tenant settings tab in the Power BI admin portal. However, some settings get defined outside of Power BI. As these settings apply to the entire organization, it becomes critical to ensure that these settings are correctly configured and that access to these settings is restricted to authorized users only.

There are three parts to configuring the tenant; these are

- Creating and configuring the tenant

- Assigning administration roles

- Tenant-level settings

© Ásgeir Gunnarsson and Michael Johnson 2020
Á. Gunnarsson and M. Johnson, *Pro Microsoft Power BI Administration*,
https://doi.org/10.1007/978-1-4842-6567-3_9

Creating and configuring a tenant

Power BI is not the only subscription found within a tenant. Other subscriptions such as Office 365 or Power Apps are also likely to be in the tenant. Therefore, the role of creating and administering the tenant does not belong to the Business Intelligence team. This role may belong to a core infrastructure team or to a team dedicated to the management of the organization's Microsoft tenant. We will refer to the tenant administrator. In a small organization, it is possible that the tenant and Power BI administrators are the same person or that the role is shared among a small team. If Power BI is the first subscription used by such an organization, it is likely that you, as the Power BI administrator, will need to guide the tenant creation process.

When starting the Office 365 journey, the tenant administrator will encounter one of three scenarios:

- **A managed tenant already exists**: If the organization is already using Office 365, then it is likely that the tenant is already managed. Many of the configuration choices will have been made.

- **No tenant exists**: Power BI has been a fantastic growth product for Microsoft, and for many organizations, Power BI may be the first time they have consumed a Microsoft cloud product. Such an organization would therefore not have a tenant in place and would need to create one before getting started.

- **A tenant exists, but no administrator has been declared**: It is possible that users within the organization have begun to use Power BI without a managed tenant being created first; this is simple to do as Microsoft allows the creation of Power BI accounts to be created using only an email address. This results in an unmanaged (also called a shadow) tenant being created. Before being able to effectively administer the tenant, you would first need to declare an administrator for this tenant.

If the tenant has already been created and administered, then there are no further actions required, and you can move onto the next section on assigning administration roles. If, on the other hand, a tenant has not been created or no administrator has been declared, then there are several steps required to set this up. Then either a tenant needs to be created or needs to be taken over by the administrator. The following two sections will describe at a high level how this can be done.

Creating a new Office 365 tenant

If your organization is new to Office 365, then the first task is to create a tenant. Each tenant is assigned a unique DNS entry of the form *TenantName*.onmicrosoft.com. This name must be unique, but don't panic if it does not align with your organization's name or domain; you will be able to assign your organization's domain to the tenant at a later stage by assigning one or more custom DNS names to the tenant. All this can be done during or shortly after the creation of the tenant.

The easiest way to set up a tenant is to sign your organization up for an Office 365 trial. During this process, the region in which the tenant is located will be chosen. This is a crucial decision as it will affect not only where your data is stored but also the legislation that will affect the tenant. Choosing the wrong region can also result in higher costs associated with moving data between your data centers and the tenant. You are not given a list of data centers to choose from but rather the country that is used during signup.

Note   It is not easy and may not even be possible to move a tenant once it has been created.

Once the tenant has been created, you will be able to log into it using a *yourUserName@YourTenantName*.onmicrosoft.com. After logging into the portal, you will be able to assign a custom domain to the tenant and will then be able to login using your regular email address. Behind the scenes, what this has done is created a new Azure Active Directory. It is possible to synchronize the users between your on-premises active directory and your new Azure Active Directory, but that is outside the scope of this book.

Step-by-step   For detailed instructions on how to add a domain, see `https://docs.microsoft.com/en-us/microsoft-365/admin/setup/add-domain`.

Taking over a shadow tenant

If a tenant was created automatically by a user signing up for a free trial using their organization email address, then the tenant already exists. When this happens, no users will be assigned the administrator role for the tenant.

A tenant without an administrator is called a shadow tenant. An administrator can take ownership of such a tenant by navigating to `https://portal.ofice365.com` and logging into the portal using their work email address. If you have not done this before, you will be prompted to create an account. Once signed into the portal, you would select the admin option on the top left or by browsing to `https://admin.microsoft.com/`. If no administrator has been declared for the tenant, then this page will simply ask if you would like to become the administrator for this tenant. To complete this process, you need to prove that you are in control of the domain by creating a txt record in the DNS settings for this domain. After this process is complete, you will be the administrator for the tenant. Having this administrator role assigned is essential because only the administrator has the necessary rights to assign other administrator rights.

Assigning administration roles

Once the administrator of the tenant has been identified, then we can begin to assign the required permissions. As this book focuses only on Power BI administration and not an administration of the entire tenant, we will only discuss the roles critical for this.

Two roles allow the administrator to make changes to the tenant-level settings and one that allows the user to view settings only.

- **Global admin**: The Global admin role is the highest level setting in Office 365, and there is no setting or function that such a user cannot modify. Such modifications include deleting users, reports, and entire workspaces. For this reason, the Global admin role should be given to as few people as possible.

Tip   Create a separate user account to be assigned to the Global administrator role. This account should not be used for any other purpose other than managing the tenant. Azure Active Directory which will be discussed later can also be used to prevent the unauthorized use of this account. We will discuss how to lock down this and other accounts in Chapter 12 on security.

- **Global viewer**: The Global viewer role is a role that has the ability to view all settings in the tenant but not to change them. This is a preferred role for both administrators and roles such as "Risk and Compliance" or "Internal audit" who are tasked with ensuring conformance to the group policy but do not have authority to make changes. Using this role permission can be granted to teams in a governance or audit role that need to validate the configuration without being able to change it.

- **Power BI admin**: The Power BI admin role is a superuser role only applicable to the Power BI subscription. The role includes the ability to change Power BI tenant settings and create and delete workspaces; however they cannot create users or assign and remove licenses.

These roles can be assigned by the global administrator, whom, up until now, we have referred to as the tenant administrator; this tenant administrator can assign global admin rights or Power BI admin rights to other users. They would do this by updating the roles assigned to users in the Users tab in the Office 365 admin portal.

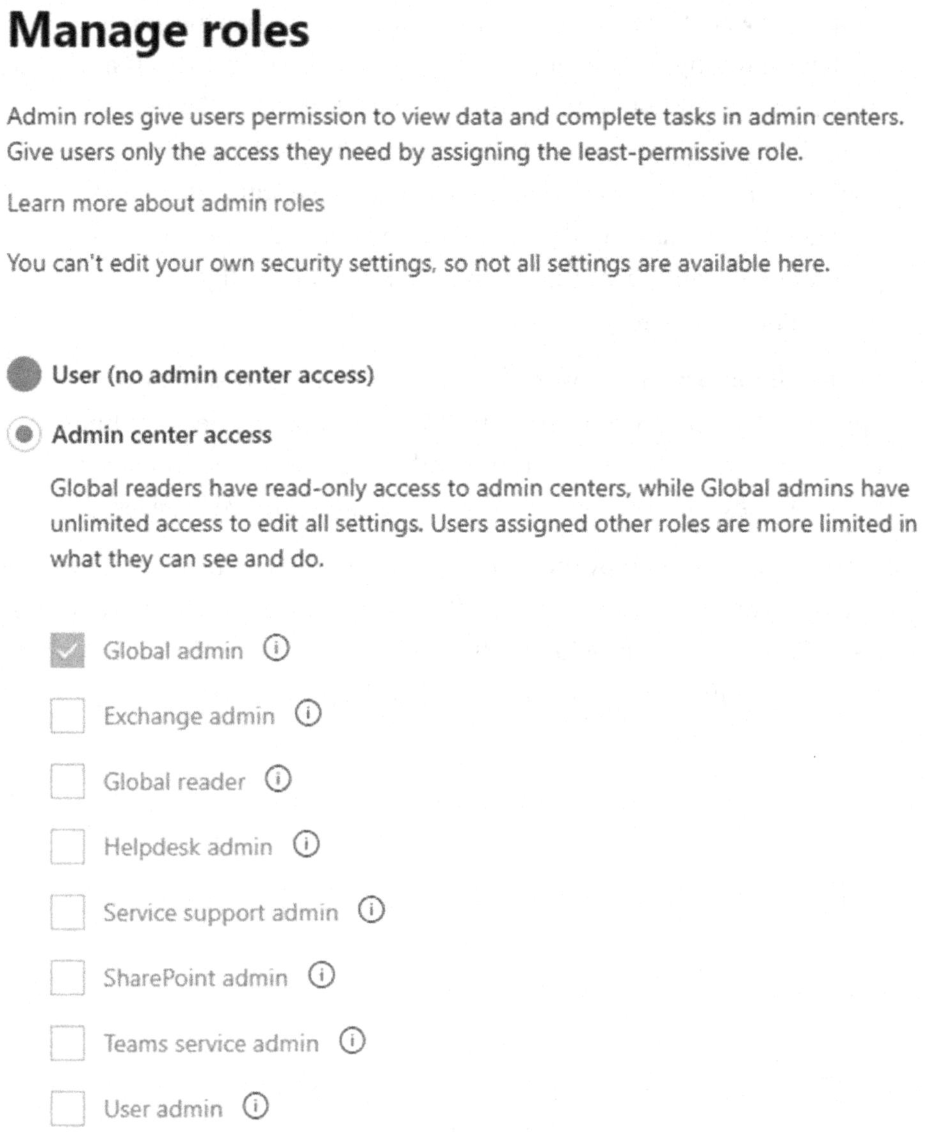

Manage roles

Admin roles give users permission to view data and complete tasks in admin centers. Give users only the access they need by assigning the least-permissive role.

Learn more about admin roles

You can't edit your own security settings, so not all settings are available here.

● User (no admin center access)

◉ Admin center access

Global readers have read-only access to admin centers, while Global admins have unlimited access to edit all settings. Users assigned other roles are more limited in what they can see and do.

☑ Global admin ⓘ

☐ Exchange admin ⓘ

☐ Global reader ⓘ

☐ Helpdesk admin ⓘ

☐ Service support admin ⓘ

☐ SharePoint admin ⓘ

☐ Teams service admin ⓘ

☐ User admin ⓘ

Figure 9-1. *Enabling Global admin role*

With an Office 365 tenant and an administrator now in place, the Power BI administrator can begin to set the appropriate administration settings in Power BI admin portal.

Power BI admin portal

The power BI admin portal is where much of the Power BI governance policies are implemented. The Power BI admin portal can be accessed via the Power BI portal by first selecting the gear icon and browsing down to the "Admin portal," or browsing directly to `https://app.powerbi.com/admin-portal`. If this page is empty, then your user has not been assigned the necessary roles to access this portal.

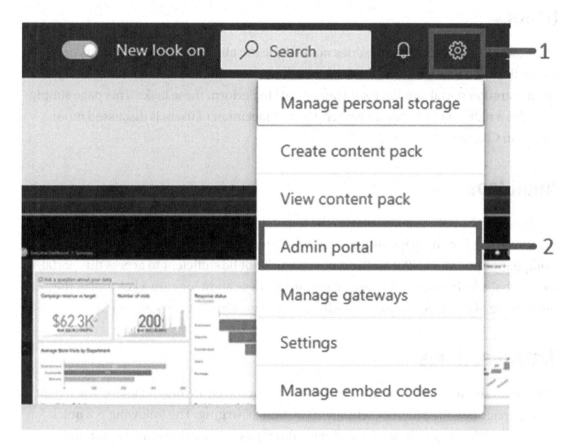

Figure 9-2. *Accessing the Power BI admin page*

Within this portal, there are several options to be configured; we will look through many of these options and discuss some of the things that you want to consider when making these settings.

Usage metrics

The Usage metrics is a great tool to quickly get an overview of the most popular reports and most active users. While this is great for a small team with few users and reports, the usage metrics report does not provide the necessary depth required to manage the system effectively. In Chapter 16 we will discuss how to do more advanced monitoring.

Users

The Power BI administrator role does not include the ability to create new users or assign licenses to users. To perform these tasks, one would need to access the Office 365 administration portal and have sufficient rights to perform these tasks. This page simply provides a redirect to the admin center. The management of users is discussed more deeply in Chapter 12.

Audit logs

Auditing in Office 365 is performed at the tenant level. Similar to the users' page mentioned earlier, this page simply provides a redirect to the Office 365 Security and Compliance portal. The Power BI admin role will not be sufficient to access this portal, so a Global admin or similar roles are required. These audit logs are a key tool in the monitoring of the system and will be discussed in greater detail in Chapter 16.

Tenant settings

The tenant settings are where we set the policies for the entire organization. The tenant settings page has 40+ different settings at the time of writing. The following is a quick summary of the major categories and critical settings that we think are important to highlight.

Help and support settings

The help and support settings collection enables the administrator to configure how users access help. In a larger organization with their own support channels, help and support can be configured to redirect users to internal support as opposed to Microsoft's general support channels.

- **Publish "Get Help" information**: If your organization would like to provide custom help resources or to redirect users to a different channel when they need to make requests, then this can be done by enabling this setting option and providing alternative resources. While the default help options are well done, being able to redirect users to your own organizational helpdesk or request portal can be invaluable.

- **Receive email notifications for service outages or incidents**: In the rare event that there are issues in the Power BI Service, a mail can be sent to a designated security group. Incident response can then deal with the disruption according to your organization's own policies. It is recommended that this be set to a small group of people who can better determine the appropriate actions to be taken.

Workspace settings

Workspaces are the containers within Power BI where report artifacts are grouped together; the processes of administering workspaces will be covered in more detail in Chapter 11. Still, there are a few key settings that control the behavior of how workspaces can be created and access across the entire tenant. These settings are

- **Create workspaces**: In a true self-service environment, users would create workspaces as they are required. This however can lead to many workspaces being created. These workspaces may also be duplicates of other workspaces and may not conform to the naming convention. Using this setting, the ability to create workspaces can be restricted to certain groups or opened up to the whole organization. It is recommended that this setting be disabled with only certain users given permissions to create new workspaces.

Note   Users always have their own personal workspaces to create content should they need to; sharing directly from these workspaces should be discouraged.

- **Use datasets across workspaces**: It is possible for reports in one workspace to access the datasets in other workspaces. The ability to access datasets across workspaces allows for significant reuse of existing work. When combined with certified datasets, this can become a powerful feature allowing for faster report creation. Great care and governance however needs to be applied as any change to the underlying dataset may break reports in workspaces that the dataset owner may not be aware of.

Information protection

Microsoft Information Protection, also known as Azure Information Protection (AIP), helps organizations classify and protect information within the tenant. This is done by applying labels to datasets and reports; these labels can mark data as being sensitive. The Power BI Service can then control how that data is accessed and used, for example, preventing the exporting of data where that data has been marked as sensitive. This is an important feature when it comes to compliance with regulations such as GDPR or HIPAA.

- **Connect Power BI to Microsoft Information Protection sensitivity labels**: Microsoft Information Protection is a new feature of Power BI (still in preview at the time of writing) that allows datasets and reports to be tagged as containing sensitive information. Group policies can then determine the extent that this information can be shared or exported.

Export and sharing

Ideally, all reports would be accessed through the Power BI portal. However, there is often a need to export or share this data within the organization, or even people outside of the organization. Power BI supports many modes of sharing, and having control of who can share data and how they can do it is one of the best tools the administrator has to ensure that they are compliant with the governance policy. Some of the most critical settings to be managed are

- **Share content with external users**: Azure B2B (Busines to Business) allows users from outside of the organization to access reports; this was a significant development as it was one of the drivers behind the misuse of the "Publish to web" feature. By allowing external users to connect using their own Microsoft accounts, this also removed the need to create a user account in the organization's Azure Active Directory for these third-party users. By adding these users as **guest accounts** within your Azure Active Directory, Power BI is also able to use their Power BI license. This can result in significant savings as it removes the need to license these individuals again, although this can still be done if required. Adding guest accounts will be covered further in Chapter 12 on security.

- **Publish to web**: Publish to web is one of the features that require the most care; many security breaches have been unintentionally caused, often by well-meaning individuals looking to share reports or information with people outside of the organization. These well-meaning users mistakenly believed that only people with the link would be able to access the report. Microsoft has made several changes to how this functionality works, including turning this feature off by default. Administrators can turn this feature on for restricted groups where appropriate.

- **Export data**: Most visuals in Power BI support the ability to export the summarized or underlying data to either a CSV or Excel file. This can be useful for users who would like to see the underlying data, or use it for further downstream manipulation. When this feature was first released, only CSV files were supported with Excel files being added later; because of this, there is a separate function to control the ability to export to excel.

- **Export to Excel**: Export to Excel allows the underlying result set of a visual to be exported to an Excel file; this is similar to export CSV. However, this will generate an XLSX file and also supports a higher number of rows that can be exported (150 000 as of Match 2020) opposed to the 3000 in CSV format.

- **Export reports to PowerPoint presentations or PDF documents**: Power BI can also export to PowerPoint and PDF; this exports a snapshot of the visuals only, and all underlying data and interactivity will be removed.

- **Export reports as image files**: At the time of writing, this was still a preview feature; this will allow users to render the report as an image file. This is often preferred by users who would like to add the report into another tool.

- **Print dashboards and reports**: Power BI exports can also be printed; when enabled, report browsers will be able to select the print dialog and print the page.

- **Certification**: In Chapter 15 we will discuss certification of datasets. This feature allows the organization to "certify" datasets and reports as vetted and approved for use in the organization. This option will enable you to restrict the certification of datasets to designated groups and to provide a link to documentation for the datasets.

- **Allow external guest users to edit and manage content in the organization**: It is possible to allow an external guest account to edit and manage reports. By default, it is recommended that this setting be turned off. However, if your organization uses third-party developers to develop Power BI content, then enabling this feature allows them to edit reports and other artifacts.

- **Email subscriptions**: Email subscriptions are an effective way for users to receive an extract of a report on a set schedule. It should be remembered that emails are an unsecured channel, and users can forward this information to unauthorized individuals. For this reason, one needs to refer to the organization's governance policy to determine the appropriate setting for this.

- **Featured content**: In Power BI, certain reports, dashboards, or apps can be highlighted to make them visible on the landing page of other users. We discuss this feature later in this chapter, but if your organization would like to use this feature, then it must be enabled first.

Content packs and app settings

Content packs and apps are a great way of packaging content to users without giving them direct access to the workspace.

Note   Content packs have been deprecated and should no longer be created, but they may still be in use within your organization.

- **Publish content packs and apps to the entire organization**: This setting restricts the users who are able to create and publish content packs and apps. As we discussed in Chapter 5, apps should be used as part of your Power BI Application Life Cycle Management process. Therefore the ability to create apps should be restricted to the development team.

- **Create template organizational content packs and apps**: Template apps allow Power BI developers to build Power BI apps and deploy to other Power BI workspaces for use by other departments within the organization. The ability to create template apps should be locked down to the development team.

- **Push apps to end users**: The discoverability of new reports in Power BI can sometimes be a challenge. The Push apps to end user function allows apps to be automatically installed for users without them needing to install the app form themselves. This can be an effective means of ensuring that users receive a default set of apps already installed.

Integration settings

To make data available in reports, Power BI often needs to integrate with other tools. This collection of settings allows the administrator to manage how that integration occurs. Key settings under this group of settings are

- **Use Analyze in Excel with on-premises datasets**: Analyze in Excel allows users to connect to a model hosted in the Power BI Service. If this model is backed by an on-premises analysis services database, then using this feature would result in unnecessary network movement as the user would be able to create a direct connection to analysis service from excel, removing the need to direct traffic over the open Internet resulting in higher latencies and increased bandwidth usage.

- **Use global search for Power BI**: Global search allows users, using the search bar, to search for data within the organization; this spans not only to Power BI but all subscriptions. This can be a powerful way to make content discoverable.

Customize visual settings

Custom visuals are used to extend the native visuals provided in Power BI; third-party providers have created many of these visuals. They may not be up to the performance and security standards set by Microsoft. The administrator can manage the number and types of visuals used in reports deployed to the service. To help, Microsoft has begun a process of certifying custom visuals, providing assurances of both its performance and security.

- **Add and use custom visuals**: The administrator can restrict the use of custom visuals to specific groups or allow all or no users to access these settings. It is a good idea to limit the visuals and as part of the governance process provide a set of approved visuals to the organization; this can be important from both a security and performance issue as well as supporting a standard look and feel across all reports.

- **Allow only Certified custom visuals**: It is also possible to limit the custom visuals to only those that have been certified by Microsoft. This is a recommended setting for any organization working with sensitive data.

Audit and usage settings

The usage and audit settings play a vital role when it comes to monitoring. There are several settings under the admin portal that control how much data is collected about different activities that users can take when using the Power BI Portal.

- **Usage metrics for content creators**: The Power BI Service can also collect and display usage metrics for reports and dashboards. This can be invaluable for the report developers, so it should and is enabled by default.

- **Per-user data in usage metrics for content creators**: Usage metrics can be set up to include the identity of report viewers; this may expose sensitive data to the report creators. Therefore, your organization's governance policy needs to determine if this data is made available to content creators.

Dashboard settings

Dashboards are a great way of consolidating visuals from across multiple reports for a single view across various reports. Additionally, they support additional reporting options that also need to be managed.

- **Web content on dashboard tiles**: The web content dashboard tile allows users to embed HTML code into a dashboard. This can be helpful in adding additional functionality; however, the introduction of external code into the portal can create a security challenge. Therefore, consider restricting this feature.

- **Data classification for dashboards**: As we were able to classify reports, we can also classify dashboards as containing sensitive data; this will prevent the export or sharing of data.

Developer settings

Power BI is sometimes referred to as a low-to-no code solution; this is because, with little or no coding knowledge, users can create rich reports. However, it is often useful to extend the capabilities of Power BI through other solutions; this can be done by allowing external tools or services to access Power BI or host content.

Note   This does not refer to Power BI embedded, which is a Platform As A Service (PAAS) service where developers can integrate Power BI directly into their solutions.

- **Embed content in apps**: This feature allows dashboards and reports to be inserted into other SaaS applications such as SharePoint or Teams. Allowing for these Power BI reports to be placed inline with other business applications allows them to be more easily discovered and used.

- **Allow service principals to use Power BI APIs**: In Chapter 15, we will discuss many of the tools available to aid the Power BI administrator; this includes functionality that is not available using the portal. A service principal is an identity within the Azure Active Directory that can be granted permission to perform specified actions without the need for users to log into the portal using their credentials. If you or anyone in the organization intend to use these APIs using a service principal, then this feature needs to be enabled. We will discuss what a service principal is and why we would want to use it in Chapter 12.

Dataflow settings

Dataflows are a collection of entities that can be created and managed within a Power BI workspace. These entities are similar to tables loaded into a staging area, where they can be reused by multiple report datasets. We will discuss dataflows in more detail in Chapter 13. At the time of writing, the only setting available in the portal is the ability to allow or disallow users to create these dataflows.

- **Create and use dataflows**: This single setting enables or disables the creation and use of dataflows. It is not possible to limit the ability to create dataflows to designated groups.

Template app settings

This collection of settings is similar to the content pack and app settings and controls how users can create and distribute Template apps:

- **Publish Template Apps**: The ability to create app workspaces to develop app solutions for distribution to clients outside of the organization. This type of functionality should only be enabled to Power BI developers who are creating content that will be shared or sold to other organizations. While it is enabled by default, consider disabling this option if your organization does not distribute Template Apps.

- **Install Template Apps**: Template apps created outside of your organization can also be installed. If your organization does make use of Template Apps, then this would need to be enabled but should be restricted to a controlled group.

- **Install Template Apps not listed in AppSource**: If Template Apps are supported, it is a good idea to consider only apps that have been listed in AppSource, which is a Microsoft repository of applications.

Q&A

Q&A is a Machine Learning (ML) feature in Power BI that allows users to ask questions of a report in a natural language; only English is fully supported at this time.

- **Review questions**: The questions asked in the report can be made available to the dataset owner; this can be useful in determining if the report is useful or if further refinement is required.

Capacity settings

The management of capacities is a detailed topic and will be discussed in greater detail in Chapter 10.

Embed codes

The Publish to web feature allows users to share content outside of the organization without the need for a Power BI license or any user authentication. As there is no authentication, all other security measures that were put in place to protect data are effectively ignored. Earlier in this chapter, we discussed the tenant-level setting that allows this feature to be disabled or restricted. If Publish to web has been enabled, then this screen provides a list of all currently published reports and who published them. It is a good practice to periodically review the currently published reports to ensure that this public sharing is appropriate. Reports that should not be shared using this feature can be revoked.

Organizational visuals

Power BI supports a rich collection of visuals out of the box and can be extended through the use of custom visuals; the Power BI market place has several visuals that can be incorporated into reports. It is possible for administrators to restrict the visuals used; this would generally be done for one of two reasons. Some visuals, such as mapping visuals, make external calls to third-party APIs. Depending on the type of data being transmitted, this may be a violation of the organization's governance policy, or even laws such as GDPR. Secondly, restricting visuals to a subset of visuals leads to a more consistent report experience within the organization.

Dataflow settings

Dataflows are a capability within Power BI that allows data to be ingested into a staging area. This setting allows the administrator to use custom storage using Azure DataLake store Gen 2. We will discuss the administration of data, including dataflows, more in Chapter 13.

Workspaces

Workspace administration is another important topic that is worthy of its own chapter. In Chapter 11, we examine the correct administration of Power BI workspaces.

Custom branding

As a Software as a Service (SaaS) solution, users of Power BI access reports and dashboards through the Power BI portal found at `https://app.powerBI.com`. By default, this portal uses the standard Microsoft Power BI branding. To aid in creating a more familiar look and feel, the portal can be configured to use a limited set of client branding elements; these include

- **Logo**: A corporate logo can be configured; this image must be of the specified size (200x300); this logo is placed in the upper left-hand corner, replacing the Power BI Logo.

- **Cover image**: The cover image can be replaced with a company banner; like the logo this image has to be a specific size (1920x160).

- **Theme color**: The top banner can have its color set to align with the corporate brand giving the Power BI portal the appearance of being part or your organization's corporate web portal.

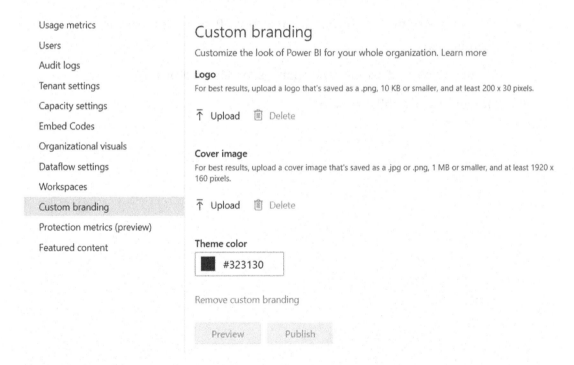

Figure 9-3. *Power BI custom branding configuration*

Featured content

If the **allow featured content** setting has been enabled, then reports and dashboards that have been selected to be featured are listed here. Content will only be featured to users who have access to the content, so there is no risk of a security breach occurring from the use of this feature.

Summary

In this chapter, we reviewed a number of the settings available to the administrator to help them to secure their Power BI environment. In the following chapter, we will look at how capacities can be administered.

Call to action (TBD)

- Identify who the administrator for your tenant is.

- Ensure the Power BI admin role is assigned appropriately.

- Align tenant settings with your organization's Power BI governance documents.

- Document current settings and changes to those settings.

- Monitor use of Publish to web.

CHAPTER 10

Administering Power BI Capacities

Read this chapter if you would like to find out more information about

- What is Power BI premium

- What features does it enable

- How to get Power BI premium

- How to manage Power BI premium

When Microsoft released Power BI, they created it a Software as a Service (SaaS) application. SaaS applications allow new customers to quickly and easily set up and use the application while also keeping the per head cost low for clients with a smaller number of users. SaaS applications also allow for more frequent deployments, allowing the product to evolve at a faster pace. This fast development cycle has allowed Power BI to move up the Gartner rankings, where it has now been number one for the last few years. As a SaaS application, it is the responsibility of Microsoft to manage the underlying platform, including the provisioning of hardware, installing and patching the software, and taking care of all the high availability and resiliency requirements needed for an enterprise-grade solution.

The advantages of this shared platform are clear. However, a shared platform also creates new challenges and limitations. One of these challenges is how to allocate costs. As there is no underlying hardware or software explicitly dedicated to a single customer, the cost of these resources is not easily passed onto the customer. To simplify the licensing structure, Power BI started with a per-user model where all users would pay the same price. This is advantageous for a smaller customer as they can share overhead costs with other customers bringing down the cost.

© Ásgeir Gunnarsson and Michael Johnson 2020
Á. Gunnarsson and M. Johnson, *Pro Microsoft Power BI Administration*,
https://doi.org/10.1007/978-1-4842-6567-3_10

A second challenge with a shared pool is that as all customers share the same underlying platform, guaranteeing performance becomes difficult with customers experiencing what is known as the noisy neighbor problem. This occurs when other users of the platform consume a disproportionate amount of resources leaving less for other users of the platform. This inconsistency in performance is usually all right for smaller and occasional users but may present more significant challenges for mission-critical enterprises. A third challenge with having a shared pool of resources is that it introduces a number of restrictions on the new features that could be built into the product, since it has the ability to affect other tenants negatively because of the increased resource demands.

To address the challenges of Power BI as a shared platform, a new Power BI implementation was created based on a Platform as a Service (PaaS) approach, in which customers can provision a dedicated allocation of resources. The customer then takes responsibility for correctly sizing and monitoring resources on the platform but still leaves the management of the underlying infrastructure to Microsoft. This gives customers some level of certainty of the performance that they can expect and also allows larger organizations to adopt a different licensing model than the per-user approach, which may not provide as much value with a large number of users. Finally, because resources could be dedicated to a single tenant, new features that consume more significant resources can be introduced.

Note   For a complete list of features available, please look at the following Microsoft site `https://powerbi.microsoft.com/pricing/#powerbi-comparison-table`.

Once the need for a dedicated capacity has been established, the next step is to create the additional capacity and add it to the organization's tenant.

Adding additional capacities to your tenant

Dedicated capacities can be added in one of two ways; the first and more common approach is to add a Power BI Premium capacity within Office 365. The second approach is to create a Power BI Embedded capacity within Azure. It is also possible to add multiple capacities both from Office 365 and Azure simultaneously.

Power BI Premium in Office 365

Purchasing a Power BI Premium capacity follows a similar path to purchasing Power BI Pro licenses in the Office 365 admin portal. You can find this option under Billing ➤ Purchase services, then browsing through the services or searching for Power BI. Under this option, you will find two Premium SKUs available:

P SKU: The Power BI Premium P SKU is the premier Power BI Premium SKU. It comes in sizes ranging from P1 to P5, which represent 8 to 128 v-cores and between 25 and 400 GB RAM, respectively. Premium P SKUs support all enterprise features as well as embedding. Power BI Premium also includes a license for Power BI Report Server, which is an on-premises subset of the Power BI Service. A P SKU can be purchased on either a monthly or annual commitment with a reasonable discount available for the longer commitment.

EM SKU: The EM SKU was designed for organizational embedding, allowing reports to be embedded into applications such as SharePoint and Teams. While the EM SKUs support free accounts, these reports can only be accessed via embedding and not via the Power BI portal or mobile apps. EM1 and EM2 are only available through volume licensing agreements with EM3 available in the Office 365 admin portal. The EM SKU is only available on an annual commitment.

Find out more   For more detail on what is included in the Premium SKUs, go to `https://docs.microsoft.com/power-bi/admin/service-premium-what-is`.

To purchase a capacity through the Office 365 portal, you require either of the following two roles, **Microsoft Office 365 Global administrator** role or the **Billing administrator** role, as discussed in Chapter 2.

When a Power BI Premium plan is purchased, a corrosponding number of v-cores is added to the number of available v-cores. These v-cores are then used to create the required premium capacities. This means that a Power BI Premium P2 representing 16 v-cores can be used to create one P2 capacity or two P1 capacities. Two separate Premium P1 plans can also be combined to create a single P2 capacity. To create such capacities, the tenant administrator would chose the "Set up new Capacity" option; they would then assign the capacity an appropriate name, nominate the capacity administrators, and choose a geography if the tenant is to be used for multi-geo which will be discussed shortly.

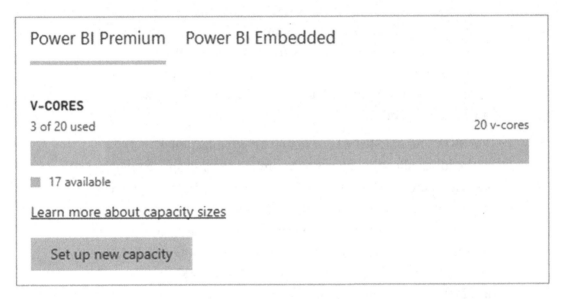

Figure 10-1. *Create new Power BI Premium capacity using available v-cores*

Before creating a new capacity, the location of the capacity needs to be considered, especially when regulations require data to be stored or processes within certain geographies that may not be in the same region as the tenant. For such scenarios Power BI Premium supports multi-geo functionality.

Multi-geo

Large multinational organizations often face restrictions on the geographies in which data can be stored and processed; this is a challenge for many SaaS solutions including Power BI, as the servers and data centers in which their data is stored are abstracted away from them.

The multi-geo feature in Power BI Premium allows the administrators of the Power BI tenant to create capacities in a region that is not the same as the region in which the tenant has been created. By assigning workspaces to this capacity, the organization has the tools to ensure that the datasets in that workgroup is restricted to that geography. When this is done, all Power BI datasets, Query caches, and R and Python images are stored only in that assigned geography, helping the organization abide by any industry or regional data residency requirements.

Azure

Power BI Embedded was created primarily for Independent Software Vendors (ISV) who need to embed Power BI reports or even report parts directly into their application without the Power BI portal. This method of embedding is often known as App-Owns-Data Embedding. In such scenarios, the ISV is responsible for much of internal plumbing of the system, including the authentication of the user. In the App-Owns-Data scenario, the identity of the end user may not be known to Microsoft or even the ISV. Therefore, per-user licensing becomes impossible, so licensing of a capacity is necessary.

While not explicitly designed as an alternative to Power BI Premium, the alternate billing model that Azure uses in which resources are billed for the duration of time that they are in use (often per second) makes this an attractive way to experiment with the Power BI Premium features. It is important to note that while Azure Power BI Embedded supports the full feature set of Power BI premium at the right capacity levels, workspaces assigned to such capacities do not benefit from sharing content with Power BI Free users. In other words, only Power BI Pro users would be able to access this functionality.

Azure Power BI Embedded currently comes in 6 tiers known as the A tiers, the smallest tier, the A1 is equivalent to a single v-core, and the largest tier being the A6 which has 32 v-cores and is similar to the P3 Premium tier. Due to the heavy resource requirements of many of the Premium features, many of them, such as paginated reports, require at least an A4 tier. A quick exercise will confirm that the cost of running an A4 Power BI Embedded capacity will be greater than the cost of a P1, which is equivalent in resources. This means that it would not make sense to run such workloads for an extended amount of time but can be an effective way to evaluate Power BI Premium and is now a recommended practice by Microsoft for customers.

Find out more   For more information of what is included in Azure Power BI Embedded as well as pricing, go to `https://azure.microsoft.com/en-us/pricing/details/power-bi-embedded/`.

Before provisioning a capacity in this way, there are a few important elements to consider. First, the Azure tenant must be part of the same active directory as the Power BI tenant. Second, and unlike Power BI Premium, the Azure Power BI capacity that is created within Azure cannot be configured within the Power BI Portal into multiple smaller capacities nor can the region be changed. Finally, the administrators of the capacity will need to be assigned in the Azure portal.

Once the capacity has been created through either channel, the administrator can then configure the capacity.

Configuring capacities

Once the capacity has been created either in the Office 365 and Power BI portals or through Azure, there are a number of configuration options to manage. The primary configuration we will look at is the workspace settings, which manages how resources are distributed across features in the capacity.

Workload settings

Workload settings allow the resources provided to the capacity to be distributed among the different features, or to simply disable some of the features in the capacity.

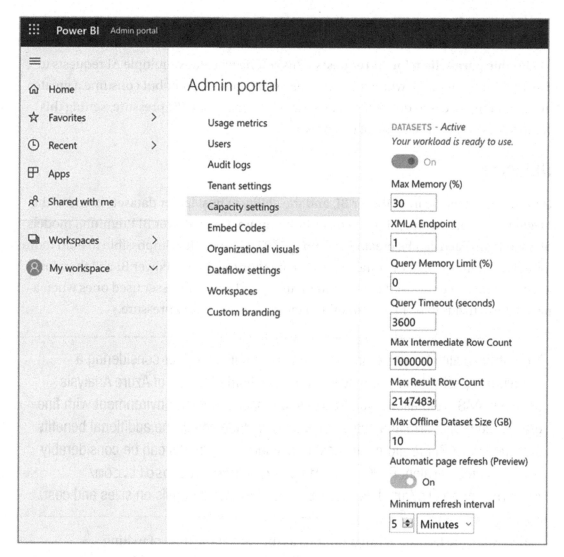

Figure 10-2. *Configuration settings for capacity*

Artificial Intelligence

The Artificial Intelligence features in Power BI Premium allow organizations to integrate Azure Cognitive Services and Auto ML Features. These features can be resource intensive so ensuring that they are properly limited is important.

Max Memory (%): This setting limits the amount of memory available to the AI features.

Allow building machine learning models: Determines if analysts and developers are able to create, train, and validate models for Power BI.

Enable parallelism for AI requests: This setting will allow multiple AI requests to execute simultaneously; when this happens, results return faster but consume a greater number of resources to do so. If you experience memory or CPU pressure, setting this value to false may relive some of this pressure.

Datasets

Datasets are at the heart of Power BI, and the ability to host larger datasets is one of the bigger drivers for the adoption of Power BI Premium. Using Power BI Premium, models of up to 10GB each can be created and up to 100TB in total. It is impossible to hold more models in memory than the total amount of memory available. Power BI will therefore keep the most recently used datasets in memory and evict the lesser used ones when a new dataset needs to be loaded or other factors cause memory pressure.

Tip   If the ability to host a large model is your only driver for considering a Premium capacity, then you may want to investigate the use of Azure Analysis Services (AAS). AAS allows you to create a model in a PaaS environment with fine-grained control of size and scale but will not include any of the additional benefits of using Power BI Premium. The cost of a single large model can be considerably less than an equivalent P SKU. See `https://azure.microsoft.com/pricing/details/analysis-services/` for more details on sizes and cost.

Below are the Dataset settings options as they are at the time of writing.

Max Memory (%): Using this setting the administrator can limit the maximum amount of memory that can be used by models loaded into memory. This setting does not limit the total size of all datasets that can be stored on the capacity but rather limits the number that is active in memory at any given time. If this memory limit has been reached and a request is received for a dataset that is not in memory, another dataset will need to be evicted before a new one can be loaded. If this setting is made too low or there are too many models in memory, then report rendering times will be severely impacted because of the constant switching of datasets in and out of memory. To remedy this the value could be increased, additional capacity could be made available, or work undertaken to reduce the number and size of models in memory.

Max Intermediate Row Set Count: When using Power BI in direct query mode, it is possible to generate queries that would require a large number of rows to be returned from the source system. An example of such a query may be for the total value of an invoice from all invoices in the system. Setting limits to the number of records that can be returned for such a query can reduce the number of long running queries but may also result in incorrect results being returned. The default for this setting is 1,000,000 and can be set as high as 2,147,483,647.

Max Offline Dataset Size (GB): In the shared tenant, Power BI datasets have a 1GB limit. Capacities allow for datasets of up to 10GB to be created depending on the SKU. The administrator can choose to reduce the maximum size as large infrequently used models can result in a high number of models being moved in and out of memory.

Note   Power BI Premium also supports large models; this allows datasets up to the maximum amount of RAM on the capacity to be created. This needs to be enabled per dataset and is not a capacity-wide setting.

Max Result Row Set Count: When Power BI receives a query, it returns a result set. This result set is like a table; depending on the query, this result set may potentially contain several million or more rows. Power BI will restrict the number of rows that can be returned in a single query; this is to prevent Power BI queries running too long. The default for this setting is 10 000 and should not be changed without good reason.

Query Memory Limit (%): Power BI not only requires memory to store the data model but also requires memory to store intermediate results of both DAX and MDX queries. Queries that consume large amounts of memory are often less performant and may also cause memory pressure in the capacity causing datasets to be evicted from memory. Capacities have different default values depending on their size and are represented by a default value of 0. It must be noted that this limit does not only apply to queries but also data load operations, so setting this value too low may result in data load failures.

Query Timeout (seconds): Long-running queries can negatively affect the performance of the capacity consuming large amounts of CPU and memory. This Capacity level setting limits the duration of a single query, but not necessarily long-running reports that may consist of several slow queries. Lowering this may result in fewer resources being overconsumed but may result in failed data loads. Power BI reports also have an internal timeout for individual queries, typically set to 3 minutes.

Automatic page refresh: A new feature in Power BI premium is the ability to refresh a report on a schedule automatically. This setting is useful when used on dashboards where the most up-to-date reports are displayed. These features, however, have the potential to flood the service with many expensive queries. It is essential for the administrator to understand how this feature is going to be used before enabling it.

Note   This feature is also available in Power BI Pro.

Minimum refresh interval: If Automatic page refreshes are enabled, then the minimum refresh schedule can also be set. When selecting a value for this setting, the frequency of data loads should be taken into consideration. For example, refreshing every 5 minutes from a source that only updates every hour may not add any value while introducing a higher workload.

Dataflows

Dataflows allow business analysts and data engineers to create and store curated datasets, making them available to model developers for further processing. This creates a new environment in which the mashup engine transforms data. Dataflows in Power BI Premium include the enhanced Dataflow Compute Engine, which replaces the traditional CSV backed datastore with a SQL backed engine. Storing data in a SQL table allows for significant performance improvements during data transformations and also supports the ability to create direct query connections directly against the dataflow, functionality that is not currently available in the shared capacity.

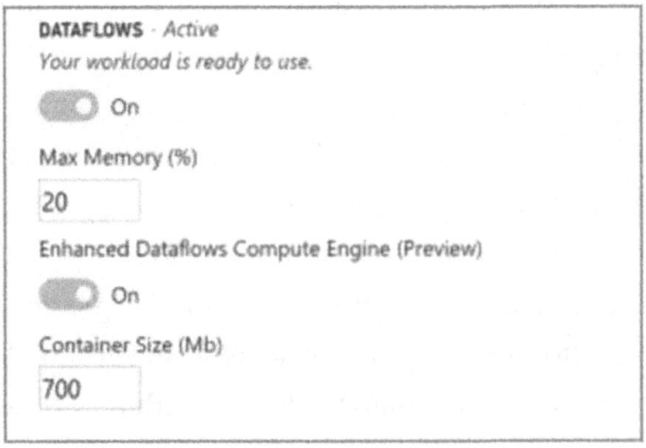

Figure 10-3. Dataflow settings for capacity

Max Memory (%): This setting represents the maximum amount of memory that can be consumed by dataflows.

Enhanced Dataflows Compute Engine: By enabling the Enhanced Dataflow Compute Engine, dataflows are stored within a SQL backed engine instead of file-based storage. This engine requires additional resources that may otherwise be used by other features. Still, it can speed up the processing of specific workloads significantly, which may ultimately reduce the overall resources required to perform data loads.

Container Size: Dataflows create a container per entity within a dataflow; this setting limits the size of these containers; the default value is 700MB.

Paginated reports

Paginated reports are a relatively new feature in Power BI, first appearing in 2019. The execution engine for paginated reports runs outside of the Power BI engine; therefore, resources need to be allocated before it can function. If this feature is being used with Power BI Embedded, then at least an A4 tier is required.

Max Memory (%): This setting limits the total amount of memory available to the paginated report service. Like the other features, this setting needs to consider the workload on the capacity.

Bring Your Own Key

All data at rest in Power BI is encrypted before it is stored to disk. This encryption helps Microsoft and its customers meet many of their security and regulatory requirements. This encryption and the management of these keys to perform this encryption are all part of the Managed SaaS solution that Power BI provides and is transparent to the client. Some regulations, however, go a step beyond and require that the data is encrypted using the customer's key and managed in such a way that even the cloud provider wouldn't be able to access the data.

Power BI Premium provides a solution to this with the ability for clients to provide their own key, and have the Power BI Service use that key instead of a Microsoft key to encrypt the data. This is made possible through the use of the Azure Key Vault. Azure Key Vault is a service that provides a secure mechanism to securely store secrets such as usernames and passwords or, in this case, an encryption key. This key is then only available to approved users or services. The Power BI Service only supports RSA keys with a length a 4096-bit length. This key can either be generated externally and imported into Azure Key Vault, or new keys can be generated in Azure Key Vault itself. A critical setting to enable in Azure Key Vault is the soft delete feature. With this feature, keys that have been deleted, possibly by mistake, can be restored. This is important because if the key is lost, Microsoft will be unable to restore this key, and the organization will lose access to all data encrypted with that key.

Step-by-step   A guide to configuring BYOK can be found here `https://docs. microsoft.com/en-us/power-bi/service-encryption-byok`.

Enabling the Power BI Premium Capacity Metric App

When a Power BI capacity is added to the tenant, the ability to install the Power BI Premium Capacity Metric App is enabled. Installing this application gives the administrator a quick view of the activities and will become an important tool for monitoring. To enable the App, a capacity administrator can select the install app button in the capacity admin screen. The Power BI Premium Capacity Metric App can also be installed using AppSource.

Hello Michael,

CHECK OUT THE LATEST VERSION OF THE POWER BI PREMIUM CAPACITY METRICS APP

The app provides up to seven days of comprehensive system, refresh, and query metrics history for your Premium capacities

[Get the app now] [Watch a video] [Dismiss]

Figure 10-4. *Enable the Power BI Premium Capacity Metric App*

Setting up the App will require you to first authenticate your user. Once set up the App will become available in the Apps menu in the Power BI portal.

Managing capacities

Once configured, general day-to-day tasks still remain that are required of the capacity administrator. The biggest of these tasks is monitoring, which will be discussed in its very own chapter later in this book.

Resizing the capacity

If the demand on the capacity grows to the point in which performance begins to degrade, then it is possible to grow the capacity. This is done differently depending if the capacity was created in Office 365 or Azure.

In Office 365, the tenant administrator is able to change the size of the capacity; this is only possible if there are enough v-cores available.

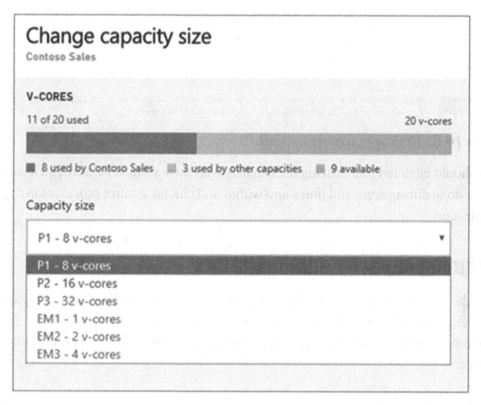

Figure 10-5.   *Resizing capacity in Power BI*

In Azure, the size of the capacity can be increased, decreased, or even stopped if need be. This can be an effective way of ramping up performance when needed, such as at month-end or reduced to save costs, possibly even by stopping the service on weekends or non-business hours.

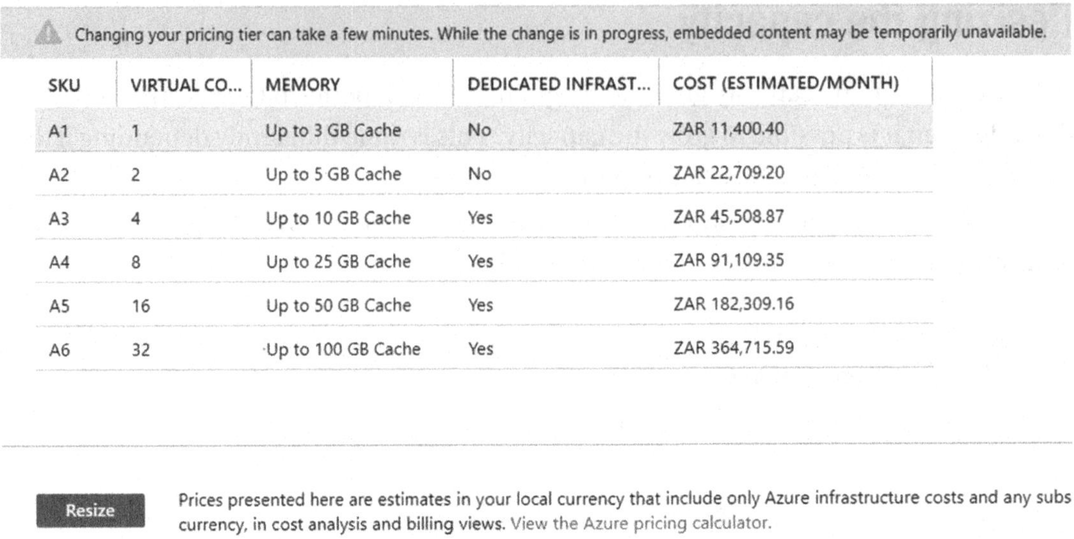

⚠ Changing your pricing tier can take a few minutes. While the change is in progress, embedded content may be temporarily unavailable.				

SKU	VIRTUAL CO...	MEMORY	DEDICATED INFRAST...	COST (ESTIMATED/MONTH)
A1	1	Up to 3 GB Cache	No	ZAR 11,400.40
A2	2	Up to 5 GB Cache	No	ZAR 22,709.20
A3	4	Up to 10 GB Cache	Yes	ZAR 45,508.87
A4	8	Up to 25 GB Cache	Yes	ZAR 91,109.35
A5	16	Up to 50 GB Cache	Yes	ZAR 182,309.16
A6	32	Up to 100 GB Cache	Yes	ZAR 364,715.59

Resize   Prices presented here are estimates in your local currency that include only Azure infrastructure costs and any subs currency, in cost analysis and billing views. View the Azure pricing calculator.

Figure 10-6. *Resizing capacity in Azure*

It should be noted that resizing the capacity will cause some downtime, so it should only be done during approved times and within and change control processes in the organization.

Assigning capacity administrators

When the capacity is created, the capacity administrators are declared for the capacity. However, it is possible to add additional administrators, and the process differs depending on whether the capacity was created through Power BI Premium in Office 365 or Azure.

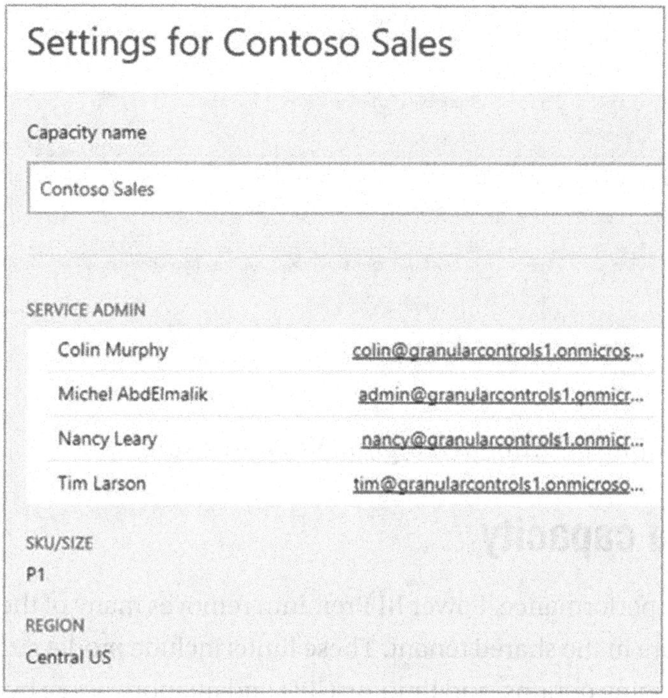

Figure 10-7. *Adding additional capacity administrators*

If the capacity was created in Azure, then capacity administrators need to be added using the Azure portal.

Users with assignment permissions

It is not only tenant and capacity administrators that can assign workspaces to capacities. The ability to assign workspaces can be delegated to other users, groups, or even the entire organization. Except for the small well-coordinated organizations, assigning these permissions to the entire organization would not be advisable as the capacity may soon fill up with non-critical workloads. If the capacity was provisioned and paid for by a business division within the organization, it might be appropriate to assign this assignment permission to a member of that business division to manage.

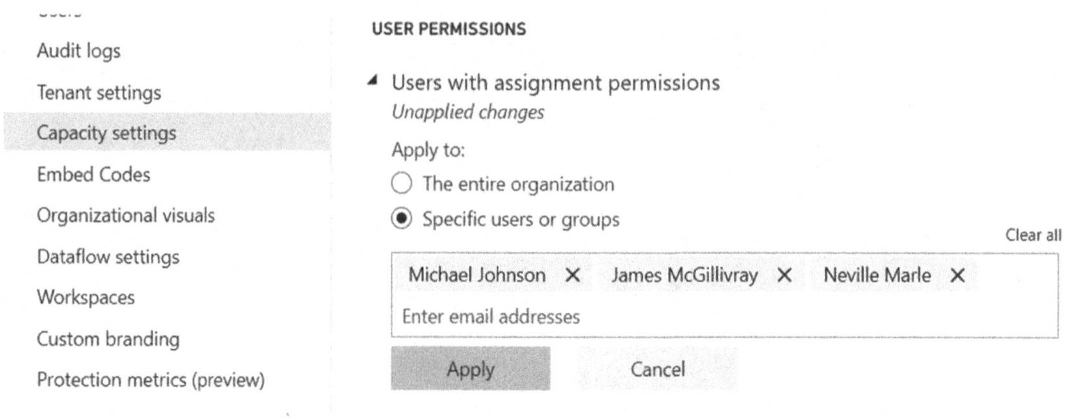

Audit logs

Tenant settings

Capacity settings

Embed Codes

Organizational visuals

Dataflow settings

Workspaces

Custom branding

Protection metrics (preview)

USER PERMISSIONS

◢ Users with assignment permissions
Unapplied changes

Apply to:

○ The entire organization

◉ Specific users or groups

Clear all

| Michael Johnson ✕   James McGillivray ✕   Neville Marle ✕ |
| Enter email addresses |

Apply   Cancel

Figure 10-8. *Adding additional assignment permission*

Restarting a capacity

To enable greater performance, Power BI Premium removes many of the restrictions on datasets that are in the shared tenant. These limits include model size, number of concurrent processing options, and limiting CPU and memory usage by individual reports. These limitations serve to protect the tenant, and without them, it is possible that the tenant can become overloaded, and response times may be affected. On rare occasions, the system may even become unresponsive. In this event, it may become necessary the restart the Capacity. In the event of a restart, unsaved work will be lost, but datasets and reports will be available after the restart without the need for a reload of the datasets.

During the restart reports would not be available until the service has restarted; scheduled refreshes will also resume after the restart. It should also be taken into consideration the effects of the restart on the business and should only be performed as a last resort.

To prevent the need for restarts, the capacity should be proactively monitored, and poorly performing models should be identified and addressed before the need for a restart arrives. Monitoring is discussed in greater detail in Chapter 16.

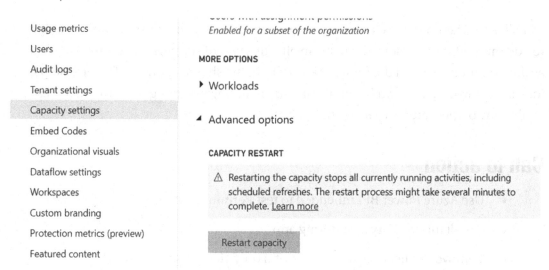

Figure 10-9. *Restarting a capacity*

Capacity limitations

Although capacities create a dedicated resource in which workspaces can be assigned (more on that in the next chapter), not all report artifacts are stored on the capacity itself. It can be easier to think of a capacity as additional memory and compute that can be assigned to certain workloads. There are a number of workloads that cannot be assigned to the capacity. These include

- Excel workbooks

- Push datasets

- Streaming datasets

This has two important considerations. First, these artifacts will not benefit from the additional resources made available by the capacity. Second, if you have used the multi-geo feature of the capacity to ensure data residency, then these datasets will not honor that assignment, and will instead be stored and processed in the home region of the tenant.

Summary

Not all organizations have or need additional Power BI capacities. However, the ability to add this additional resource can be an effective way of supporting new workloads or scaling solutions beyond the limits of Power BI in the shared capacity. The next step is to look at how workspaces can be administered, including assigning them to capacities to enable any of the features that we spoke about.

Call to action

- Use Azure Power BI Embedded to test Permium features.

- Install the capacity monitoring app

- Remove Pro licenses from users who only view content from Premium backed workspaces to reduce costs.

- Use multi-geo to store datasets in regions other than your tenant region when needed.

- Carefully manage workspaces assigned to Premium capacities.

CHAPTER 11

Workspace Administration

Read this chapter if you would like to find out more information about

- Creating workspaces

- Different types of workspaces

- Understand the roles within workspaces

- How to assign workspaces to a premium capacity

In the Power BI Service, workspaces are collections of artifacts such as dataflows, datasets, reports, and dashboards. Workspaces are used to create logical groupings of these objects. These groupings are often related to a real-world entity such as projects, departments, or products. Workspaces are used to facilitate collaboration, providing easy navigation and control access to reports and report artifacts.

Private and shared workspaces

Broadly speaking, there are two types of workspaces in Power BI, private workspaces called My Workspace and shared workspaces. Private workspaces exist for users to create and test their content without sharing it. The aim is that these workspaces are not shared with other users but used very much like we use the "My Documents" folder on a Windows computer. While it is not possible to add other users or groups to personal workspaces, it is possible to share reports and dashboards directly from a "My workspace" of a user. Sharing in this way is not advisable for two reasons. Firstly, there is very little visibility as to which users have access to what content. Currently, the only way to find out who has access is to iterate through each object and check manually.

© Ásgeir Gunnarsson and Michael Johnson 2020
Á. Gunnarsson and M. Johnson, *Pro Microsoft Power BI Administration*,
https://doi.org/10.1007/978-1-4842-6567-3_11

This is not an effective or sustainable approach to managing access. Secondly, private workspaces are bound to individual accounts. If the user assigned to that workspace were to leave the organization, the workspace would eventually be deleted, and other users would lose access to that content.

Note   It is possible to recover the content of a workspace for a short time after it has been deleted. Workspace content is kept for 30 days after the user account is deleted and can be restored.

The second type of workspace is a shared workspace. Shared workspaces facilitate collaboration between teams within an organization and externally using guest accounts. In a well-governed environment, each workspace represents a collection of related report artifacts and should be guided by the Power BI governance policy. Examples of such collections could be workspaces dedicated to departments such as Human Resources or Finance. Over the last few years, workspaces have evolved to support new functionality, and the underlying mechanisms behind the workspaces have changed such that we now have two versions of workspaces, classic workspaces and app workspaces.

Classic workspaces and workspaces

When the Power BI Service was released in 2014, it used what is today known as a classic workspace (also referred to as group workspaces). These classic workspaces were built on top of Office 365 groups. However, they introduced some challenges in the management and maintenance of these groups. In late 2018 a new type of workspace was introduced, the app workspace. App workspaces introduced new features and an improved security model. As each tenant can have a mix of classic and app workspaces, the administrator must understand the difference between the two.

Classic workspace

Classic workspaces, also known as V1 workspaces, were released in 2014. These workspaces functioned as the primary mechanism for sharing content throughout the organization. Classic workspaces are tightly bound to Office 365 groups such that whenever an Office 365 group is created, a Power BI workspace will also be created. The inverse is also true: when a Power BI workspace is created, a new Office 365 group is created. This tight coupling between groups and workspaces works well for organizations with a good governance structure around the creation of groups and workspaces. However, organizations with less discipline saw an explosion in the number of Office 365 groups being created. On top of this, each Office 365 group would result in the creation of SharePoint and OneDrive sites resulting in further proliferation of unused and unmanaged objects.

Office 365 groups only support the addition of individual users, meaning that users needed to be managed individually and not using groups. For smaller organizations, this may not be a problem, but in a larger organization where team movement happens more often, maintaining users becomes a more considerable challenge. It is not uncommon to find that users still have access to workspaces that they should no longer have access to. Effective administrators quickly learned to leverage the Power BI APIs and PowerShell module to help. Tools and automations are discussed in Chapter 15.

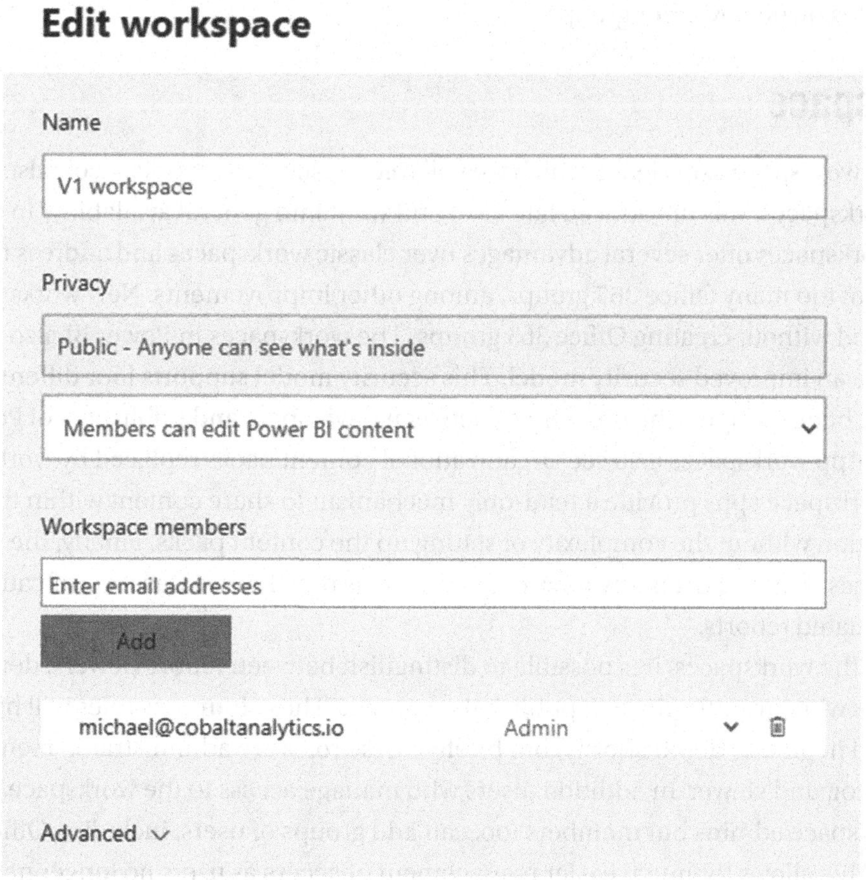

Edit workspace

Name

V1 workspace

Privacy

Public - Anyone can see what's inside

Members can edit Power BI content ⌄

Workspace members

Enter email addresses

Add

michael@cobaltanalytics.io   Admin   ⌄   🗑

Advanced ⌄

Figure 11-1.   Configuring access for a V1 workspace

Classic workspaces leverage two privacy settings in the Office 365 group. The first setting determines who can view content in the workspace, and this value can be public or private; the second setting determines what actions members of that group can take. There are only two values available under this setting. The first value is that users only view content but may not edit content. The second option is that members can edit all content in the workgroup; this includes publishing organizational content packs.

This all or nothing approach makes it difficult for administrators to separate content creators from publishers. As we will discuss shortly, the new workspaces address this by introducing additional roles to address the different roles played by members of a reporting team.

To create content to be shared with users outside of the workgroup, the Power BI team introduced organizational content packs. Organizational content packs allow the reporting team to package dashboards, reports, and datasets into a package that can be distributed within an organization. These content packs could then be installed into workspaces owned by other groups.

Workspace

The new workspace experience which we will refer to simply as workspaces, also known as V2 workspaces, was introduced late 2018 and went into general availability in early 2019. Workspaces offer several advantages over classic workspaces and address the creation of too many Office 365 groups, among other improvements. New workspaces are created without creating Office 365 groups. The workspaces in Power BI also introduce an improved security model. This security model supports four different roles that better support the differences between developers and publishers of Power BI content. App workspaces also see Organizational content packs replaced by workspace apps. Workspace apps provide a read-only mechanism to share content within the organization without the complexity of setting up the content packs. Finally, the new workspaces also support many new features such as dataflows, dataset certifications, and paginated reports.

With the workspaces, it is possible to distinguish between report viewers, developers, and users who are authorized to publish the content. These four new roles will be discussed in greater depth shortly, but briefly, these roles are administrator, member, contributor, and viewer. In addition, users who manage access to the workspace, not just workspace admins but members too, can add groups of users, including Office 365 groups. This allows for much easier management of access as users no longer need to be added one at a time and can leverage existing collections of users.

The new workspaces also enable new features such as dataflows as well as the ability to share access to datasets and dataflows across workspaces. These two features together allow for better consolidation and reuse of data assets across the organization. Datasets and dataflows are covered in greater detail in Chapter 13.

Creating a workspace

Administrators and users do not have to plan for the creation of users' private My Workspaces as these are automatically created when new users are added to the Power BI tenant. The private workspace does not require a Power BI Pro license either, and free users are also assigned a private workspace. All private workspaces are given the name "My workspace" and are only visible to the user logged into the Power BI portal. Administrators can view but not access the private workspaces of other users through the Power BI admin panel or using the Power BI APIs to pragmatically access the workspace. We discuss the Power BI APIs in Chapter 15.

Name and Description: The name of a workspace is required to be unique, although names of deleted workspaces can be reused. The organizations' governance policy should guide naming conventions for the workspace name. Workspace names should also be kept short as when viewed in the Power BI navigation pane; only the first 25 characters are visible. Hovering over the name will reveal the full name, but it can be tedious for the user to do if there are a lot of workspaces beginning with the same 25 characters. The description should also be given to each workspace; this description is displayed under the workspace's name when a user is in that workspace, and it will aid users with the context of the workspace and the reports and dashboards contained in it.

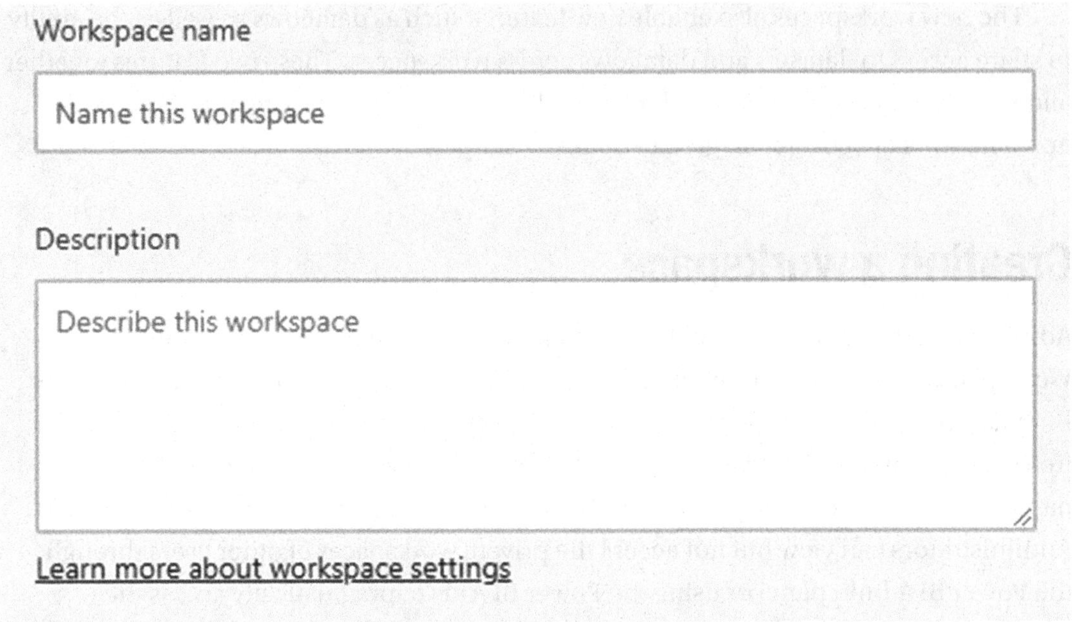

Workspace name

Name this workspace

Description

Describe this workspace

Learn more about workspace settings

Figure 11-2. *Name and Description of workspace*

Revert to classic: Today, the default workspace type is the new app workspace. However, it is possible to still create a classic workspace if required. This is done by selecting the "Revert to classic" option at the top of the "Create new workspace" pane. When you change the workspace type to classic, the available configuration options which change to reflect the differences between classic and app workspaces, and the different V1 and V2 options will be called out below.

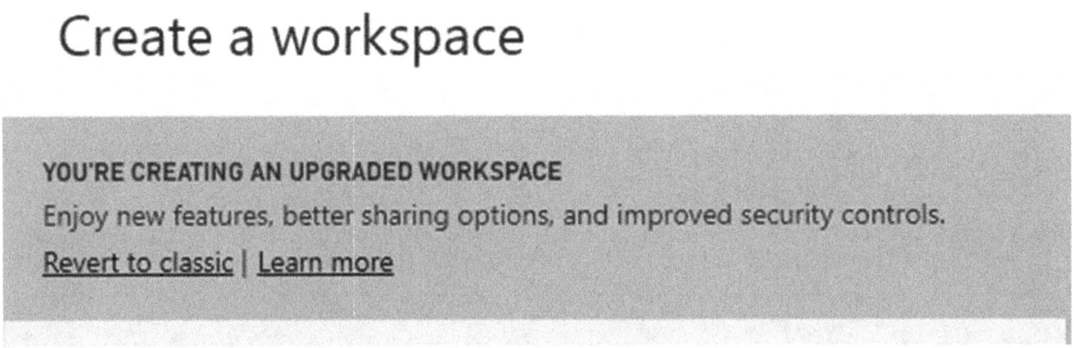

Create a workspace

YOU'RE CREATING AN UPGRADED WORKSPACE
Enjoy new features, better sharing options, and improved security controls.
Revert to classic | Learn more

Figure 11-3. *Reverting a workspace back to classic*

Workspace image: When creating a V2 workspace, an image can be assigned to the workspace. While it is still possible to assign a workspace image in a V1 workspace, this has to be done outside of Power BI on the Office 365 group administration page. Images can be used in several ways to help users quickly identify workspaces if the applicable logos or brands can be used per workspace. Colors and logos can also be used to separate Development, Test, and Production workspaces. As with names, how logos and colors are used should be driven by the Power BI governance document to ensure consistent use throughout the organization.

Contact list: The contact list is another V2 feature; this allows for a customized list of users or groups to be notified in the event of any issues occurring in the workspace. By default, such notifications will be sent to the group administrators; however you may need to provide notifications to other key stakeholders. Some of the groups of people who you may consider adding to this contact list may be a general IT alert group and the business owners of that workgroup who may need to be made aware of issues early.

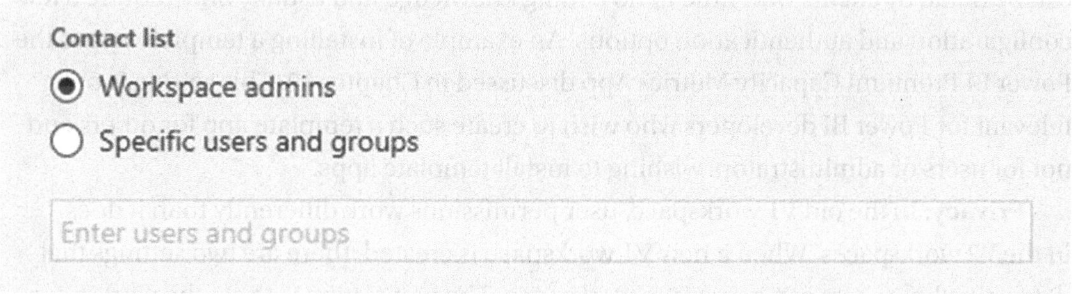

Figure 11-4. Contact list for notifications

Workspace OneDrive: One of the benefits of the V1 workspace is that when the workspace was created, several other objects were created. One of these objects was a OneDrive folder. This folder is an effective place to store files related to a division or group that the workspace relates to. OneDrive is also an effective way of versioning Power BI Files, as files in OneDrive have a built-in versioning system.

Dedicated capacity: To make use of the many benefits of Power BI Premium or Embedded capacities, a workspace needs to be assigned to that capacity. This is done by enabling the "Dedicated Capacity" slider. This option is only available to users who are part of the Capacity administrators' group or have been granted assignment permissions in the capacity management page within the Power BI admin portal. Available capacities, as well as the region they are hosted in, are displayed in the dropdown list. When leveraging the multi-geo capabilities of Power BI, the administrator needs to ensure that the assigned region complies with the organization's governance policies.

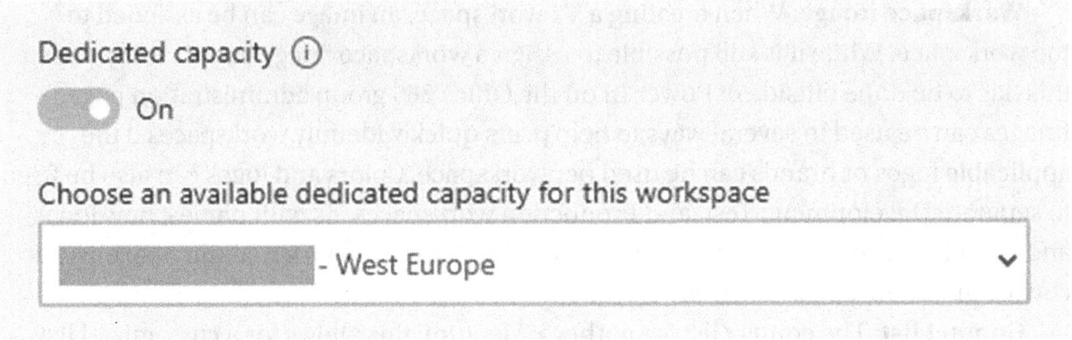

Dedicated capacity ⓘ

⬤◯ On

Choose an available dedicated capacity for this workspace

▨▨▨▨▨▨▨▨ - West Europe   ⌄

Figure 11-5. *Assigning a workspace to a capacity*

Develop template app: Power BI template apps allow Power BI partners to build apps that will be shared with clients outside of their organization. Template apps can then be installed from AppSource or even through a custom portal. Such installations can be made by clients with little to no coding knowledge and usually only require a few configuration and authentication options. An example of installing a template app is the Power BI Premium Capacity Metrics App discussed in Chapter 10. This setting is only relevant for Power BI developers who wish to create such a template app for others and not for users or administrators wishing to install template apps.

Privacy: In the old V1 workspace, user permissions work differently than it does in the V2 workspaces. When a new V1 workspace is created, there are two settings that determine how users can access the workspace. The first setting is to set the workspace to be public or private; in a public workspace all users in the organization are able to see the content inside of the workspace. Once this setting has been set, it is not possible to revert back, so it is important to fully understand how access to the workspace was to be accessed. Once the access type has been set, the next setting is to determine what actions members of the workspace have. The two options here were to allow members to only view the content in the workspace; the second option allows these members to view and edit content. Only users could be added as members, which can result in a large administrative burden on the Power BI administrator. In addition to the administrative burden, this security model restricted the abilities of the administrator to distinguish between view only and editing users without granting Admin access to the workspace itself. For this reason alone, V2 workspaces are recommended over V1 workspaces.

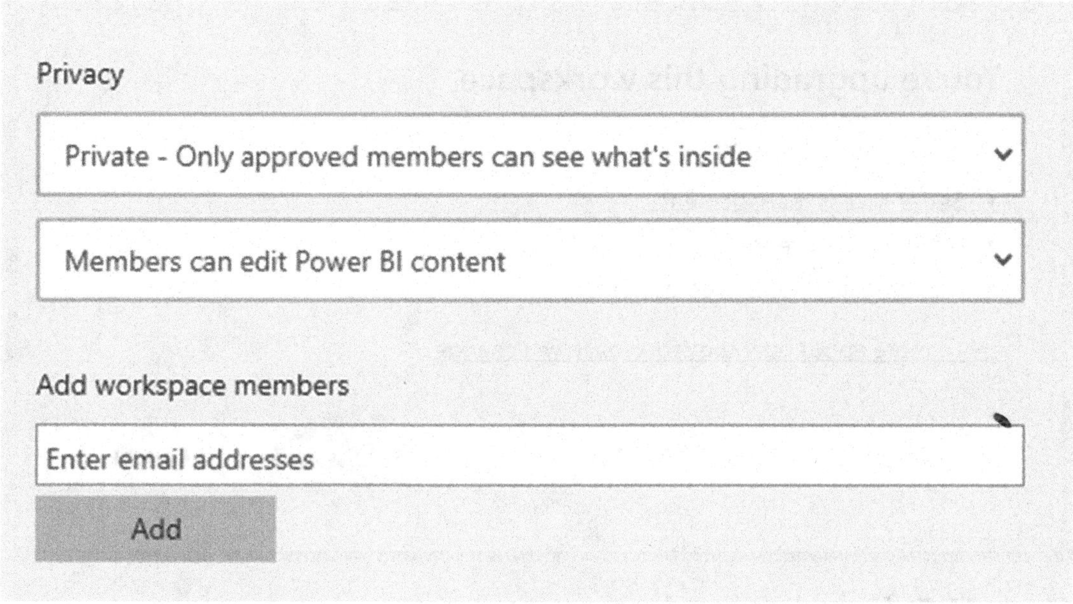

Figure 11-6. *Configuring a classic workspace*

Upgrading a workspace from classic to the new workspace

Workspaces that were created using the V1 workspace model can be upgraded to the new V2 workspace model. This migration is easily done by navigating to the "Edit this workspace" tab, and then scrolling down to the upgrade this workspace (preview) option under the advanced tab. This will begin a simple wizard-style approach to the upgrade; the tab provides an overview of the changes that should be expected. It is recommended that you read through this fully before migrating the workspace. Before the upgrade option can be selected, the workspace administrator will need to confirm they are ready to migrate the workspace by ticking the "I'm ready to upgrade this workspace" option.

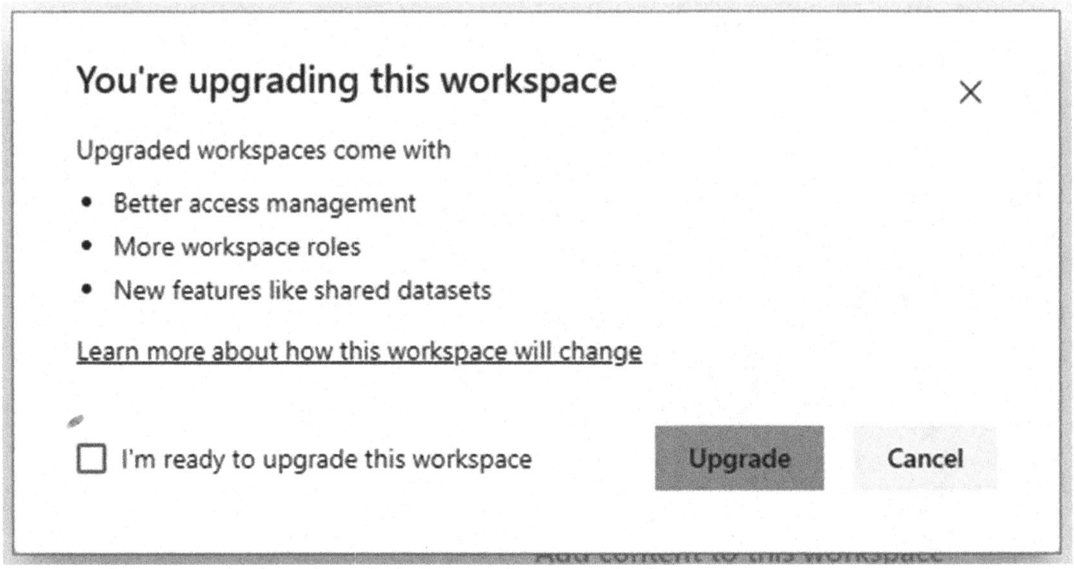

You're upgrading this workspace   ✕

Upgraded workspaces come with

- Better access management
- More workspace roles
- New features like shared datasets

Learn more about how this workspace will change

☐ I'm ready to upgrade this workspace   Upgrade   Cancel

Figure 11-7. *Upgrading a workspace*

Once the migration is complete, a dialog confirming the upgrade was successful will be displayed.

Before migrating the workspace, it is recommended that you notify the users of the workspace about the upcoming change, and it is recommended that you perform this migration after hours if possible. Users who have the workspace open during the migration will be asked to refresh their browsers. Users who are editing reports using the online report editor will be prompted to save their changes before refreshing.

The names and IDs of workspaces will not be changed during this migration, and all links previously sent out to users will continue to work. The OneDrive folder for the migrated V2 workspace will be automatically bound to the OneDrive folder for the Office 365 workgroup.

As content packs are not supported in the new V2 workspaces, they will be removed. Published content packs will be removed and will no longer be able to be installed. Installed content packs will remain in the workspaces in which they were installed; however, they will no longer be updated. Links to this content will also change, and resharing these links is required.

While it is possible to revert a V1 workspace that has been upgraded to a V2 workspace back to a V1 workspace, it is not possible to migrate a new V2 workspace back to a V1 workspace. It is only possible to revert the workspace if a number of conditions are met; the first of these conditions is that the underlying Office 365 group was not deleted. The content of the workgroup will be kept for 30 days, after which the workspace cannot be reverted back to a V1 workspace.

Users roles in a workspace

Power BI v2 workspaces introduce four roles that provide better control over the permitted actions that a user can take. These roles are as follows:

Viewer: The viewer role primarily allows users to interact with reports. The viewer role should be the default role assigned to people who are not expected to edit content in the workspace, for example, those who are not report developers. For users who are assigned to this role, thought should be given to rather sharing the workspace content via a workspace app. The workspace app provides a few additional benefits over the viewer's roles, such as custom navigation and links that make for better user experience.

Contributor: The contributor role should be the default role assigned to users or groups who are expected to create content in the workspace. Members of this role can create new datasets and reports, schedule data set refreshes, and publish dashboards. The purpose of this role is to allow content creators to create content but not have the ability to publish these changes themselves.

Member: The member role should be restricted to a small subset of the Power BI report developers. Members of this role can add additional users but not with permissions higher than the member role itself. Members of the member role can publish a workspace app and can promote items within the workspace. This role should be limited to members of the reporting team who are authorized to accept and promote the changes made by other users, or users who need to manage other members of the team.

Admin: The workspace admin role is not to be confused with the Power BI admin role. Users or groups assigned the workspace admin role are granted full control of the workspace only and will not have control over objects outside of the workspace. The primary actions that a workspace admin can take are to modify settings of the workspace itself (such as name and description) and moving the workspace between capacities if an appropriate capacity assignment is also held by the user.

These roles are cumulative, and only a single role can be assigned to a user, although it is possible that a user may inhabit multiple roles by being a member of multiple groups that are assigned different roles within the workspace; in this case the higher of the roles will apply. A summary of the permitted actions per role is presented in Table 11-1.

Table 11-1. *Permissible actions per role*

Capability	Admin	Member	Contributor	Viewer
Update and delete the workspace.	X			
Add/remove people, including other admins.	X			
Add members or others with lower permissions.	X	X		
Publish and update an app.	X	X		
Share an item or share an app.	X	X		
Allow others to reshare items.	X	X		
Feature apps on colleagues' Home	X	X		
Feature dashboards and reports on colleagues' Home	X	X	X	
Create, edit, and delete content in the workspace.	X	X	X	
Publish reports to the workspace, delete content.	X	X	X	
Create a report in another workspace based on a dataset in this workspace.	X	X	X	
Copy a report.	X	X	X	
Schedule data refreshes via the on-premises gateway.	X	X	X	
Modify gateway connection settings.	X	X	X	
View and interact with an item.4	X	X	X	X
Read data stored in workspace dataflows	X	X	X	X

Assigning workspaces to capacities

While workspaces can be assigned to capacities when created, it is also common to move workspaces into and out of capacities after their creation. This will likely happen when new capacity is provisioned; Premium only features are required, such as paginated reports and larger data sets, or when users assigned Power BI Free licenses are required access to the reports in those workspaces. The process of migrating a workspace requires a workspace administrator as well as being a capacity administrator or having assignment rights to that capacity (see Chapter 10 for more detail).

Restoring a deleted workspace

In the event of a workspace being deleted, it is possible for a Power BI admin to restore the workspace. This can be done by using the Power BI APIs or by searching for the workspace in the workspaces tab in the Power BI admin portal.

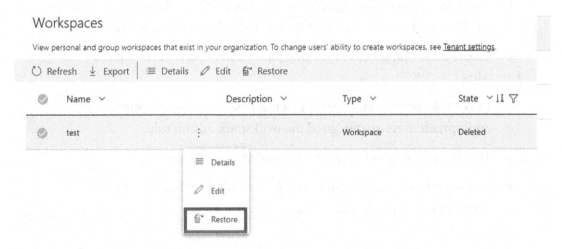

Figure 11-8. *Restoring a deleted workspace*

When restoring the workspace, you are allowed to choose a new name for the workspace. A new name is required if a new workspace has since been created using that name. Before the workspace can be restored, a new administrator needs to be assigned.

Note   When restoring a workspace, all previous user role assignments are deleted and will need to be recreated.

Summary

Workspaces are the primary mechanism for sharing content with other users and groups in the organization. Each user is assigned their own private workspace simply called "My workspace" and should only be used by the user to develop and test their own content. When reports are to be shared, a new shared workspace should be created. To take advantage of many of the new features available in Power BI, it is recommended that workspaces be created as the new app workspace over the older classic workspace.

Access to workspaces can be controlled by adding users and groups and assigning those users and groups to appropriate roles.

Call to action

- Determine who in the organization should be allowed to create workspaces. Creating a group for this can make it easy to manage.

- Create a naming scheme for workspaces and ensure it is complied with.

- Check role assignments for users within workspaces to ensure only appropriate users are assigned the workspace admin role.

- Migrate workspaces to the new V2 workspaces if possible.

- Ensure only workspaces that need to use Premium features are assigned to premium capacities.

CHAPTER 12

Managing users and security

Read this chapter if you would like to find out more information about

- How Power BI implements user authentication
- Enhanced security options

Security, like many features in Power BI, leverages other infrastructure components in the Office 365 and Azure platforms. In the case of Office 365, including Power BI, security is implemented using Azure Active Directory (AAD), which is a web-scale Platform as a Service (PaaS) in Azure. Azure Active Directory is built on the foundations of Microsoft Active Directory, which is used for identity access management in organizations the world over. One of the primary benefits of AAD is that it can be seamlessly integrated with an organization's on-premises implementation providing a single set of user credentials for both on-premises and cloud applications.

The primary goal of AAD is to ensure users can be productive whenever and wherever they are while still ensuring that the organization's assets, including its data, are secure. The AAD tenant is created as part of the Office 365 tenant creation process and is the engine behind actions like creating users. AAD comes with many features, and like Power BI enhanced enterprise-grade features, these are available through the purchase of higher tiers of the product.

Editions of Azure Active Directory

Azure Active Directory is available in four different editions with each edition having additional features on top of the previous version.

The editions of AAD are

© Ásgeir Gunnarsson and Michael Johnson 2020
Á. Gunnarsson and M. Johnson, *Pro Microsoft Power BI Administration*,
https://doi.org/10.1007/978-1-4842-6567-3_12

Free: When signing up for Power BI without any other services, your AAD tenant will use the free edition of Azure Active Directory. This free tier supports all the core features required of an authentication service. In addition to the comprehensive identity management, the free edition also supports Two-Factor Authentication also known as 2FA, as well as Azure AD Connect Sync allows active directory to be synchronized with a compatible version on the on-premises version allowing you to use a single login for both on-premise networks and the cloud.

Azure AD for Office 365: This edition was designed especially for uses of Office 365 products and is only available if your organization has purchased an E1, E3, E4, E5, or F1 subscription. In addition to all the benefits of the free edition, Azure AD for Office 365 also includes custom branding on the login screen, an SLA on the availability of the AAD service of 99.9%, and support for two-way synchronization of AAD and on-premise active directory.

Premium P1: The P1 Premium edition is required if your organization has more complex security requirements such as Conditional Access. Conditional access allows the creation of rules-driven authentication processes that can be used to enforce organizational access policies. An example of such a policy includes requiring users not on the corporate network to use Two-Factor Authentication before gaining access to corporate applications.

Premium P2: The P2 Premium edition of AAD contains advanced features such as Vulnerabilities and Risky Accounts Detection and Risk-Based Conditional Access policies which make use of machine learning to provide proactive threat detection.

P1 or P2 Premium plans can be purchased in several ways, including through your Microsoft account representative, the Open Volume Licensing Program, Cloud Solutions Provider, and through the Office 365 admin portal.

To see a full comparison of all editions of Azure Active Directory, go to `https://azure.microsoft.com/en-us/pricing/details/active-directory/`.

Creating a new user

In a large organization, the job of creating users would not usually be assigned to the Power BI. Such tasks are sent to a security team that manages the organization's Active Directory infrastructure. In small organizations or organizations who only use Power BI and not any of the other Office 365 or Azure services, it may be required. Users can be added to the organization's directory using a variety tools including the Office 365 admin portal, the Azure Active Directory portal, and the PowerShell automation cmdlets discussed in Chaper 15. To add a user to Azure Active Directory, the administrator needs to be part of either the Global administrators or User administrator roles.

While each portal results in a new user account, the experiences do differ. In the Azure Active Directory portal, users are asked to provide the minimum information required to create a new user. In the Office 365 portal, where the intent behind the user is often clearer (they are often employees), there are greater details.

Identity

User name * ⓘ	Example: chris @ cobaltanalytics.io ∨
	The domain name I need isn't shown here
Name * ⓘ	Example: 'Chris Green'
First name	
Last name	

Groups and roles

Groups	0 groups selected
Roles	User

Settings

Block sign in	Yes No
Usage location	∨

Figure 12-1. *Adding a new user using the Azure portal*

We discuss some of these options in the following.

Required settings

User Name: Each user in Azure Active Directory is assigned a unique user name.

Domain Name: Each active directory tenant can host multiple domains.

Password: A secret known only by the user used for authentication.

Optional settings

First and Last Name: The first and last names of the user will make it easier to identify the user.

Groups: This will add the user account to any existing groups; this can also include any classic workspaces that automatically create groups.

Roles: Any roles that the user should be added to; this could include the Global admin or Power BI admin role.

Block sign in: This option will allow you to prevent the user from signing in if for some reason you needed to disable the account.

Assigning licenses

Once the user has been created, they would then need to have a Power BI license assigned to them. This could be a Free or Pro Power BI license depending on the license type.

The user would be able to sign up for a free trail license; this will revert back to a free license after the trial period has ended.

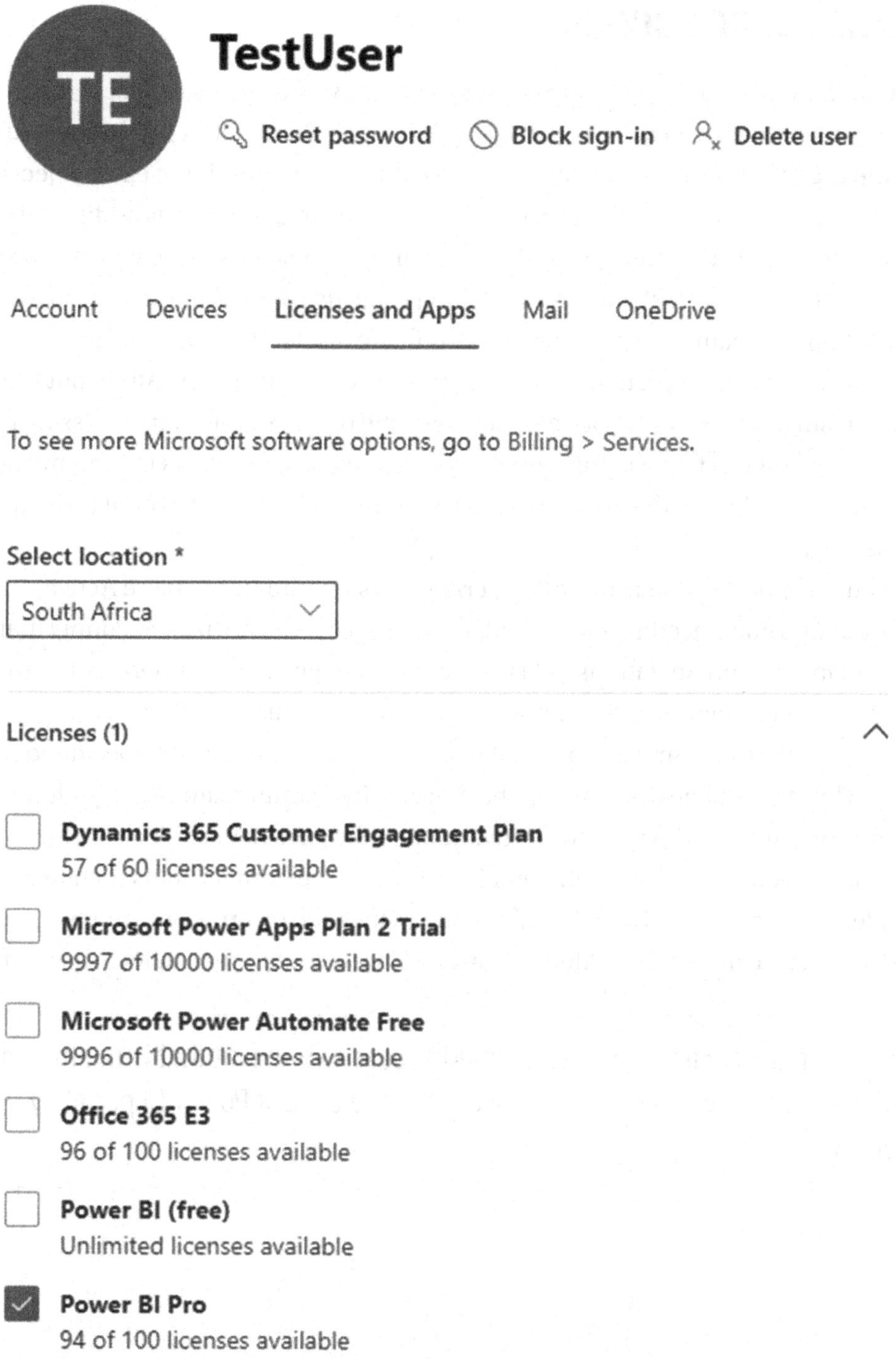

TE

TestUser

🔑 Reset password   ⊘ Block sign-in   👤ₓ Delete user

Account   Devices   **Licenses and Apps**   Mail   OneDrive

To see more Microsoft software options, go to Billing > Services.

Select location *

South Africa   ⌄

Licenses (1)   ⌃

☐ **Dynamics 365 Customer Engagement Plan**
57 of 60 licenses available

☐ **Microsoft Power Apps Plan 2 Trial**
9997 of 10000 licenses available

☐ **Microsoft Power Automate Free**
9996 of 10000 licenses available

☐ **Office 365 E3**
96 of 100 licenses available

☐ **Power BI (free)**
Unlimited licenses available

☑ **Power BI Pro**
94 of 100 licenses available

Figure 12-2. *Assigning a Power BI Pro license to a user in the Office 365 portal*

External user access

A common requirement for organizations is to allow external users to access reports. Traditionally this has been achieved in one of two ways. An account can be created within the organization's AAD tenant. However, this can create a lot of extra objects in AAD that need to be managed, and can also result in greater costs as additional subscriptions may be required. Second and a common misconception which has been spoken about previously but warrants revisiting is the use of the Publish to web (public) feature. When this feature is used, the report is made available without security. This initially meets the requirement to share reports outside of the organization, but there is no mechanism in place to stop people outside of the organization from accessing this content. Microsoft has taken a number of steps over the last few years to limit misuse of Publish to web, including the ability to turn the feature off, which is now also the default tenant setting.

To better support the sharing with external users requirement, Azure Active Directory allows guest accounts to be added. Guest accounts are user accounts that are created in other organizations' AAD tenants but are given access permission to the tenant. This level of sharing is also known as Business-to-Business B2B sharing.

Before external accounts can be used in Power BI, they first need to be added to the AAD. This needs to be done by a global or security administrator. When adding an external account, AAD will send an invitation to the external user. This means that the user does need to provide a valid email address. The external user is then required to complete the signup for this external account. Once the external account has been created, that user can then be added to Power BI in the same way that local accounts are.

Note   When guests accounts are granted access to a tenant that is not their home tenant, they will only be able to gain access to the correct Power BI portal by using a direct link.

Branding

If your AAD tenant is using any edition but the free edition, then it is possible to brand the sign-in screen. This provides a consistent look and feel throughout the sign-in process. This sign-in branding only becomes available through the portal once the user has entered their username. There are several configuration options available to customize the sign-in screen.

Language: The language used for the sign-in page can be changed from the default English language. This does not change any of the language settings of various applications and applies to the sign-in screen only.

Sign-in page background: An image can be configured as the background image for the sign-in screen. This image, no larger than 1920 x 1080, will appear on the login screen; using a similar background image as that used on the corporate intranet can help enhance that standard look and feel.

Banner logo: The banner logo, no greater than 60x280, is usually the organization's logo. Again this helps provide a consistent look and feel.

Sign-in page text: Custom text, up to a length of 265 characters, can be provided; this text could be a disclaimer or a link to a corporate help desk.

Multi-Factor Authentication

Multi-factor authentication improves the security of accounts by requiring the user to not only know the password and a shared secret but also to possess something that only the user would have access to. This could be a physical token such as access to a device or a physical characteristic such as a biometric token. The following forms of authentication can be used with AAD:

- Microsoft Authenticator app
- OATH Hardware token
- SMS
- Voicemail

Multi-factor authentication can be made compulsory for all users in the organization or can be used as part of AAD conditional Access.

Conditional Access

Conditional Access policies are if-then statements in which the organization can build a set of authentication flows to enforce organizational policies and ensure that the correct access controls are put in place. Conditional Access is only available through the P1 and P2 AAD premium editions or Microsoft 365 Business Licenses.

Conditional Access works by taking in several inputs known as signals and then making a decision on whether they accept, deny, or challenge the authenticating user.

Signal

Some of the signals available are

User or group membership: Policies can be set up so that they apply to certain users or groups; a typical example of this may be to apply a different conditional access policy to external users.

IP location: IP location can be used in a number of authentication scenarios. Examples of such include determining if the authentication request is coming from the corporate network. IP location also is used to determine if the authentication is coming from certain geographies. A simple policy may be to deny authentication requests from countries that your organization does not have a presence in.

In the event of employees traveling to such countries, a group can be created, and employees can be added to that group to allow only them to connect.

Device: Organizational policies can also be created to prevent users from connecting to the service using devices that do not meet a set of requirements. These requirements could specify that the user be joined to the domain or that they comply with some minimum set of criteria, such as having BitLocker installed.

Application: It is also possible to use the application as a signal; this could be used to drive a policy in which certain applications are only available while the user is on the origination network. Such a policy could be used to limit admin access to users who are on the corporate network.

Decision

Once AAD has received the signals, such as the identity of the user, their location, and what application they are using, AAD will be able to make a decision.

Deny: A simple decision can be made to deny the authentication attempt; an example of such a policy may be to deny all incoming authentication requests from known "Hacking hotspots" or denying access to users who are or are not part of certain AD groups.

Challenge: Certain signals can trigger the need for additional authentication challenges. An example of this may be requiring users to use multi-factor authentication if the user is part of an administrative role.

Grant: The authentication request is approved, and the user is given access to the application.

Real-time and calculated risk detection

Integration with Azure AD Identity Protection allows Conditional Access to identify risky sign-in behavior. When risky behavior is identified, AAD can force users to perform extra security checks, force them to change their password, or even disable the account until an administrator can take action.

Microsoft Cloud App Security

Microsoft Cloud App Security allows organizations to create Conditional Access policies using real-time session controls. This can help ensure that Power BI analytics are kept secure and give administrators the ability to monitor in real-time the activities of users.

As of this writing Microsoft Cloud App Security is still in preview and is limited in its actions. Currently there are two detections for Power BI:

Suspicious share: Detects when a report is shared with an unusual external user; this can be combined with sensitivity labels to detect when users attempt to share with users outside of the organization.

Mass share of reports: Microsoft Cloud App Security can also be used to detect occurrences of several reports being shared in a short amount of time; this may be a sign of a compromised account.

Summary

Azure Active Directory provides several configurable options to enhance the security position of the organization and thereby Power BI itself. Using Conditional Access fine-grained policies can be enabled, allowing the organization's user to work both safely and productively.

Call to action

- Consider enabling Two-Factor Authentication (2FA) for added security.

- Use guests accounts to enable external access rather than creating a separate account.

- Set up Conditional Access for enhanced user security.

CHAPTER 13

Datasets and Dataflows

Read this chapter if you would like to find out more information about

- How to deploy and manage datasets and dataflows
- Configure data refreshes
- Enable large models in Power BI Premium
- Enable and use the XMLA endpoint

As part of the Application Lifecycle Management process, administrators are often responsible for the deployment and management of report artifacts. Datasets and dataflows are two important artifacts that often require more care than reports and dashboards would. Critical tasks relating to the management of datasets and dataflows include

- Publishing to the service
- Configuring data sources
- Refreshing data
- Managing access
- Promoting and certifying data

In this chapter, we discuss some of these key administration activities as they relate to Power BI datasets and dataflows.

© Ásgeir Gunnarsson and Michael Johnson 2020
Á. Gunnarsson and M. Johnson, *Pro Microsoft Power BI Administration*,
https://doi.org/10.1007/978-1-4842-6567-3_13

Power BI datasets

Power BI datasets, also referred to as the Power BI model, consist of tables, relationships, calculations, formatting, and data. Datasets are created in Power BI Desktop together with a report as part of a single PBIX. When a report is published to the Power BI Service, the dataset is included as part of that deployment, assuming that the report was not built on a dataset that has already been published to the power BI service. These reports are sometimes referred to as lean reports as they do not contain an embedded data model. Once the PBIX file has been published, the model gets separated from the report, and both will inherit the name of the PBIX file. It is possible to change the name of the report but not the dataset.

Publishing to the service

Depending on the deployment policy of your organization, the job of publishing Power BI artifacts may become the responsibility of an administration or operations team. This separation of duties can play an essential role in ensuring that a well-governed Power BI environment is maintained.

You can read more about deployment processes in Chapter 5.

There are many ways to deploy datasets and dataflows to the Power BI environment.

- Publishing using Power BI Desktop
- Uploading from the portal
- Publishing using APIs
- Publishing using the XMLA endpoint

Publishing using Power BI Desktop

The most common approach to publishing reports is to use Power BI Desktop. When logged in, the Power BI application has a **Publish** button on the ribbon.

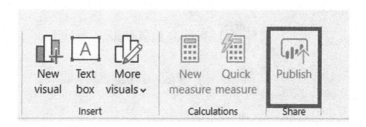

Before the PBIX can be published to the service using the Desktop application, all changes must first be saved. After selecting the Publish button, a dialog window is displayed, listing all workspaces that the user has permission to publish to. Once the workspace has been selected, the process will first ensure that there is no existing report with that name; if the report name already exists, you will be asked if you want to overwrite the published file or cancel. The PBIX is then uploaded to the service. This may take some time if the model is large. Once Power BI Desktop has completed the upload, a dialog is displayed that confirms the upload is complete along with a link to the report.

Uploading from the portal

It is also possible to upload Power BI reports using the portal. This option is useful when the administrator does not have the Power BI Desktop installed, such as if they are using an operating system that is not supported.

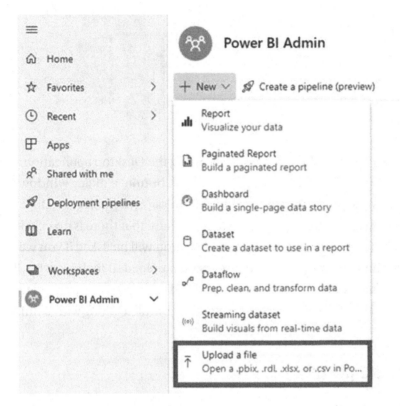

Figure 13-1. Uploading a PIBX file using the portal

Using this option, the administrator must ensure that they are in the correct workspace before uploading the report.

Publishing using the REST APIs or PowerShell Cmdlets

Manual deployments may be appropriate for small organizations with few reports, but in any large organization with many reports and datasets, an automated approach to these deployments is preferable. The Power BI Service provides REST APIs that can be used to perform many operations including the publishing of PBIX files. Many of these functions are also available as PowerShell Cmdlets. Chapter 15 discusses these APIs in more detail.

Using these automated tools, it is possible to upload many reports in a consistent manner. These automation options can also be integrated with many of the automated deployment tools that your organization may already use.

Publishing using the XMLA endpoint

If your organization uses Power BI Premium, it is also possible to create and modify datasets directly using the new XMLA endpoint functionality. This endpoint is discussed in more detail later in this chapter. The XMLA endpoint exposes the underlying Analysis Services service, allowing traditional tools such as Visual Studio or Tabular Editor to make changes to the model. This is the preferred way to deploy large models as this approach may not force the upload of all data, making it a faster way to apply changes.

Keeping data up-to-date

Once a dataset has been deployed to the Power BI Service, often the next step is to ensure that the dataset is kept up-to-date. This is done by ensuring that the dataset can connect to its source systems and load the latest data. To achieve this the user configuring the report needs to

- Configure data sources and gateways for the dataset

- Invoke data refresh

Configuring data sources

When Power BI reports and their underlying datasets are published to the Power BI Service, the credentials for the associated data sources are not included. This means that the credentials need to be provided before data access can occur. For datasets using DirectQuery or live connections, this means that the reports will remain unusable and reports using import mode that the data will become stale. Configuration of the datasets data sources can be accessed via the settings table on the dataset.

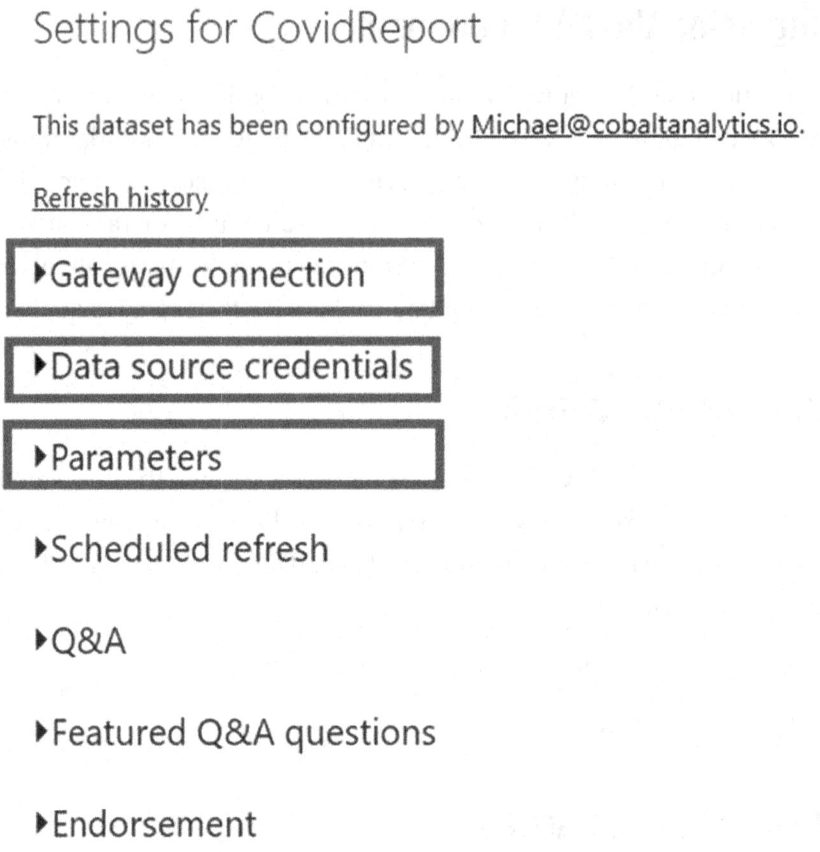

Settings for CovidReport

This dataset has been configured by Michael@cobaltanalytics.io.

Refresh history

▸Gateway connection

▸Data source credentials

▸Parameters

▸Scheduled refresh

▸Q&A

▸Featured Q&A questions

▸Endorsement

Figure 13-2. *Data source configuration for datasets*

There are three important tabs on this menu.

Gateway connections

Gateways provide a bridge between the Power BI Service and on-premises data sources. The gateway can also be used to refresh cloud-based data sources when combined with on-premises data or when forced to. One advantage of the Power BI Gateway is that data sources can be configured once and reused by reports and datasets that have access to the data source.

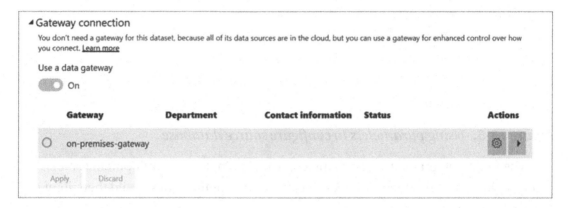

Figure 13-3. *Selecting an On-premises data gateway*

Gateways are discussed in greater detail in Chapter 14.

Data source credentials

When data gateways are not required, the data source credentials can be manually
provided per data source.

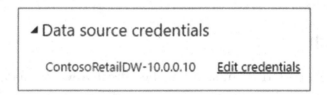

Figure 13-4. *Updating data source credentials*

Parameters

Parameters can be used in many ways to define configurable variables and are a
great way of creating dynamic connection details in Power BI datasets. This is useful
for organizations that have separate environments for development, testing, and
production. Connection strings in Power BI are embedded in the application and
cannot be changed during deployment like they can be in other tools such as SQL Server
Integration Services. Parameters can be used to dynamically modify the connection
string by providing configurable values such as in the example in Figure 13-5.

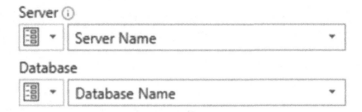

Figure 13-5. *Using parameters to configure source database*

When in development these parameters would point to the development servers, but when deployed to a production workspace, these parameter values would then point to the production data sources.

Once the data sources and gateway have been correctly configured, the next step is to refresh the data.

Data refreshes

For reports that use import mode to remain up-to-date, the data in those models must be refreshed. How these refreshes are scheduled is determined by the size, frequency, and method of change.

Manual refresh

Manual refreshes are performed by selecting the **refresh now** option for the dataset. The refresh now button adds the dataset into a queue of datasets to be refreshed, so it may not start immediately.

Figure 13-6. *Manually refreshing a Power BI dataset*

This option may be appropriate for data sources that are not expected to be refreshed often or have a data source that is not consistently online.

Scheduled refresh

Refreshing datasets manually is not a sustainable practice when your users require constant up-to-date data. For this Power BI supports scheduled refreshes. Scheduled refresh can be configured to trigger refreshes multiple times per day. The capacity type determines the number of times a dataset can be refreshed. Datasets inside of a shared capacity can be refreshed up to 8 times per day. Datasets published to Premium workspaces can be refreshed up to 48 times per day.

Schedules can be created to run either daily or weekly, with time of day set at intervals of 30 minutes. This means that a dataset could be set to refresh every hour during core business hours, once every 3 hours throughout the day, or whatever custom refresh schedule works for your business. Premium backed workspaces can be set to refresh every 30 minutes throughout the day. In Figure 13-7 you see how to schedule a data refresh twice daily at 8:00AM and 10:30:AM in the selected timezone.

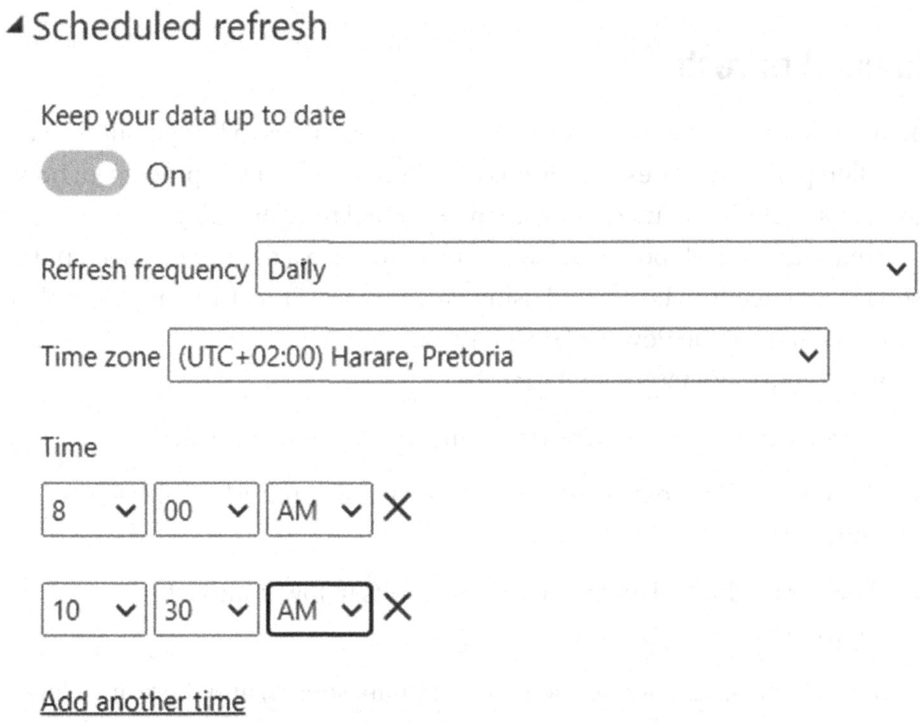

Figure 13-7. *Creating a refresh schedule*

> **Warning**   While it is be possible to process the model every 30 minutes, careful attention needs to be paid the added load that these refreshes place on the source systems, as these refreshes can cause high resource usage. If this is the case, then as the administrator, you may want to recommend the use of incremental refresh.

Automated refresh

Some data sources may not support refreshes at set times during the day. For example, if your organization runs a large end-of-day process that completes at inconsistent time intervals, then it is not possible to know when the best time to schedule the load is. In this case, it is possible to invoke a dataset refresh using the Power BI APIs. Using the APIs it is possible to include the Power BI dataset refresh as a step in your ETL process. This ensures that the refresh happens as soon as new data is available, while not being called repetitively or before the data is ready.

Incremental refresh

Incremental refresh is a feature in Power BI that allows tables to be split into smaller sections called partitions. These partitions can then be selectively processed; how these partitions are selected is defined using an incremental refresh policy.

An incremental refresh policy cannot be created once a dataset has been published to the service and needs to be created using Power BI Desktop. Creating this policy may be the responsibility of the Power BI developers.

Reasons to consider incremental refresh:

- Smaller volumes of data retrieved mean faster data refreshes.

- A shorter refresh period results in more reliable refreshes with fewer timeouts.

- Fewer rows loaded during refreshes results in lower impacts on source systems.

Incremental refresh cannot be used on every data source, and there are a few limitations.

Incremental refresh requirements:

- Table must include a date or datetime field.

- Refreshes can only work on dates in the past.

- The data source should support Query-folding such as SQL server.

Step-by-step   For step by step instructions on how to set up Incremental refresh, see `https://docs.microsoft.com/en-us/power-bi/admin/service-premium-incremental-refresh`.

Alerting

With any automated solution, it is essential to ensure that the appropriate people are notified of any errors with the refresh so that these issues can be addressed promptly to minimize user impact. When creating the refresh schedule, it is possible to supply a list of email addresses that should be notified in the event of an error.

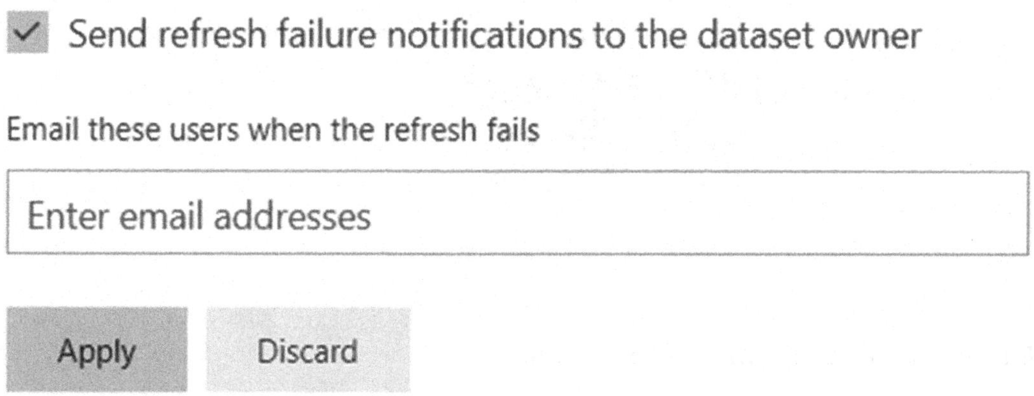

☑ Send refresh failure notifications to the dataset owner

Email these users when the refresh fails

Enter email addresses

Apply   Discard

Figure 13-8.   Configure Failure notifications

It is also possible to send such notifications using the APIs by passing the list of user to be notified. See Chapter 15 for more on the Power BI APIs.

XMLA endpoint

As of March 2020, the Public preview for the read-write XMLA endpoint became available for premium capacities (the read XMLA endpoint has been available for a few more months). The XMLA endpoint supports programmatic access to the underlying dataset in much the same way as we are able to connect directly with Azure Analysis services. Before being able to use the XMLA for a workspace hosted on a premium capacity, it first needs to be enabled in the Capacity admin portal.

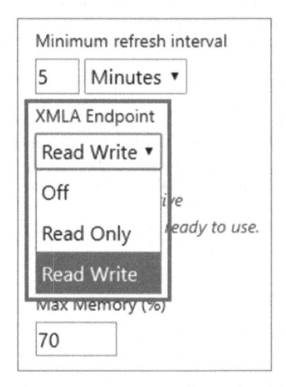

Figure 13-9. *Enabling the XML endpoint*

There are many reasons why an organization would want to enable the XMLA endpoint. We look at some of the features that the XMLA endpoint enables.

Read-only XMLA endpoint

Using the read-only XMLA endpoint, it is possible to use several common tools to connect directly to the dataset; tools such as SQL Management Studio can be used to query the metadata of the database. More practically, other reporting tools that support XMLA can query the model directly. Such tools include Excel and Tableau, allowing business users to continue using the tools that they know while supporting a single version of the truth across the enterprise. When using the XMLA endpoint, authentication is still managed through Azure Active Directory, and users still need to be given access to the underlying workspace.

To be able to use the XMLA endpoint, all that is needed is a valid user account and the URL for the endpoint. The URL for the endpoint can be obtained by navigating to the Premium tab of the workspace and copying the workspace connection. An example of this endpoint can be seen in Figure 13-10.

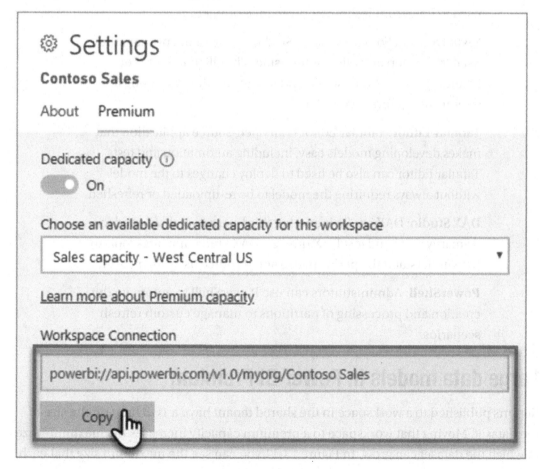

Figure 13-10. *Getting workspace connection*

Read-write XML endpoint

Setting the XMLA endpoint to read-write supports all the features available in the read-only endpoint as well as many functions that allow the dataset to be updated using either XMLA or TOM (Tabular Object Model). Some of the tools that can use the XML endpoint are

> **SQL Server Management Studio**: Management Studio is often used by SQL Server administrators and developers to connect to and manage SQL Server environments. Management Studio can be used to perform tasks such as exploring the dataset, returning metadata about the model such as its size, creating and deleting partitions, as well as procession partitions.

> **SQL Server profiler**: Profiler can be used to connect to Power BI workspaces and monitor the activities taking place. This can be used to help troubleshoot performance problems.

> **Visual Studio**: For years Visual Studio has been the primary tool used to develop any Microsoft Business Intelligence solution, including multi-dimensional and tabular models providing an easy-to-use graphical interface.

> **Tabular Editor**: Tabular Editor is an open-source application that makes developing models easy, including automation and tests. Tabular Editor can also be used to deploy changes to the model without always requiring the model to be re-uploaded or refreshed.

> **DAX Studio**: DAX studio is another third-party tool developed to primarily write and test DAX queries. DAX Studio includes tools to help understand the performance and resource usage of measures.

> **PowerShell**: Administrators can use PowerShell to automate the creation and processing of partitions to manage custom refresh scenarios.

Large data models in Power BI Premium

Reports published to a workspace in the shared tenant have a 1GB limit on the size of the dataset. Moving that workspace to a premium capacity increases the maximum size to which the dataset can grow. In Figure 13-11 you can see the maximum size that each SKU supports.

SKU	Dataset Size limit
Shared Tenant	< 1GB
P1	< 3GB
P2	< 5GB
P3, P4, P5	< 10GB

Figure 13-11. *Maximum dataset size per SKU*

Using Power BI premium, it is possible to publish data models larger than these limits. Using the large models feature in Power BI, it is possible to grow the model to the maximum amount of memory available to the capacity.

SKU	Available Memory
P1	25 GB
P2	50 GB
P3	100 GB
P4	200 GB
P5	400 GB

Figure 13-12. *Memory limits per Premium SKU*

This means that it is possible to support datasets up to 400 GB using a P5 Premium SKU, although this would not be advisable as this would not leave any memory for other processes. Enabling of large datasets is done per dataset and can currently only be done using the Power BI PowerShell Cmdlets.

```
PowerShell
Set-PowerBIDataset -Id <Dataset ID> -TargetStorageMode PremiumFiles
```

Figure 13-13. *Enabling large datasets using PowerShell*

When large datasets are enabled, the file upload sizes are still limited to the sizes listed in Figure 13-12. However, refreshes on that dataset are supported up until the max memory size for the capacity. For this reason, it is recommended that large datasets be combined with an incremental refresh or custom partitioning.

Managing access

Controlling access to data is an essential administrative function; datasets can contain data that is sensitive and must not be accessible by unauthorized users. There are two primary mechanisms that we use to secure data. The first is by limiting users to workspaces or workspace apps that require access. Secondly, row-level security is used to prevent legitimate users from accessing data that they should not view, such as limiting a sales agent from seeing the sales of other agents.

In Chapter 11, we looked at how access to workspaces can be managed by assigning roles to users for that workspace. To promote reuse of datasets within an organization, it is possible to build reports on top datasets that are published in other workspaces. This promotes the idea of having one central model that serves as a single version of the truth. To enable this feature, a Power BI administrator needs to enable this setting in the Tenant settings portal.

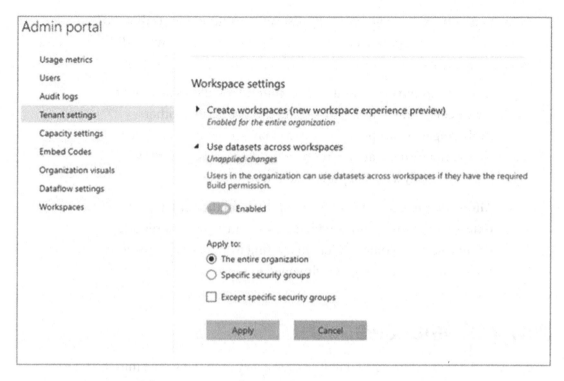

Figure 13-14. *Enabling cross workspace datasets*

Once this setting is enabled (it may take up to 15 minutes to take effect), users can be added to the dataset by selecting the **Manage Permissions** option on the dataset. A new dialog is displayed where you can capture the user or groups that you wish to grant access to.

Add user
CUSTOMER PROFITABILITY SAMPLE

Grant access to

| Michael Johnson   ✕ | Enter email addresses |

☑ Allow recipients to reshare the artifact

☑ Allow recipients to build new content from the underlying datasets

Figure 13-15. *Adding a user to a dataset*

Users or groups who are added to this list can consume reports that are based on datasets that are in workspaces that they do not have access to. Two additional settings are available for this:

> **Allow recipients to reshare the artifact**: This allows users who have been granted access to reshare this access with others. Resharing may be appropriate in a smaller organization, but should not be delegated in more controlled environments where there is usually a formal process to request access.

> **Allow recipients to build new content from the underlying dataset**: With this option enabled, users can build new reports connected to the data model, this setting would be required for Power BI report developers who need to reuse existing datasets.

Power BI dataflows

Like Power BI datasets, Power BI dataflows are a way to moving data into the Power BI Service. However, unlike datasets, Power BI reports cannot be built directly against dataflows. Instead, dataflows provide an easy-to-use self-service data preparation process that allows for the creation of standardized entities that can be reused as the source for multiple datasets.

Advantages of using Power BI dataflows:

- Consolidate and standardize repeated data transformations

- Reduce impact on source systems

- Uses the Common Data Model to create standardized entities

The development process for Power BI dataflows differs somewhat from that of Power BI datasets. The only supported development environment for dataflows is Power Query online, which is a web-enabled version of the Power Query editor that we see in Power BI Desktop. The code to import datasets is identical, and it is even possible to copy and paste the code directly from Power BI Desktop into a dataflow.

When Power BI dataflows ingest data, the data is not loaded directly into a dataset. Instead the data is landed as a CSV file together with metadata about the data, its source query and its storage location. By default, the data is stored within the Power BI Service and is not accessible through any other mechanism. This can be changed to allow the storage of dataflows within an Azure Data Lake Storage Gen 2 account that is linked to the organization's Azure account.

Configuring dataflows to use external storage

By default, all dataflows are stored within the Power BI Service and managed by Microsoft. Therefore, it is not possible to interact with these datasets in any way except through the Power BI Service. It is possible to change the storage location of the dataflows to an Azure Data Lake Storage (ADLS) Gen 2 storage account in your organization's Azure Subscription. When this is done, it is possible to

- Extend the amount of storage available for dataflows

- Access the dataflow storage directly through other tools such as Azure machine learning

- Create CDM folders using external tools such as data factory, data bricks, or any other tool

Before the external storage can be set up, the ADLS account needs to be configured. This is a task that cannot usually be performed by a Power BI administrator so the details are not discussed here. See the link to the step-by-step instruction later in this section for details on how this can be done. The next step is to configure the dataflow settings in the Power BI admin portal. This needs to be done by someone with Global administrator permissions on the tenant.

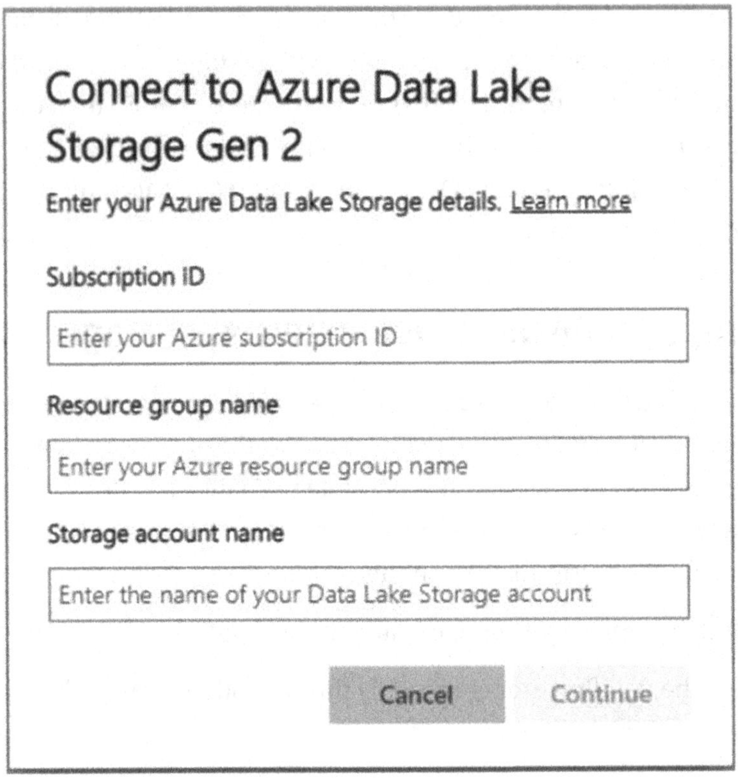

Connect to Azure Data Lake Storage Gen 2

Enter your Azure Data Lake Storage details. Learn more

Subscription ID

Enter your Azure subscription ID

Resource group name

Enter your Azure resource group name

Storage account name

Enter the name of your Data Lake Storage account

Cancel   Continue

Figure 13-16. Configuring ADLS details

Provide the details to the

- Subscription ID

- Resource Group

- Storage Account

Once this step is complete, Power BI is connected to the ADLS. The next step is to enable workspace administrators to assign workspaces to this storage account.

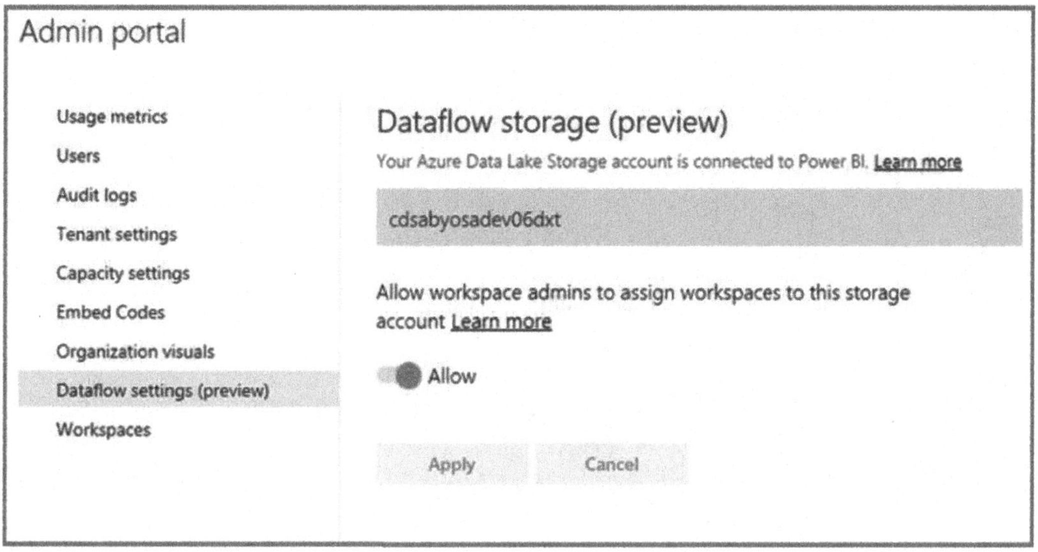

Figure 13-17. *Allowing workspace admins to use the storage account*

Step-by-step   For detailed instructions on how to set up external storage, see
`https://docs.microsoft.com/en-us/power-bi/transform-model/`
`service-dataflows-connect-azure-data-lake-storage-gen2`.

Enhanced compute engine

The enhanced compute engine allows Power BI Premium users to optimize the
performance of their dataflows by changing the underlying storage mechanism. The
primary benefit of this is

- Faster loads

- Using Query directly against dataflows

The enhanced compute engine can be configured for the tenant in the Power BI
Premium Capacity admin portal.

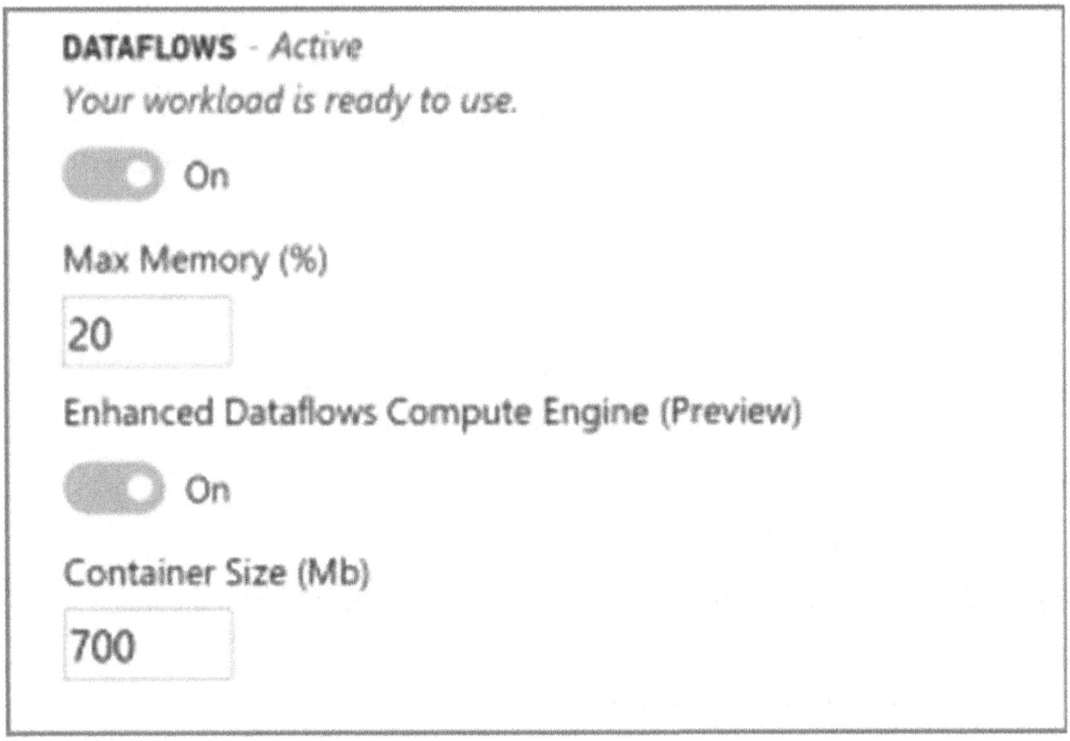

DATAFLOWS - *Active*
Your workload is ready to use.

⬤ On

Max Memory (%)

20

Enhanced Dataflows Compute Engine (Preview)

⬤ On

Container Size (Mb)

700

Figure 13-18. Configure enhanced compute engine

In addition to enabling the enhanced compute engine, you also need to set the container size, this is the container that executes the enhanced compute engine process. If this process is given too little memory, then there will be a large amount of paging between the container and disk, which results in slower dataflows.

Publishing dataflows

Unlike Power BI reports and datasets, dataflows are authored in the Power BI Service using Power Query Online. Suppose the dataflow needs to be moved from one environment to another. For example, when moving the dataflow from development to production, the dataflow can first be exported to a JSON file that contains definitions for the entities as well as the M code for those data sources. It is important to note that, like the PIBX file, there are no credentials stored in the file.

Once the dataflow has been exported to this .json file, it should also be checked into your organization's source code repository.

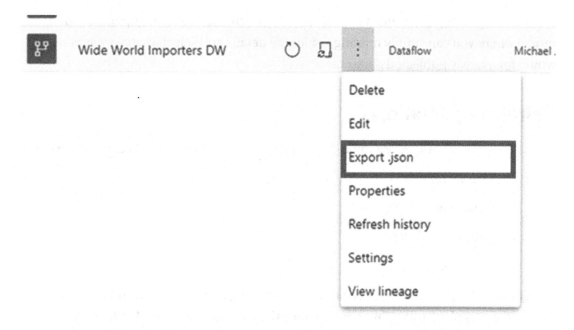

Figure 13-19. *Exporting a dataflow to a .json file*

Uploading the dataflow is not like uploading a PBIX file. Instead, you select the option to create a new dataflow inside of the workspace in which you want to upload the dataflow. You are then given four options, the third of which is to import a model.

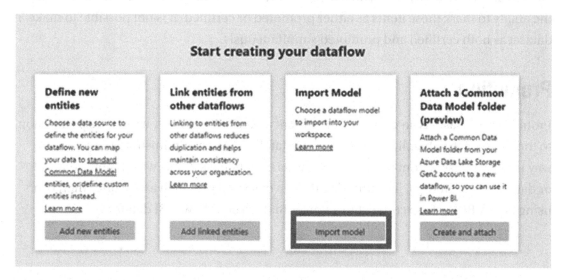

Figure 13-20. *Uploading a dataflow model*

After importing the model, you will then be directed to the settings page for the model where you can supply missing credential details and select a gateway as you would for a newly published dataset.

Refreshing dataflows

Refreshing a dataflow is very similar to the dataset refresh process and can be done by

- Manual refresh

- Scheduled refresh

- Automated refresh

- Incremental refresh

The only significant difference between refreshing datasets and dataflows comes from incremental refreshes. Incremental refresh is only available for dataflows when using Power BI Premium.

Endorsing datasets or dataflows

To increase the visibility, use, and trust of datasets and dataflows, Power BI introduced the ability to mark these items as either promoted or certified. It is not possible to make a dataset as both certified and promoted simultaneously.

Promotion

Promoting a dataset is an easy way for content creators or any user with write permission to the workspace to highlight the dataset or dataflow. As an administrator, there is no way to prevent users from promoting datasets or dataflows in this way. When a dataset or dataflow is promoted, it is moved to the top of search lists such as the one when users using Power BI Desktop connect to a Power BI dataset or Power BI dataflow.

Figure 13-21. *Promoting a dataset*

As a Power BI administrator, you would want to monitor the use of this functionality to ensure that it is not being abused, as promoting too many or even all datasets would have the same effect as not promoting them at all. To manage this, a policy on the use of this feature and how long a dataset or dataflow should be promoted should be decided.

Certification

The certification of a dataset or dataflow is to signal to users that the data within is safe and should be considered as a proven data source. Unlike promotion, the process of certifying a dataset should be more strenuous and cannot be done by anyone but designated individuals, if at all. Before being able to certify a dataset, there is a setting in the Power BI admin portal that first needs to be enabled and configured.

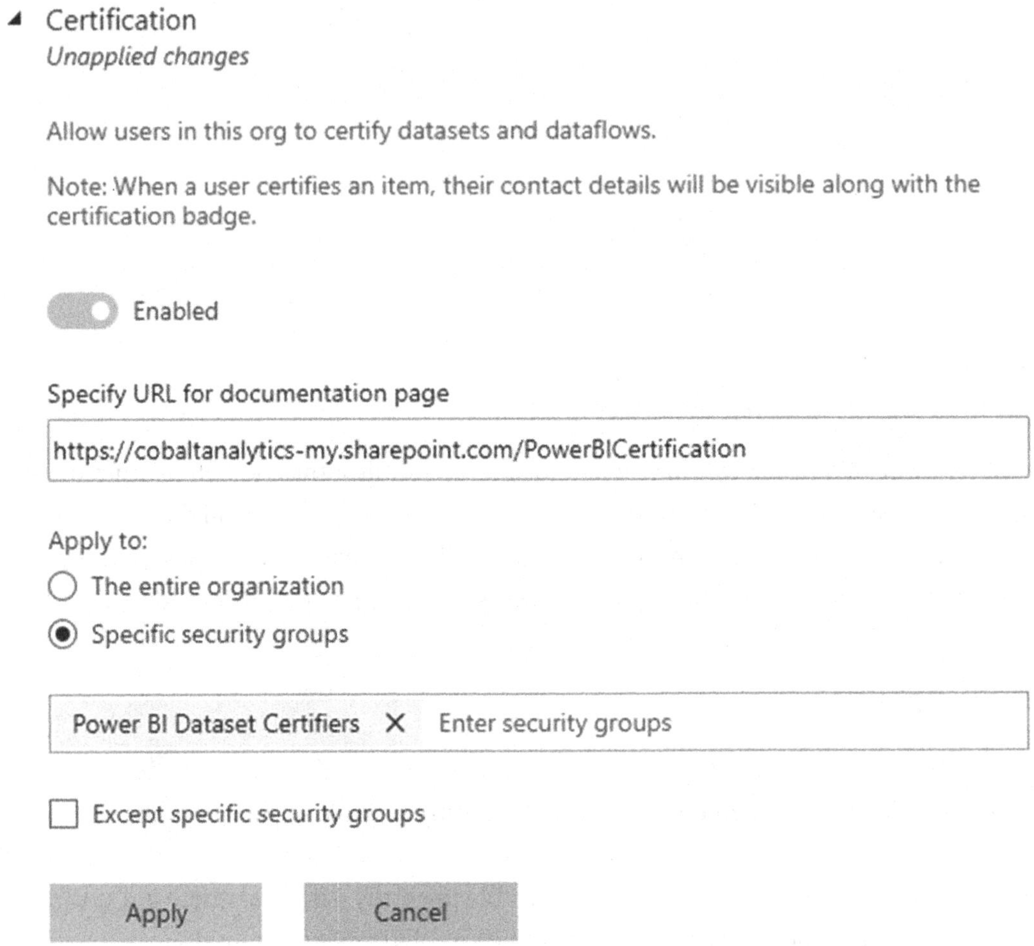

◢ Certification
Unapplied changes

Allow users in this org to certify datasets and dataflows.

Note: When a user certifies an item, their contact details will be visible along with the certification badge.

◖◗ Enabled

Specify URL for documentation page

https://cobaltanalytics-my.sharepoint.com/PowerBICertification

Apply to:
○ The entire organization
◉ Specific security groups

Power BI Dataset Certifiers ✕   Enter security groups

☐ Except specific security groups

Apply	Cancel

Figure 13-22. Enabling certification of datasets

URL for documentation: You can provide a link to a knowledge repository such as SharePoint, confluence, or even a workflow tool where users can find out more about getting their datasets certified.

Apply to: It is possible to specify who can certify datasets and dataflows. It is not recommended that you enable this for the entire organization. The second option is to specify a list of security groups that are either able to or prohibited from using this functionality. It is important to note that this requires security groups and Office 365 groups; otherwise individuals cannot be captured here like other options in the Power BI admin portal.

The key to this setting is having a formal process that developers need to go through to certify their datasets. This process could be as informal as sending an email to the members of the certification team, or the creation workflows to manage this process.

Part of your organization's Power BI governance document needs to specify how the certification is done and how these are evaluated and monitored. Once a policy for certification has been established, and the certification functionality is enabled, it is then possible to certify the dataset or dataflow by navigating to the settings page for the dataset or dataflow. This is done by expanding the endorsement pane and selecting the certify option. A description should also be provided to aid users in understanding how this dataset should be used.

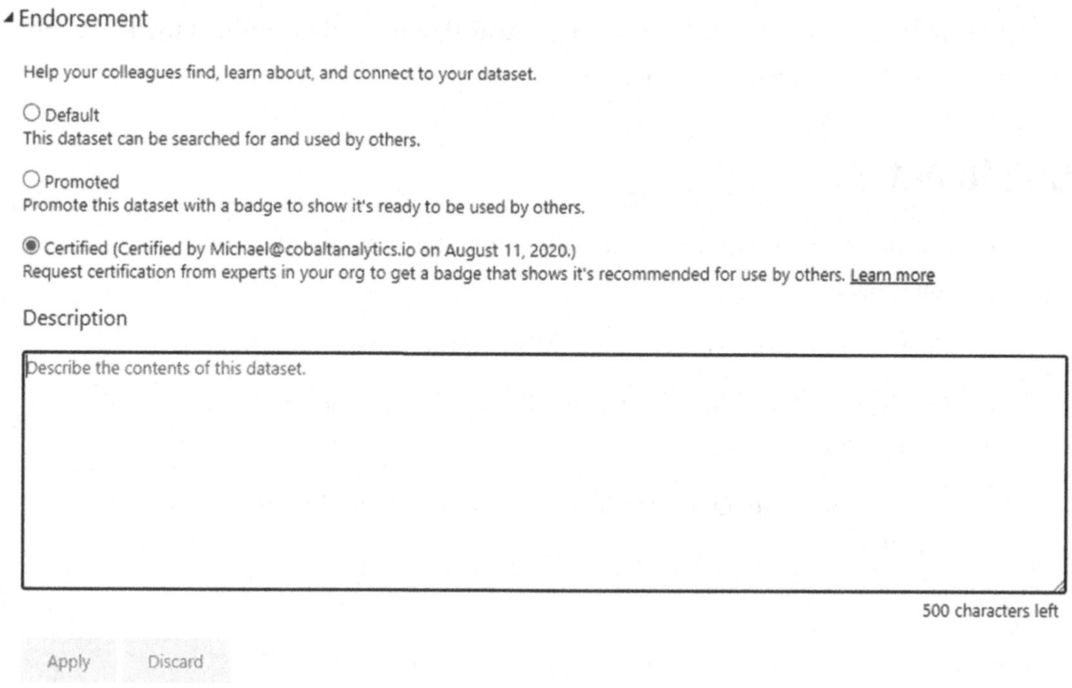

⊿ Endorsement

Help your colleagues find, learn about, and connect to your dataset.

○ Default
This dataset can be searched for and used by others.

○ Promoted
Promote this dataset with a badge to show it's ready to be used by others.

◉ Certified (Certified by Michael@cobaltanalytics.io on August 11, 2020.)
Request certification from experts in your org to get a badge that shows it's recommended for use by others. Learn more

Description

> Describe the contents of this dataset.

500 characters left

Apply   Discard

Figure 13-23. *Certifying a dataset*

Once certified, the dataset will appear at the top of the search list when browsing available datasets.

Certification and promotion is a great way to enhance the usage and trust in the datasets and dataflows built by your organization.

Summary

The creation of datasets and dataflows is primarily a development task, but managing these artifacts once they are in production is an administrative one. The two key responsibilities here are

- Ensuring that the data is accessible and up-to-date

- Ensuring that the impact on the source system is acceptable and does not affect the operations of the organization.

There are many tools available to the administrator to help ensure the availability of data.

Next, we look at the On-premises data gateway that is used to connect the Power BI Service to your on-premises data sources.

Call to action

- Formalize deployment and monitoring process for datasets and dataflows

- Ensure appropriate refresh schedules for datasets and dataflows.

- Configure external storage for dataflows to enable new enhanced data preparation functionality.

- Monitor for large data refreshes and evaluate if incremental refresh is possible.

CHAPTER 14

On-Premises Data Gateway

Read this chapter if you would like to find out more information about

- What the On-premises data gateway is

- When a gateway is needed

- How to set up the gateway

- Managing the gateway

- Monitoring the gateway

- Troubleshooting the gateway

When Power BI report developers build reports, they do so using the Power BI desktop application. This application is usually run within an organization's network and has access to resources such as databases and file systems. When these reports are published to the Power BI Service, the service may not have the same access to local resources as the developer had. When this happens, a mechanism to provide the same level of access to these local resources to the Power BI Service is required. This mechanism is the On-premises data gateway that we will refer to simply as the gateway. The gateway acts as an agent that runs securely within the organizational network or on a standalone machine and provides the Power BI Service access to the required resources.

© Ásgeir Gunnarsson and Michael Johnson 2020
Á. Gunnarsson and M. Johnson, *Pro Microsoft Power BI Administration*,
https://doi.org/10.1007/978-1-4842-6567-3_14

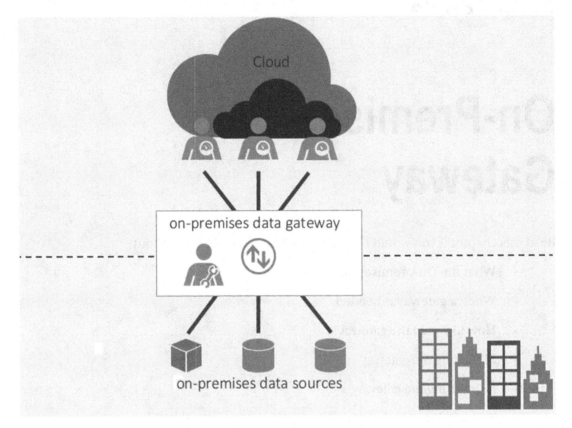

Figure 14-1. *Role of the gateway*

The gateway is not only used for Power BI but also supports a growing number of services running in Azure. Some of these applications include

- Power Apps

- Power Automate

- Azure Logic Apps

- Azure Analysis Services

Many principals that apply to Power BI also apply to these other services. In this chapter, before embarking on a process of setting up the gateway, it first needs to be established if the gateway is even required.

When is a gateway needed?

Gateways are required whenever the source of data, required by the Power BI Service, cannot be accessed directly over the public Internet. This can generally be for one of two reasons.

- The data source resides on a private network

- The data source is not supported directly by the service

The data source resides on its own private network

The Power BI Service is cloud-based, meaning that it was built to run only in the cloud. The service also assumes that other services are available over the Internet. While this is true of many Platform-as-a-Service (PAAS) and Software-as-a-Service (SAAS) applications, it is not always the case with on-premises and Infrastructure-as-a-Service (IAAS) applications.

Example of data sources that require a gateway:

- On-premise databases such as SQL Server, MySQL, and Oracle

- Files and folders stored in a local file system or network share

- ODBC

- SQL Server installed on an Azure Virtual Machine

The data source is not supported in the service

The gateway is also required when Power BI uses a data source that is not supported directly by the Power BI Service. An example of this is the R and Python data sources. Each of these languages supports a variety of versions and libraries that are not compatible with each other, and are thus not supported in a shared infrastructure environment like the Power BI Service and require the gateway to be set up and configured on servers for this use.

Examples of data sources not supported by the service

- Python scripts

- R scripts

- Web data source using the Web.Page() function

> **Note**   R and Python scripts are not supported on the standard gateway. Therefore they need to be set up using the personal gateway.

A full list of data sources and their need for a gateway can be found at `https://docs.microsoft.com/en-us/power-bi/connect-data/power-bi-data-sources`.

Gateway architecture

When we speak of the gateway, we usually think of the application that is installed in the organizational network. The gateway is actually a collection of applications and services that work together to facilitate the movement data. Each data movement follows a simple pattern that we discuss after we look at the components that make up the system.

Components of the gateway

The gateway consists of three core systems that create a secure and reliable communication channel between the Power BI datasets and their data sources. Each of these services contains multiple components, but we will not go to that level of detail.

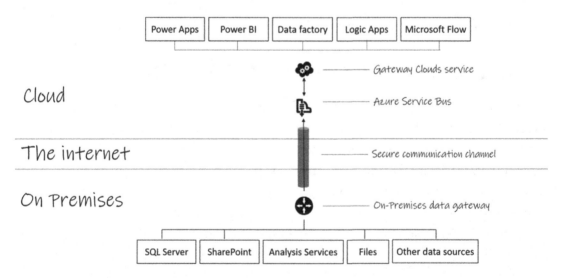

Figure 14-2. *Power BI gateway architecture*

Figure 14-2 shows the basic layout of the gateway; the three components are

- **Gateway Cloud Service:** is responsible for handling all requests for data from the Power BI Service; such requests occur during on-demand or schedule refreshes, reports using DirectQuery and live connections, and when using Power Query online such as when designing a dataflow. The gateway cloud service is responsible for scheduling data requests as well as securing the credentials used to perform the refresh.

- **Azure Service Bus:** Provides secure and reliable messaging between the Gateway cloud service and the On-premises data gateway. This simply means that the On-premises data gateway and the Gateway cloud service never communicate directly with one another, but rather pull and push messages off the Service Bus. These messages can be requests for data as well as the results of these data requests.

- **On-premises data gateway:** Receives requests for data over the Azure Service Bus. These requests are processed and then returned to the Power BI Service.

With a secure and reliable channel created through which data requests get submitted, we look in more detail how those requests are processed.

Typical steps for a data request

All requests for data follow a similar pattern, whether they are from scheduled data imports or reports using DirectQuery or live connections. These steps are

1. Gateway Cloud Service receives a request for data from the Power BI Service.

2. Gateway Cloud Service packages the data request together with credentials required for the query.

3. The package gets placed on the Azure Service Bus.

4. An available Gateway member pulls data requests securely from the Azure Service Bus.

5. On-premises data gateway decrypts query and credentials.

6. On-premises data gateway executes the query; this can be a DirectQuery or a Live connection query in which case it is sent directly to the data source or an import query, in which case it will invoke the mashup engine to perform the data import.

7. On-premises data gateway returns the results of the request to the Gateway Cloud Service via Azure Service Bus.

This process is the same for both the standard or personal gateways.

Power BI Gateway workloads

Power BI supports three storage modes; each storage mode stores and queries data differently and, therefore, has different data access requirements. The first storage mode is called import mode and is a cached model, meaning that it imports and stores data. When a report uses import mode, Power BI imports all the data it needs into its own internal storage called Vertipaq engine using a process known as the mashup engine which executes the Power Query commands. When users interact with reports, the reports generate queries against the xVelocity engine. The other two modes are called direct and live storage modes. We refer to these two modes collectively as the non-cached modes. In the non-cached modes, Power BI generates queries for each visual that needs to render at the time of the report execution, meaning that there is no need for periodic refreshing of the datastore.

The gateway enables the data movement requirements for all workload types in which the data is not available in the public cloud. Each workload type consumes CPU, Memory, and network differently. Therefore a gateway that is optimal for one workload type may not be ideal for another.

A full list of data sources, their support for the gateway, and support for live connections and DirectQuery is found at `https://docs.microsoft.com/en-us/power-bi/connect-data/power-bi-data-sources`.

Cached workloads

Cashed datasets are the most common workload types in Power BI and include all reports built using an imported data source as well as all dataflows. In a cached dataset, all data, defined by the source queries (written in Power Query) are imported and stored in the model first. This transformation, performed by the mashup engine, is the same process used by Power BI desktop. The dataset needs to be loaded first before it can be queried and needs to be periodically refreshed for the report data to remain current. Because cached datasets store data in their internal data store, they tend to be much larger than non-cached datasets that store only metadata. When a cached dataset is refreshed, the required processing commands are sent from the Power BI Service to the gateway. Each request is then processed in three distinct steps.

Connect

Before the gateway can transform data, it first needs to connect to and download the data sources. Before connecting the gateway retrieves the authentication credentials required to connect to the data source; these credentials are securely stored in Azure Key Vault, which can be used to securely store keys and other secrets.

Note   You can read more about Azure Key Vault at
`https://azure.microsoft.com/en-us/services/key-vault/`.

Integration with Azure Key Vault is seamlessly built into the Power BI Service and does not need to be managed by the organization or administrator. With the authentication details, the gateway can then authenticate against the data sources using one of many authentication protocols, including OAuth, basic or Windows authentication. Once the data has been securely copied to the gateway, it can then be transformed.

Transform

Once the data has been loaded into the gateway, the Power Query command is executed by the mashup engine. Such commands include the creation of new columns, rows, and even tables. These operations can be very resource heavy, including the use of a lot of memory. Ensuring that data is filtered as close to the source as possible reduces the amount of data that is processed by the mashup engine. Only planning and monitoring can correctly determine the correct amount of resources required for this step. During the transform phase, data may be spooled to disk; in the event of large datasets being used, it is recommended that high throughput storage be used, such as solid-state storage.

Transfer

Once all transformations have been completed by the gateway, the result sets need to be returned to the Power BI Service either for further processing or to be loaded into either Power BI data models or dataflows. This transfer is made securely over an encrypted channel. Before transmission, the result set is compressed to reduce the amount of data that needs to be moved over the Internet. Both the compression and encryption of this data require CPU and a good network to ensure data is moved quickly to the service.

Non-cached workloads

Power BI supports two non-cached storage modes, Live connections and DirectQuery. In both these storage modes, no data is sourced from the data source before it is queried. Instead, queries are generated and executed at runtime.

- **Live connections:** Connections made against an Analysis Services model; this can be a tabular or multidimensional model. Internally, Power BI also uses an analysis service tabular model, so there is no need for the service to translate the underlying DAX queries into another query language.

- **Direct Queries:** Made against data sources that have a compatible query language and are supported in Power BI; such data sources include relational databases, Hadoop, Spark, and others. The primary reason report designers use DirectQuery is because of large data sizes or the need for near real-time results.

Both storage modes use the gateway as an agent to relay queries from the Power BI Service to their on-premises data sources. Similar to the cached dataset, the gateway fist needs to access the credentials required by the data source before opening a connection. There is no transformation step involved, so the mashup engine is not invoked. The result set for the query is compressed and encrypted. Non-cached workloads, therefore, do not have the same requirement for large amounts of memory, but a good CPU and network connectivity are vital as these directly affect report performance.

On-premises data gateway modes

The gateway is available in two modes; each of these modes has a different target audience. The gateway installed in **standard mode** is the recommended gateway mode; this mode was initially known as the enterprise data gateway as it made more of the features that enterprises are looking for. The second mode is called **personal mode** and was designed for users who need to easily set up gateway but are not very concerned about the availability of the gateway.

Note   While it is possible to install both a standard and personal gateway on a single computer, this is not generally recommended as both gateways will consume the same resources which may result in poor performance.

Personal gateway

The personal mode gateway exists primarily as an easy to configure and run version of the gateway. There are instances where it is required over the standard gateway. In personal mode, the gateway is installed as a user application. As a user application, local administer rights are not required, and the application runs under the identity of the user who executed it. By running as the user, the gateway mostly has access to everything that the user has access to, making setup and configuration easy. This is useful, as many organizations do not grant local administrator rights to users on their computers; configuring additional service accounts and granting those accounts access to the data source are also something that users are not able to do without the help of IT. This lower barrier to entry makes the personal gateway ideal for developers and other power users.

The personal gateway can only be used by the owner of that gateway. The use of that gateway is also dependent on that gateway being available. If it has been installed on a laptop or similar type device, then it is unavailable while the machine is in sleep mode or has been disconnected from the network, including any required VPN connections.

Advantages of the personal gateway

- Easier to set up

- Supports sources such as R and Python that are not supported in the standard gateway

- Easy to use permission as the application runs under users account

213

Disadvantages of the personal gateway

- No support for High Availability

- Can only be used by a single user

- Does not support other Power Platform applications such as Power Apps and Power Automate

- Does not support Dataflows and Paginated reports

Step-by-step   For instructions on how to install the personal mode On-premises data gateway, go to `https://docs.microsoft.com/en-us/power-bi/connect-data/service-gateway-personal-mode`.

When reports are promoted to a production-like environment, ensuring access to the gateway becomes very important, if not critical. In these instances, the personal gateway is not sufficient, and a reliable version of the gateway is required; this is where the standard gateway comes into play.

Standard gateway

The standard gateway was built to provide a reliable gateway for use throughout the entire organization. The Standard gateway is the recommended gateway mode for use for anything that is deemed "in Production."

Tip   Don't set up a single gateway to be shared by development, testing, and production. Instead, set up three separate gateways. This will avoid any impact that test and development may have on production and allows you to test new versions of the gateway before upgrading your production environment.

Unlike the personal gateway, the standard gateway is installed as a service, preferably on dedicated machines running windows server. The standard gateway supports clustering and load balancing, helping organizations ensure reliable and consistent performance, making it the preferred choice for production workloads.

As a service, the standard gateway will run under its own local account; by default, this is *NT SERVICE\PBIEgwService.* This service account can be changed to another local or domain service account.

Advantages of the standard gateway

- Supports gateway members running in a cluster for high availability.

- Report load can be distributed across nodes in the cluster.

- Support for DirectQuery and Live Connections.

- Supports dataflows.

- Supports Paginated reports.

- Can be used by multiple users.

Disadvantages of the standard gateway

- Often requires members of the IT department to install.

- Service account required for windows authentication SSO through Kerberos to be used.

- Does not support R and Python; therefore there is no high availability option for these data sources.

Step-by-step   For instructions on how to install the standard On-premises data gateway, go to `https://docs.microsoft.com/en-us/data-integration/gateway/service-gateway-install`.

Regardless of which gateway mode is installed, the underlying architecture of the gateway remains the same.

High availability and scaling workloads

When Power BI is being used to support business-critical reporting, it is essential that the service be reliable and available. High availability in the Power BI Service is managed by Microsoft, but ensuring the availability of the gateway falls on the organization and the gateway administrators.

The standard gateway enables high availability using gateway clusters. Gateway clusters are collections of standard gateways that form a single logical gateway in the Power BI Service. If for some reason, a cluster member were to become unavailable, for example, during a software update or hardware failure, then other members in the cluster would seamlessly take on the activities of the unavailable node, ensuring uninterrupted service.

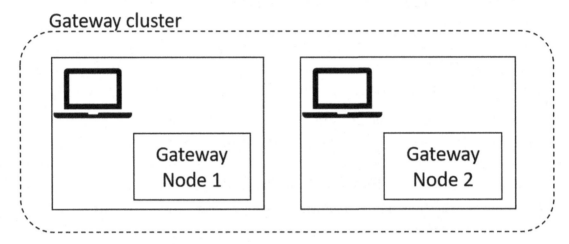

Figure 14-3. *Gateway cluster*

The creation of a gateway cluster is straightforward and does not rely on technologies such as Windows Failover Clustering to work. All gateways setup in standard mode are actually created as clusters of one member. We will discuss how to set up the gateway and clusters later in this chapter.

Once the gateway is set up, each member in the cluster polls the Azure Service Bus for new data requests. These data requests are not allocated to specific nodes but instead assigned to the first available node to pull them off the bus. While it is not possible to allocate rules to each node based on a source or workload type, it is possible to manage the load balancing of each node to ensure that a node is not overworked. This is done by setting the CPU and memory thresholds.

- **CPUUtilizationPercentageThreshold:** This is the maximum amount of CPU that the gateway can consume while still accepting data requests. A value of 0 indicated that throttling does not take place.

- **MemoryUtilizationPercentageThreshold:** This is the maximum amount of memory that the gateway can consume while still accepting data requests. A value of 0 means that there will be no throttling.

- **ResourceUtilizationAggregateionPeriodInMinutes:** This number sets the time that the memory and CPU are aggregated by. This is important, especially in the case of CPU, where short bursts of 100% CPU usage are common on an otherwise idle processor. The default is set to 5 minutes; this effectively means that if one of the threshold values is breached, then the gateway will not accept new requests for at least 5 minutes.

See the section on configuration on how to adjust these settings.

When these limits are breached, the gateway will not accept any requests until this value falls below the threshold. If none of the gateway nodes in the cluster are able to process the data request, then the request fails.

Advantages of gateway clusters

- Removes a single point of failure.

- Requests can be distributed among all gateway nodes in the cluster, ensuring balanced workloads.

- By updating only a single node at a time, the administrator can ensure that the clusters remain online.

With a little theory about the gateway architecture complete, next, we can look at how to set up the gateway.

Setting up the On-premises data gateway

Unlike most of the infrastructure used in Power BI, gateway administrators or users are fully responsible for setting up and maintaining the gateway. It is essential that administrators set up the gateway correctly to ensure that reliable and timely data requests are performed.

Users will often install the personal gateway on their own personal devices. While this is unlikely that these setups conform to best practices, this may be all right for these occasional ad-hoc users. Plus ensuring that standard gateways are correctly configured and maintained is one of the primary responsibilities of the gateway administrators. We begin by looking at some of the requirements for the gateway.

Requirements

At the time of writing, the Power BI gateway requires a compatible windows 64-bit operation system, which can be at least Windows 8 or Windows Server R2 with .Net 4.6 installed. Newer versions of the gateway require .Net 4.7.2. It is recommended to check on the minimum versions of both the .net framework and OS before installing the gateway. This does mean that unsupported OSs such as Linux will not work, and it is not uncommon to find a lone Windows machine in a predominantly Linux environment set up to act as the gateway.

The gateway has the following requirements:

- Windows x64 (Windows 8 or Windows Server 2012 R2).

- .Net 4.6.

- Cannot be installed on Windows Core.

- It can be run in a virtual environment.

- The machine cannot be a domain controller.

Sizing

Apart from the OS and .Net requirements, there isn't much documentation on the minimum hardware specs required to run the gateway. However, the gateway does come with the following recommended requirements:

- 8-core CPU.

- 8 GB of memory.

- Solid-state drive.

- Where possible, install the gateway on a dedicated computer.

- Although it is possible to install a gateway in both personal and standard mode on a single computer, this is not recommended.

These are only recommendations by Microsoft, and computers that do not meet these requirements may still work, but should be tested first. These recommendations should be used as a starting point, and the computer can be upgraded if necessary. It is also important to consider the workload type. For example, in environments that use only DirectQuery or Live Connections, the gateway computers may not need as much memory or a solid-state drive, as these workload types do not consume as many resources. When import mode is used, however, ensuring that there is enough memory available helps avoid writing the content of the data transformations to disk while the mashup engine is transforming it. It should also be considered that multiple datasets may be refreshing at the same time, meaning that two, three, or more times the amount of memory may be required compared to using Power BI Desktop to load data.

Tip   Installing the gateway in a virtual machine gives you the flexibility to resize the computer when necessary.

Placement

In addition to the computer that the gateway is installed on, how the computer is connected to the network plays a big role in the overall performance. In both cached and non-cached scenarios, the latency between gateway, the data source, and the Power BI Service affects report refresh and report response times. This is especially relevant on gateways setup in personal mode, that are usually installed on desktops, or even laptops that could be using a slow LAN or even a wireless network.

The recommendation for the placement of the gateway is to set them up as close to the data source as possible, and on a network with the best outgoing Internet connection possible. Administrators may be tempted to install the gateway on the physical host of the data source; this is generally not recommended, especially in the case of services such as SQL Server that may have a high per-core cost that would be consumed by the gateway.

Downloading and installing the gateway

The install file for the gateway can is downloaded in several ways. The easiest way is to navigate to the downloads section under the settings pane and select the gateway. This directs you to a page where you can choose between the standard and personal mode gateway. Some installations will provide a single installer for both the standard and personal gateway.

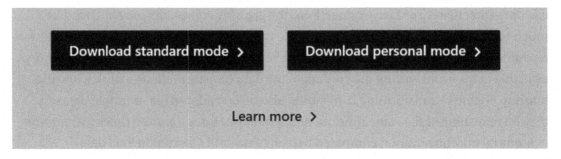

Figure 14-4. *Download Gateway installer*

Tip   It is possible to download and install the gateway using PowerShell. This is a good approach in large environments where several gateways need to be installed. See the session on automation later in this chapter for more on how to use the gateway cmdlets to install power BI.

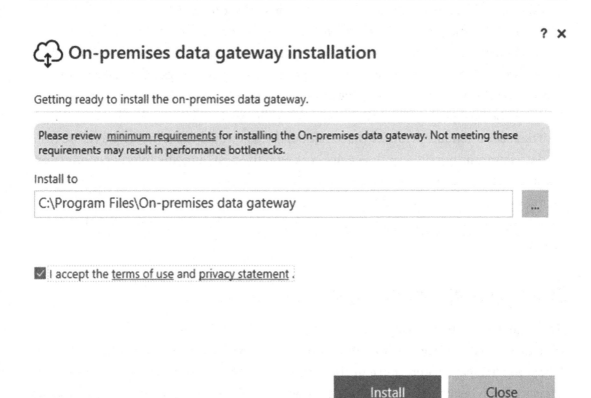

Figure 14-5. *Accept terms and install folder*

Once the gateway is installed, the setup wizard guides you automatically into the setup process. If for some reason, you are not ready to proceed with setting up the gateway, you are able to cancel. This does not uninstall the gateway but leaves it in an unconfigured state. This is the same state that that the gateway is left in when installed via PowerShell.

Configuring the gateway

Once the gateway is installed, the next step is to configure it. If you installed the gateway manually using the installer, then you are directed straight through to the configuration screen. If you installed the gateway using PowerShell or if you canceled the setup after the install, then you can enter the configuration panel by searching for the On-Premises gateway in the **Start Menu**; this is the same for when you want to change the configuration of the gateway.

Figure 14-6. *Open the On-premises data gateway configuration screen*

The first step is to provide the credentials of the user who will administer the gateway. The credentials are used to both authenticate the gateway to the service and make the user an administrator of the gateway. It is good practice to ensure that the Power BI administrators set up the gateway rather than have users or report developers perform this task to ensure a separation of concerns.

Figure 14-7. Login with Gateway administrators account

After successfully authenticating the administrators' account, the next step is to choose the configuration type:

Figure 14-8. Main setup options

- **Register a new gateway on this computer:** You choose this option if you want to create a new gateway cluster or if you want to add a new member to the cluster.

- **Migrate, restore, or takeover an existing gateway:** You choose this option if you want to

  - **Move a gateway to a new computer:** If you need to move the gateway from one computer to another, then you can use this to do so. This is particularly useful when the gateway is offline and cannot be recovered. An alternate approach to this is to add a new member to the cluster, make the new member the primary member, and then remove the old member. To do this, the primary member must be online.

  - **Recover a damaged gateway:** If the gateway has been damaged, then this option can be used to get the gateway online again.

  - **Take ownership of a gateway:** If the gateway was installed using an account that should not be a gateway administrator, then this can be used to change the account associated with this gateway.

Register a new gateway on this computer

Creating a new gateway cluster is as simple as providing a name for the gateway and choosing a recovery key. The name of the gateway should conform to the Power BI gateway naming standard that your organization has in place; it is recommended that this name include the fact that it is a gateway as well as which environment this gateway is to be used in. Although it is possible to use the same gateway for multiple environments, this should be discouraged as development or testing workloads can have negative consequences on the production environment.

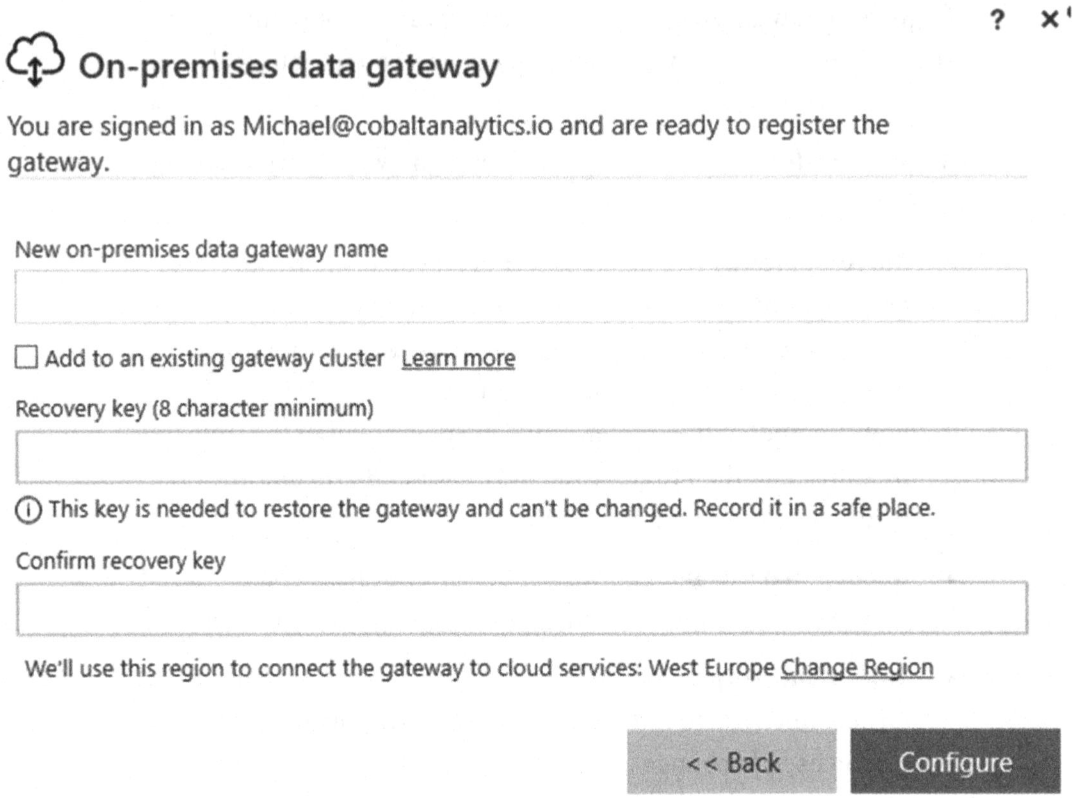

? x '

☁ On-premises data gateway

You are signed in as Michael@cobaltanalytics.io and are ready to register the gateway.

New on-premises data gateway name

[   ]

☐ Add to an existing gateway cluster Learn more

Recovery key (8 character minimum)

[   ]

ⓘ This key is needed to restore the gateway and can't be changed. Record it in a safe place.

Confirm recovery key

[   ]

We'll use this region to connect the gateway to cloud services: West Europe Change Region

[<< Back]   [Configure]

Figure 14-9. *Configuring a new Gateway cluster*

The recovery key is required for additional nodes to be added to the cluster, repair the cluster member, and/or to upgrade the gateway. Ensuring that this key is recorded and kept secure is important.

Tip   if your organization does not have a secure means of storing such credentials, then you should consider using Azure Key Vault. `https://azure.microsoft.com/en-us/services/key-vault/`

Adding a new member to an existing cluster

Adding another gateway to an existing cluster is also a relatively straightforward task. Again you are asked to provide a name for the gateway. You will then enable the "Add to an existing gateway" option that returns a list of existing gateway clusters that the user is an administrator for.

Steps

1. Capture the new name of the cluster, again applying the organization naming convention.

2. Enable "Add to an existing gateway."

3. Select the gateway cluster to add the new node to.

4. Provide the recovery key used for the gateway cluster.

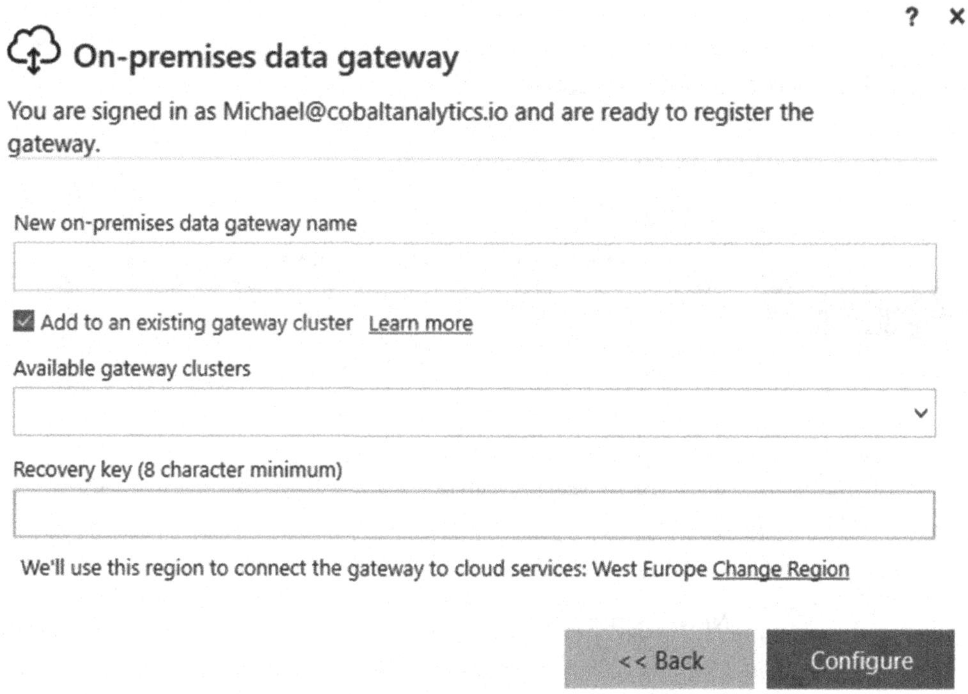

? ✗

⌂ On-premises data gateway

You are signed in as Michael@cobaltanalytics.io and are ready to register the gateway.

New on-premises data gateway name

```
[                                                          ]
```

☑ Add to an existing gateway cluster Learn more

Available gateway clusters

```
[                                                       ⌄]
```

Recovery key (8 character minimum)

```
[                                                          ]
```

We'll use this region to connect the gateway to cloud services: West Europe Change Region

```
[  << Back  ]  [  Configure  ]
```

Figure 14-10. Adding a gateway to a cluster

Network connectivity

The Power BI gateway requires connectivity to the Internet. By using the gateway, Power BI removes the need to allow incoming connections; these are connections that originate somewhere on the Internet and would need to pass through the corporate firewall. For good reasons, most organizations prohibit such connections. Instead, the gateway makes an outgoing connection to the Power BI Service via the Azure Gateway Service and uses Azure Service Bus as a messaging system.

Depending on how the setup of your network is configured, you may need to request that the firewall administrator open up certain ports and URLs to allow outgoing connections. This is common in secure environments such as banks and other regulated environments. All traffic passes through port 433, and a list of URLs can be found at

```
https://docs.microsoft.com/en-us/power-bi/admin/power-
bi-whitelist-urls
```

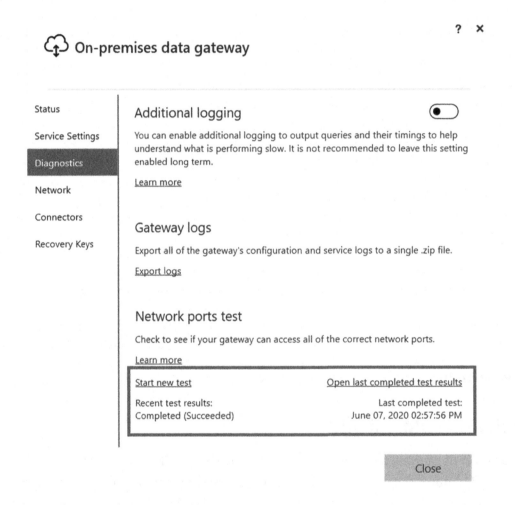

Figure 14-11. *Testing network access for the gateway*

There is an option to run a network diagnostic assessment that will let you know of any problems.

If your organization uses a proxy to access the Internet, you can read how to configure that here `https://docs.microsoft.com/en-us/data-integration/gateway/service-gateway-proxy`.

Updating the gateway

New versions of the gateway are often released, and the administrator must ensure that these are kept up-to-date. New releases of the gateway not only provide performance and security enhancements but also enable new functionality by updating the gateway to use the latest mashup engine that may be required by datasets built using the latest version of the Power BI desktop application.

It should be noted that the gateway becomes unavailable for at least the duration of the upgrade and possibly longer if issues are experienced, so upgrading the gateway should only be done during approved windows for business-critical workloads. If the gateway is installed as part of a gateway cluster, then this upgrade procedure is simpler as each node in the cluster can be upgraded independently of one another, reducing the risk of an outage. It is recommended that you first upgrade one of the non-active nodes in the cluster first.

Warning   As the personal gateway does not support clustering, all updates result in some downtime.

Data sources

After the gateway has been created, data sources can be added to the gateway. Data sources are preconfigured connections to on-premise data sources such as files, local intranet, or databases that can be reused by datasets written against those data sources. Data sources give the gateway administrators control over the data sources used via the gateway. To create a data source on a gateway, the user needs to be a gateway administrator. Adding a data source can be done before a report is deployed or while setting up the dataset connection settings.

Figure 14-12. *Add or remove a data source from the gateway*

Tip   The option to add a data source or remove the gateway can be hard to find as ellipses (…) only show when hovered over at the end of the gateway pane.

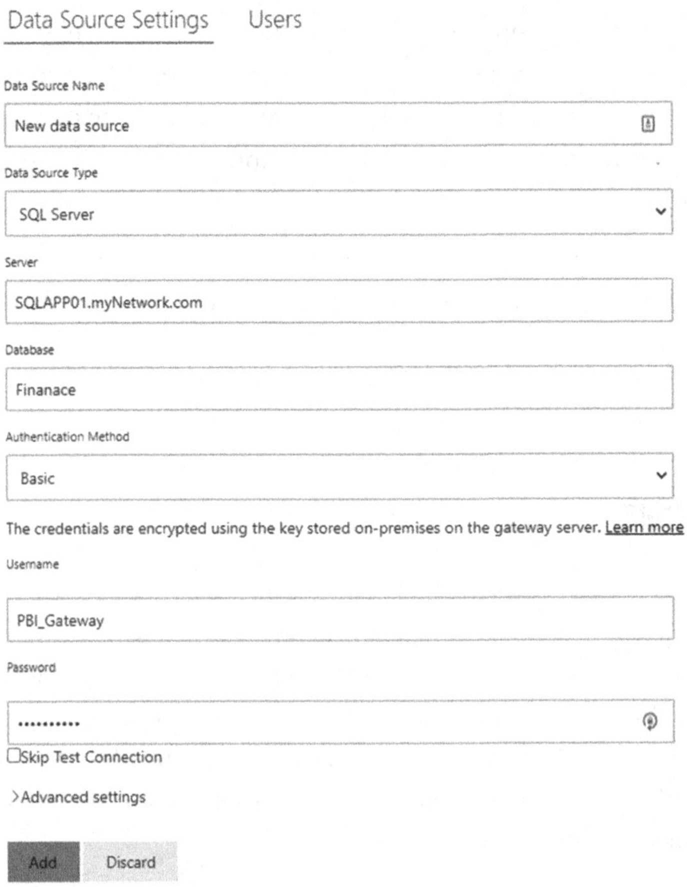

Data Source Settings   Users

Data Source Name

New data source

Data Source Type

SQL Server

Server

SQLAPP01.myNetwork.com

Database

Finanace

Authentication Method

Basic

The credentials are encrypted using the key stored on-premises on the gateway server. Learn more

Username

PBI_Gateway

Password

••••••••••

☐Skip Test Connection

〉Advanced settings

Add   Discard

Figure 14-13. *Configuring a new data source*

Report writers are then able to use those data sources by selecting the gateway that they want to use, then mapping the connection to a data source using the "Maps to" dropdown that lists available sources.

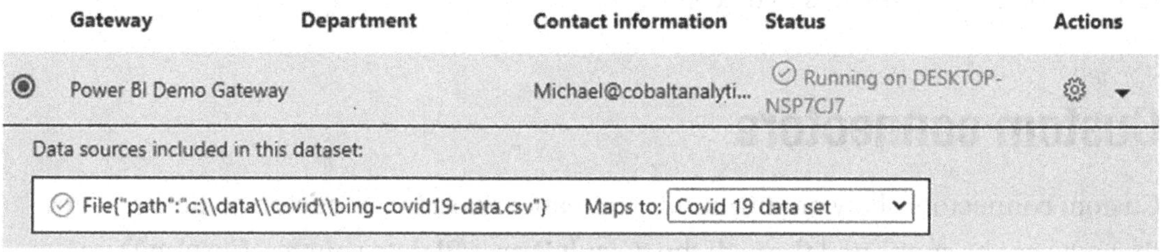

Gateway	Department	Contact information	Status	Actions
◉ Power BI Demo Gateway	.	Michael@cobaltanalyti...	⊘ Running on DESKTOP-NSP7CJ7	⚙ ▾

Data sources included in this dataset:

⊘ File{"path":"c:\\data\\covid\\bing-covid19-data.csv"}   Maps to: | Covid 19 data set   ⌄ |

Figure 14-14. *Mapping data sources in the gateway*

If the user who is mapping the data source is not an administrator of the gateway, then users can be granted permission to use the gateway on the datasource settings page. This needs to be done for each datasource and does not grant the user access to all data sources on the gateway.

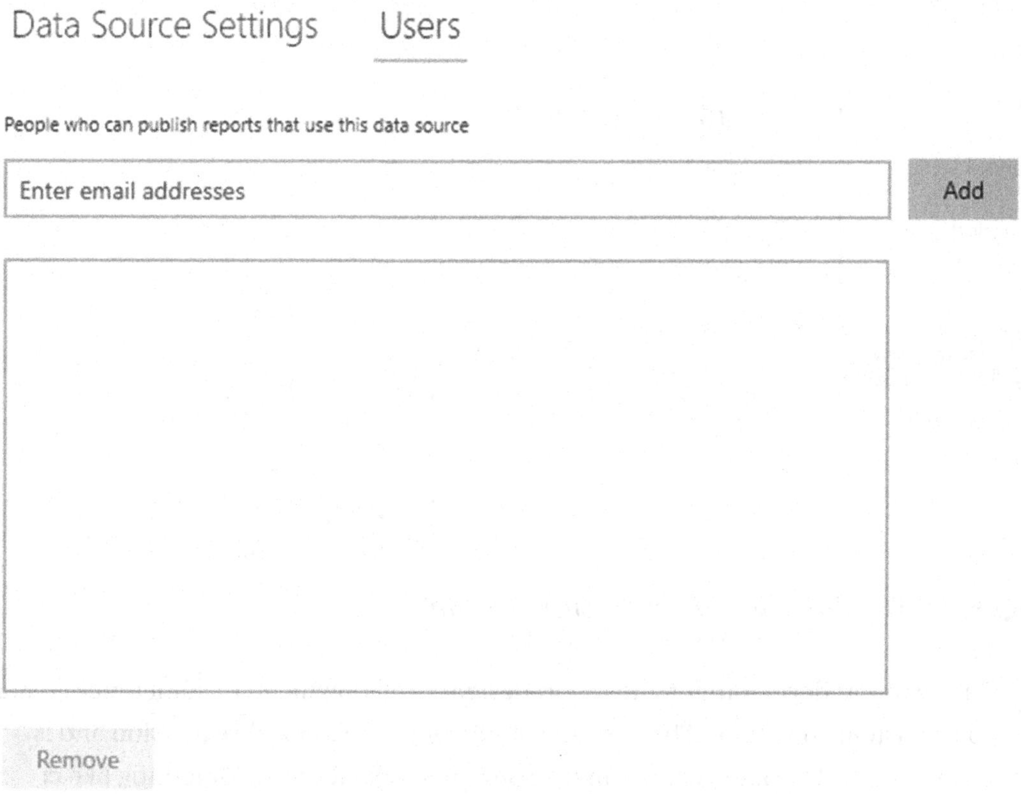

Data Source Settings   Users

People who can publish reports that use this data source

| Enter email addresses | | Add |

Remove

Figure 14-15. *Adding a user to a data source*

These users can configure reports that they manage to use the data source without requiring authentication details, providing an additional separation of responsibilities, and allowing the gateway administrator to change authentication details without requiring the report owners to take any actions.

Custom connectors

Custom connectors allow organizations to create or obtain connectors to data sources that may not be supported through the default Power BI data sources. Custom Data Connectors are usually created by Independent Software Vendors (ISVs) to allow their clients to connect to their source data. When such custom connectors are used in Power BI desktop, the use of such connectors first needs to be enabled in the desktop tool.

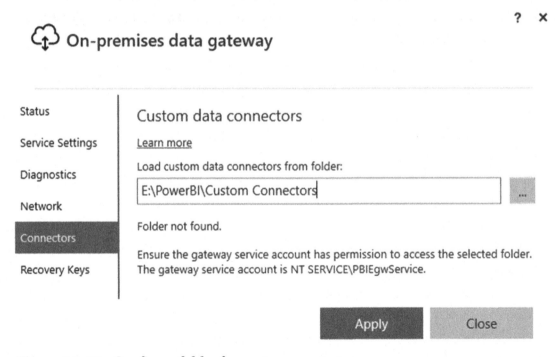

Figure 14-16. Configure folder for custom connectors

During report development, the report designer will download or sometimes create their own custom connector. The custom connector uses a .Mez file extension and is placed in a particular folder, usually in the user's personal folders. Something like **c:\ users***UserName***\Documents\Power BI Desktop\Custom Connectors**. Unlike custom visuals, the custom connector is not embedded into the.PBIX file itself. For the custom connector to work during data refresh, it needs to be available to each of the gateways. This means creating a folder on each host and ensuring that a copy of the correct .Mez file is available.

Warning   Custom connectors can be used to execute malicious code or can result in data being compromised. Custom connectors should only be used from a trusted source.

Monitoring and troubleshooting

Monitoring the performance of the gateways is an essential administrative task. An effective monitoring strategy ensures that you not only understand how the gateways are performing but also when action should be taken for a poorly performing gateway. There are two levels of monitoring that need to be performed:

- **General health:** Monitoring the general health of the gateway involves monitoring not only the use of CPU, memory, disk, and network but also the number of queries being processed by the gateway. Such monitoring activities are often performed in near real-time for early detection of potential issues.

- **Query performance and troubleshooting:** Monitoring the general time taken for specific queries, groups of queries, or data sources to return as well as the frequency of failed queries and timeouts. Such monitoring is often not performed in real-time and may only be evaluated periodically or in the event of errors.

General health

Monitoring the health of the gateway is similar to monitoring other applications in the Microsoft ecosystem. Basic monitoring focuses on four primary resources:

- CPU
- Memory
- Disk
- Network

No application can function at its optimal level if any of these resources is in short supply. In addition to the four primary resources, a good general health monitor will watch out for other signs that the system is under strain or if there are other problems. In the case of the gateway, this could include query timeouts or failures. For a quick understanding of the four primary resources, many users and administrators use Task Manager.

Task Manager

Task Manager is an easy to use application that can quickly give the user an overview of the health of the system. In addition to providing system-level counters, users can drill down to specific applications and processes.

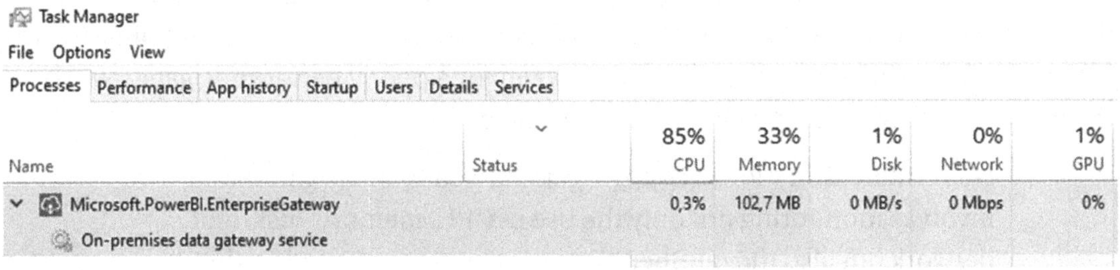

Figure 14-17. *Viewing gateway performance using task manager*

While Task Manager is simple to use, it is not a suitable candidate for reliable monitoring as it required the administrator to be logged into the terminal and monitoring the system. This is impractical for continued usage; instead, Performance monitor provides a better functionality.

Performance Monitor

Performance Monitor, also known as Perfmon, is a system monitoring tool that can be configured to provide in-depth counters on a number of key matrices. Performance Monitor works by aggregating a number of events over a given timespan. As all counters are simple aggregations, these counters are not very helpful in diagnosing specific problems but are very useful in determining if a problem exists. An example of this is monitoring failed queries; while the counter will not help you identify the failed query, it alerts you to the fact that a query has failed. While Performance Monitor can be used in a similar way to Task Manager, as a real-time display of counter values. A better solution is to create a data collector that can be used to systematically log counters and their values on a schedule. These values can then be stored to various destinations such as text files. These stored results can then be collected and analyzed on a schedule using a tool such as Power BI; however, for a real-time monitoring solution, you can log these counters directly into a SQL Database where a new real-time dashboard and alerts can be created.

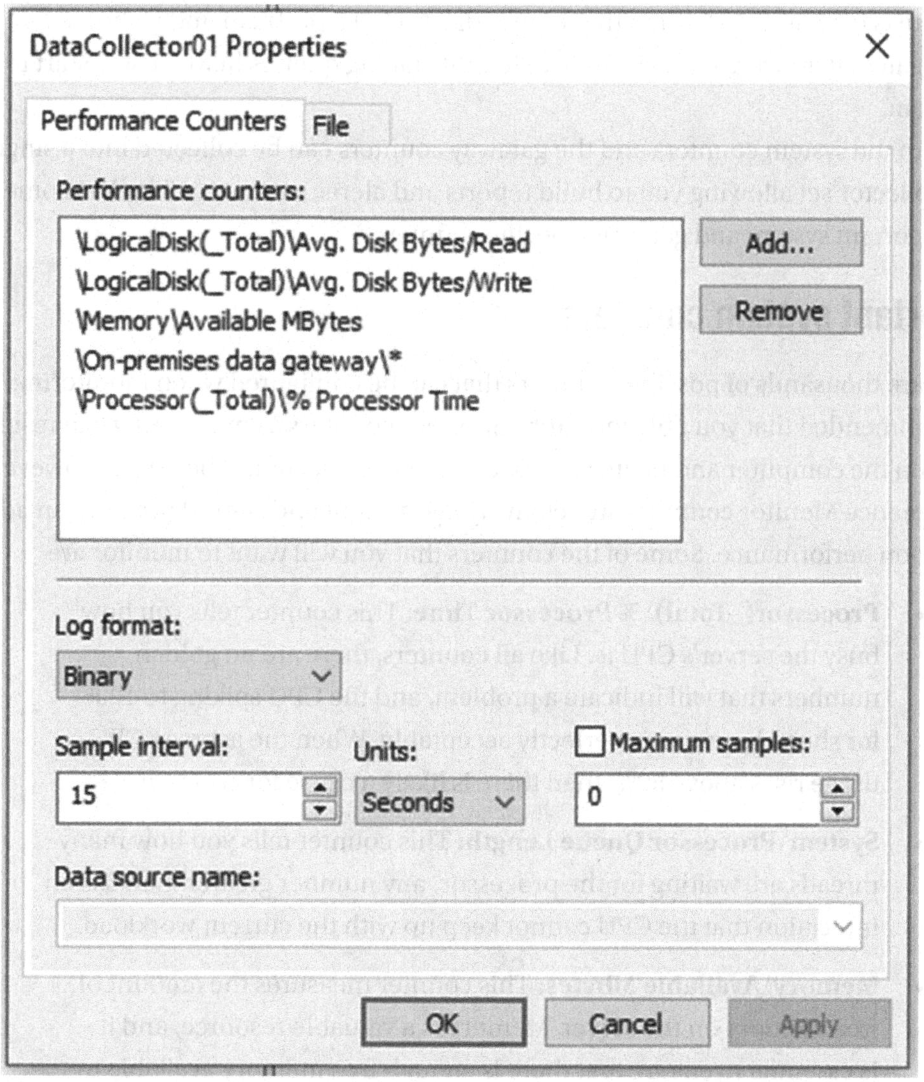

Figure 14-18. *Setting up a performance monitor collector set*

One of the core reasons for collecting these counter values is to build a baseline for the cluster. A baseline is simply an understanding of what the computer's resource usage looks like when it is stable. This becomes important during times of crisis when the administrator needs to identify the source of a problem. If you understand what the expected or baseline values are, then it becomes easier to determine if there is a problem. An example of this is finding out that the gateway is consuming 80% of the CPU; this simple measure by itself does not tell you if something is wrong, but if this measure is usually at 40%, then that is an indication of a problem and it should be investigated. It is also good to be able to identify failing queries before users start to complain.

Both the system counters and the gateway counters can be collected into a single data collector set allowing you to build reports and alerts; next we will look at some of the important system and gateway-specific counters.

Important system counters

There are thousands of possible counters that can be configured when monitoring, but it is recommended that you only monitor important counters as monitoring can result in strain on the computer and begin to impact the system. It should be noted, however, that Performance Monitor counters are relatively lightweight and should not have an adverse impact on performance. Some of the counters that you will want to monitor are

- **Processor(_Total)\% Processor Time:** This counter tells you how busy the server's CPU is. Like all counters, there are no golden numbers that will indicate a problem, and the CPU spiking to 100% for short durations is perfectly acceptable. When the average CPU usage rises above 80%, then there is likely a cause for concern.

- **System\Processor Queue Length:** This counter tells you how many threads are waiting for the processor; any number greater than 0 is an indication that the CPU cannot keep up with the current workload.

- **Memory\Available Mbytes:** This counter measures the amount of free memory on the server. Memory is a valuable resource, and it is essential to ensure that there is enough free memory available to handle requests. When there is not enough memory available, the server pages some of that memory to disk, which is much slower than a memory. Ideally, this number remains greater than 0.

- **Paging File(_Total)\% Usage:** When the operating system runs out of memory is begins to swap data out to disk. Moving data out to disk is several orders of magnitudes slower than those same operations happening in memory, so you want to avoid this happening at all if possible. If this is happening, add more memory or add more members to the cluster to distribute the load.

- **PhysicalDisk(_Total)\Avg. Disk sec/Read and PhysicalDisk(_Total) \Avg. Disk sec/Write:** This counter reports the number of read and write operations that are happening on the disk.

- **Network interface\Bytes total/sec:** This counter indicates the rate at which the network adaptors are processing data. This number should remain below 50-60% of the sustainable bandwidth of the network.

On-premises data gateway counters

The On-premises data gateway provides several gateway-specific counters that the administrator can use to monitor gateway activity.

```
1
2
3    (get-counter -ListSet 'On-Premises data gateway').counter
4
```

```
PS C:\Windows\system32> (get-counter -ListSet 'On-Premises data gateway').counter
\On-premises data gateway\# of all queries executed / sec
\On-premises data gateway\# of queries failed / sec.
\On-premises data gateway\# of ADO.NET queries executed / sec
\On-premises data gateway\# of ADO.NET queries failed / sec.
\On-premises data gateway\# of ADOMD queries executed / sec
\On-premises data gateway\# of ADOMD queries failed / sec.
\On-premises data gateway\# of Mashup queries executed / sec
\On-premises data gateway\# of Mashup queries failed / sec.
\On-premises data gateway\# of OLEDB single resultset queries executed / sec
\On-premises data gateway\# of single result set OLEDB queries failed / sec.
\On-premises data gateway\# of OLEDB multiple resultset queries executed / sec
\On-premises data gateway\# of multiple result set OLEDB queries failed / sec.
\On-premises data gateway\# of OLEDB queries executed / sec
\On-premises data gateway\# of OLEDB queries failed / sec.
\On-premises data gateway\# of items in the Service Bus pool
\On-premises data gateway\# of items in the ADO.NET connection pool
\On-premises data gateway\# of items in the OLEDB connection pool
\On-premises data gateway\# of all open connection executed / sec
\On-premises data gateway\# of all open connection failed / sec
\On-premises data gateway\# of ADO.NET open connection executed / sec
\On-premises data gateway\# of ADO.NET open connection failed / sec
\On-premises data gateway\# of ADOMD open connection executed / sec
\On-premises data gateway\# of ADOMD open connection failed / sec
\On-premises data gateway\# of Mashup open connection executed / sec
\On-premises data gateway\# of Mashup open connection failed / sec
\On-premises data gateway\# of OLEDB open connection executed / sec
\On-premises data gateway\# of OLEDB open connection failed / sec

PS C:\Windows\system32>
```

Figure 14-19. *Getting a full list of gateway counters*

235

At the time of writing, 27 gateway-specific counters can be monitored. Each counter monitors a different workload type and it is not unreasonable to monitor all 27. If, however, you know that some counters are not relevant to your environment, then you may exclude them. Some of the counters that you will want to pay attention to are

- **# of all queries executed/sec:** This counter will give you a count of the number of queries executed per second. If your organization uses only imported datasets, then this number will likely be small. For reports that use DirectQuery and live connections against on-premises data sources, this number can be a good indication of heavy use.

- **# of queries failed/sec:** Any number greater than 0 should be investigated as it may be cause for concern and indicate problems with the source system. Timeouts against the production OLTP system can be an indication report beginning to affect the operations of the system.

- **# of items in the Service Bus pool:** The gateway uses Azure Service Bus to send data requests to the gateway reliably; this counter lets you know if the gateway cluster can satisfy all incoming requests. There is no golden value here, and each environment will differ, which is why baselining this value is important. If this number begins to climb, it is an indication that more queries are being sent to the cluster than the cluster can resolve. To fix this problem, the cluster can be scaled up or out by adding more resources to the gateway computers or adding more members to the cluster. Additionally, the developer can be asked to look for more efficient ways to query the data. (Dataflows could be an appropriate solution.)

Note   Adding additional nodes to the cluster may be meaningless if the **"Distribute requests across active gateways in the cluster"** is not enabled, as queries will not scale beyond a single node.

Troubleshooting

Monitoring of a solution such as a gateway helps confirm that the environment is running as expected and that there are no errors. When errors are detected, it often falls to the administrator to troubleshoot the problem. Such problems can be reported in a few ways.

- **Power BI alerts:** Data sources should be configured to notify administrators when errors occur.

- **Monitoring:** Administrators may detect errors or degraded performance from their general health monitoring.

- **Users:** Report users may also contact the administrators directly or via a contact center to notify them about problems in the system.

Identifying the cause of problems may be challenging. Some of the questions you may consider when troubleshooting the gateway are

- Does the problem occur consistently?

- Is there a problem with a particular data source, source system, or gateway?

- Are all the gateways running the latest version of the On-premises data gateway software?

- How does the current gateway throughput compare to known benchmarks?

Here we look at some of the tools available to help the administrator troubleshoot some of these problems.

Refresh history

When a refresh fails in the service, details of the error are logged to the service. These errors can be viewed by the administrators and other users with access to the dataset. You can view these details by viewing the refresh history; if any of these jobs have failed, then details of the failure can usually be logged to the service.

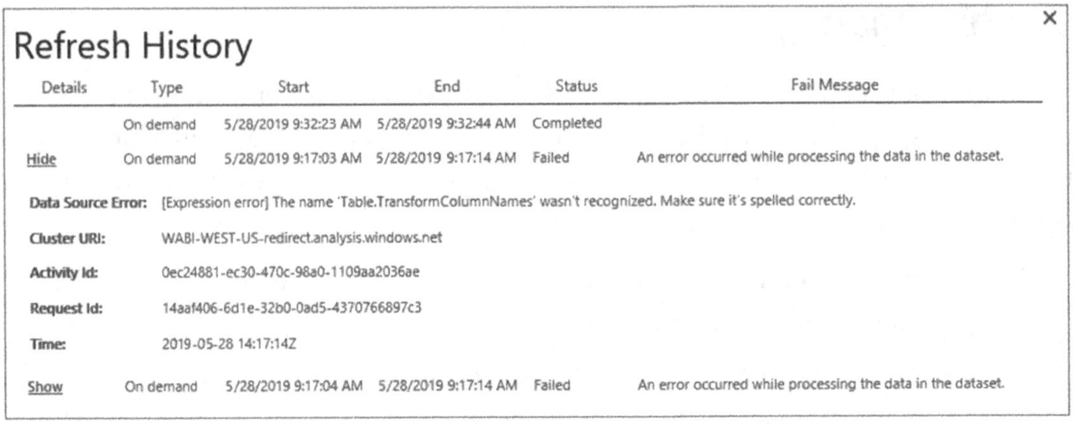

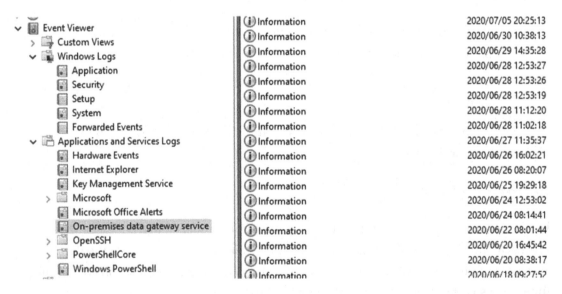

Figure 14-20. *Dataset refresh error details*

Event logs

The windows event logs can also be used to diagnose problems with the gateway. Such events are usually at the application level, so if there are problems with the gateway starting or if the gateway process suddenly terminates, then the details of the error can usually be found in the event log.

Figure 14-21. *View application events in the event log*

Gateway logs

The gateway itself also records more detailed logs. These logs are usually the best place to start. However, these logs are only available on the standard gateway. The logs can be accessed by

1. Launching the On-premises data gateway app.

2. Login (you must be logged in to view the logs).

3. Navigate to the Diagnostics.

4. Select export logs.

Figure 14-22. *Exporting gateway logs*

The application generates a .zip file on the desktop of the user who exported the log. Inside the .zip file, you find multiple files; many of these files are created daily with a date timestamp to make finding the relevant log entries easier. These files can also be accessed directly depending on the operating system the gateway is installed on. You can the log files at:

- \Users\PBIEgwService\AppData\Local\Microsoft\On-premises data gateway\Report

- \Windows\ServiceProfiles\PBIEgwService\AppData\Local\ Microsoft\On-premises data gateway\Report

By default, these logs only capture error information. However, it is also possible to capture detailed **query execution** details and **performance counters**. The detailed execution report has a wealth of information on which queries are failing or how long they take to complete. The Performance counters are the same as the Performance Monitor counters. To enable the additional logging, you need to manually update the configurations file **Microsoft.PowerBI.DataMovement.Pipeline.GatewayCore.dll.config** setting the **QueryExecutionReportOn** and **SystemCounterReportOn** values to **True.**

```
<setting name="QueryExecutionReportOn" serializeAs="String">
  <value>True</value>
</setting>
<setting name="SystemCounterReportOn" serializeAs="String">
  <value>True</value>
</setting>
```

Figure 14-23. *Update Config file*

After making the changes, you need to restart the gateway which can be done from within the On-premises data gateway app.

1. Navigate to Service settings.

2. Select Restart now.

To make analyzing these logs easier, Microsoft has created a Power BI report template that you can use to connect to these logs. At the time of witting, this report was still in preview, but as a template, you are able to modify it to meet your needs.

Additional logging

The level of logging provided by the gateway logs is often enough to diagnose most problems; however, it does not include all the information available. The gateway offers a verbose logging option than can be enabled via the On-premises data gateway app.

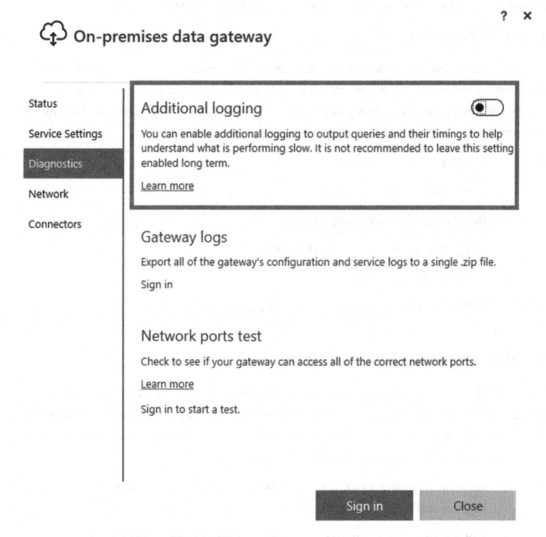

Figure 14-24. *Enable additional logging*

Like the performance logging options, the gateway needs to be restarted, so you need to consider this before enabling it during a critical time. This level of logging is also likely to cause additional load on the gateway and computer that it runs on, so leaving the gateway in this mode is not recommended.

Automation

In large organizations or those that embrace an infrastructure-as-code philosophy, the gateways can be installed and managed using the DataGateway PowerShell cmdlets. These cmdlets are not installed as part of the Power BI cmdlets and need to be installed separately. The cmdlets can be installed using the following command:

```
Install-Module -Name DataGateway
```

The DataGateway Cmdlets also require PowerShell core 6.2.2 or greater, which is a different implementation of PowerShell than the one used by the Power BI Cmdlets.

Many of the gateway admin tasks can be automated using the DataGateway Cmdlets, such as

- Getting a list of gateways

- Returning the cluster status

- Removing nodes from the cluster

- Adding new data sources to the cluster

- Deleting the entire cluster

The cmdlets can be broken down into four categories.

Cmdlets to manage policies

These cmdlets aid the administrator in managing the gateway policies; such policies include the ability to control who can install gateways and which mode they may install. This can be particularly helpful if your organization would like to restrict or eliminate the use of personal gateways. Examples of such cmdlets are

- **Get-DataGatewayInstaller:** Lists users authorized to install and register gateways within the tenant

- **Get-DataGatewayTenantPolicy:** Returns the gateway installation and registration policy for the tenant

- **Set-DataGatewayTenantPolicy:** Updates the installation policy used in the tenant

Cmdlets to manage gateway clusters and members

This set of cmdlets can be used to manage the gateway cluster itself. This can include getting a list of gateways, their status, and even removing members from the cluster. Note that there is no add-member cmdlet as members can only be added manually at this point.

- **Get-DataGatewayCluster:** Lists all gateway clusters for the current user or a specific one based on the passed parameters

- **Get-DataGatewayClusterStatus:** Returns the cluster status along with additional properties

- **Remove-DataGatewayClusterMember:** Removes a gateway member from the corresponding gateway cluster

- **Set-DataGatewayCluster:** Sets properties for an existing gateway cluster.

Cmdlets to manage users

This set of cmdlets can be used to manage users of the gateway clusters

- **Add-DataGatewayClusterUser:** Add a user to a gateway cluster.

- **Remove-DataGatewayClusterUser:** Remove a user from a gateway cluster.

Managing data sources

In addition to managing gateways, you can also automate to manage the data sources for that gateway.

- **Add-DataGatewayClusterDatasourceUser:** Adds a user with required permissions for a Power BI data source

- **Get-DataGatewayClusterDatasource:** Lists all or selected Power BI data sources on a gateway cluster

- **Get-DataGatewayClusterDatasourceStatus:** Tests the connectivity of a data source from the gateway cluster.

- **Get-DataGatewayClusterDatasourceUser**: Lists users for the data source on a gateway cluster

- **Remove-DataGatewayClusterDatasource**: Removes a Power BI data source from a gateway cluster

- **Remove-DataGatewayClusterDatasourceUser**: Removes a user from a Power BI data source

- **Set-DataGatewayClusterDatasource**: Sets properties of an existing Power BI data source

Summary

The gateway serves as an important bridge between the power BI server that runs in the cloud and the data sources that reside on private networks. Ensuring that the gateways remain available and perform well is crucial.

Call to action

- Ensure gateway is installed in a cluster with at least two nodes.

- Ensure servers with gateways installed have adequate resources.

- Monitor resource usage and query performance.

- Install the gateway cluster as close to data sources as possible.

- Ensure distribute requests across active gateways in the cluster is enabled; this needs to be done in the gateway admin portal in the service.

CHAPTER 15

Power BI Administration Tools

Read this chapter if you would like to find out more information about

- Learn about the different portals available to Power BI administrators
- Tools to help the Power BI administrator
- Tips on how to automate admin tasks

In this chapter we will look at some of the tools available to help the Power BI administrator perform their duties. If you have read the earlier chapters, you will be familiar with some of the portals that Microsoft has created to help manage important Power BI objects such as users, workspaces, tenant policies, and many others. In addition, there are several tools that can help the administrator automate many of their tasks, ensuring that repetitive tasks are performed efficiently and consistently. We will also look at third-party tools that are available outside of the Microsoft ecosystem to help extend the capability of the Power BI ecosystem.

We will discuss the following tools as well as the types of tasks that you can perform through these portals.

- Portals
- Automation tools
- Third-party tools

© Ásgeir Gunnarsson and Michael Johnson 2020
Á. Gunnarsson and M. Johnson, *Pro Microsoft Power BI Administration*,
https://doi.org/10.1007/978-1-4842-6567-3_15

Portals

Portals are where most people begin to manage their Power BI environment. There are several portals available in Azure, Office 365, and Power BI to manage various parts of the Power BI tenant. The portal that you chose and the rights that you have assigned will determine what functions you can perform. The portals that we will use are often simple and intuitive; however they do require that the user performs the tasks manually. In large organizations some tasks may need to be performed hundreds of times, making them less appropriate. We will discuss automation options after this section on portals.

The portals we will look at are

- Power BI Portal

- Power BI admin portal

- Office 365 admin portal

- Azure portal

All these portals can be accessed through a web browser, where the user is authenticated using their Azure Active directory credentials.

Power BI portal

The Power BI portal is usually the first portal used by Power BI administrators to manage their Power BI environments. The Power BI portal is easy to use and is highly coupled with the rest of the Power BI environment. This coupling is so tight that it is often difficult to separate what is an administration function and what is not, and the distinction between the different types of tasks is often guided by the Power BI governance policy. An example of such a distinction may be in the creation of workspaces or the publishing of reports. The Power BI portal can be used to perform almost any task required of the administrator, although such tasks are performed manually.

The Power BI portal is accessed using the `https://app.powerbi.com` URL.

Some of the tasks that can be performed through this portal are

- Create and update workspace

- Add users to workspace

- Create and update refresh schedule

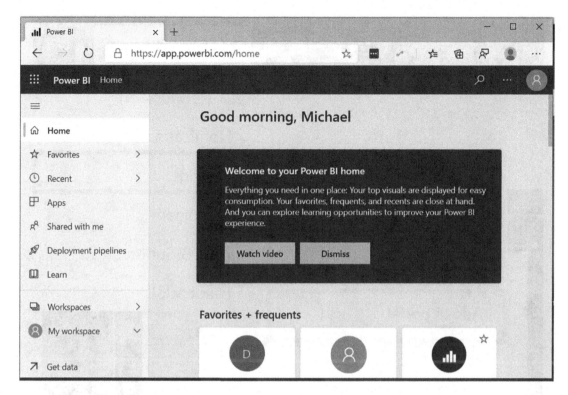

Figure 15-1. *The Power BI Portal*

Power BI Admin Portal

The Power BI admin portal is dedicated to administrative tasks and is the portal that is
used to manage many of the settings that are generally restricted to the admin role. The
Power BI admin portal can be accessed through the Power BI portal, selecting admin
portal on the settings tab or by directly navigating to `https://app.powerbi.com/admin-`
`portal`.

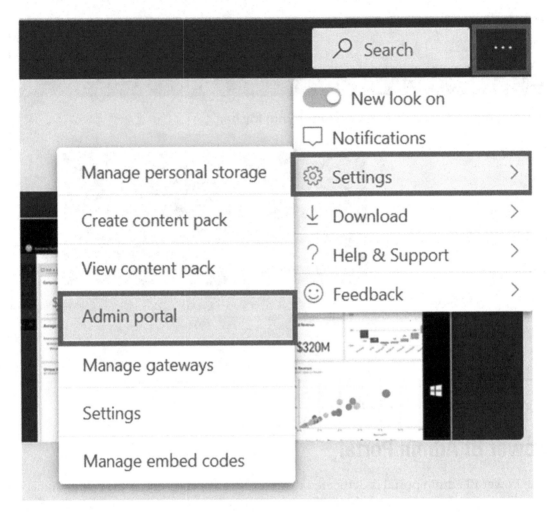

Figure 15-2. *Accessing the Power BI admin portal*

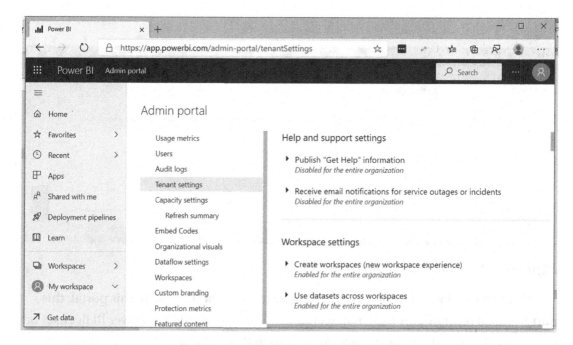

Figure 15-3. *Power BI admin portal*

Some of the tasks that can be done in the Power BI admin portal are

- Restore deleted workspaces

- Configure premium capacities

- Change tenant settings

- Configure Azure Data Lake Storage

When exploring the Admin panel, you will find that some options such as users and Audit logs only provide a link to the Office 365 portal. This is because these functions are at the tenant level and not specific to Power BI.

Office 365 admin portal

The Office 365 admin portal is used to manage the Office 365 tenant and all the services that it's comprised of, including Power BI. The Office 365 portal is not available to users who only have the Power BI administrator role and a role such as the Global administrator or Billing administrator is required to access this portal. The portal can be accessed through the https://admin.microsoft.com/ URL.

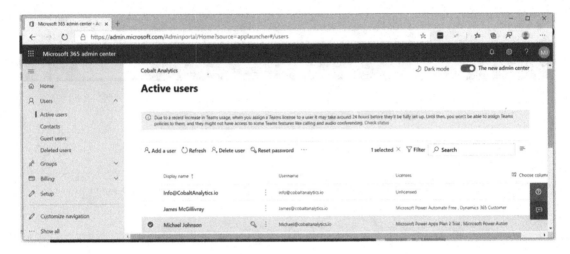

Figure 15-4. *Office 365 admin portalv*

There are no Power BI–specific functions that can be performed in this portal; this portal is used primarily for user management and the purchasing of Power BI licenses or capacities. Some of the tasks that are performed in this portal are

– Create new users.

– Assign Power BI licenses.

– Assign Power BI Admin role.

– Purchase P and EM SKU dedicated capacities.

– Access Activity logs (can also be done in PowerShell).

Azure portal

The Azure portal is used to manage Azure-specific resource but can also be used to manage users. The Azure portal can be accessed through `https://portal.azure.com/`.

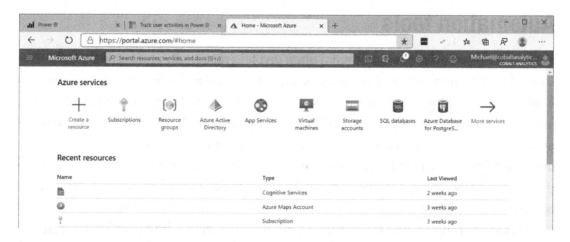

Figure 15-5. *The Azure portal*

The Azure portal is unlikely to be used by administrators in Power BI environments that do not make use of more advanced features such as Power BI embedded, or when using their own Azure Data Lake storage for Dataflows. Some of the tasks that can be done in the Azure portal include

- Provision of A SKU dedicated capacities.

- Create users.

- Assign licenses.

- Create and configure Service Principals.

- Create Azure Data Lake storage (used for Dataflows discussed in Chapter 13)

Portal Summary

So far in this chapter we have looked at the web portals available to manage the Power BI environment. All these portals are all available to the administrator using a web browser.

Automation tools

Administering a Power BI environment often involves repeatedly performing the same steps over and over. An example of such a task could include compiling a list of workspaces and datasets. While this task can be accomplished through the portal, such an exercise could take days or even weeks in a large organization. To make these possible at scale, Power BI provides several automation options for administrators to use. It is important from both an efficiency point of view and from a governance perspective that these tasks are performed consistently to ensure compliance with all policies, Power BI or otherwise.

This level of automation is not only intended for Power BI administrators but can also be used by Power BI developers and users alike.

REST APIs

The Power BI REST APIs provide a programmatic way to send queries and commands to the Power BI Service. REST APIs stand for **Re**presentational **S**tate **T**ransfer (REST) **A**pplication **P**rogram **I**nterface (API) and use commands sent over https to communicate with the Power BI Service. By using https as a protocol, it means that there are not any special security rules that need to be created and that standard tools such as web browsers, Postman, and even Power BI (with limits) can be used.

The APIs provide several methods that are not only limited to administrative tasks. These REST APIs are heavily used when building Power BI solution using Power BI embedded. Each REST API method request has four properties:

- **Endpoint**: The endpoint is simply the URL of the method; each endpoint has a single function. Object identifiers such as the workspace ID are often passed through to the service in the endpoint URL.

- **Method**: HTTP supports several methods, but the Power BI REST APIs are limited to using the GET and POST methods. The GET method is used when the request fetches data such as a list of workspaces. POST is used when the request performs an action such as adding a user to a workgroup.

- **Header**: The header contains the authentication details.

- **Body**: The body may contain additional information required by the API.

Each of these requests returns a json object; this object will contain the results of the request. An example of such a request is

```
GET https://api.powerbi.com/v1.0/myorg/groups
```

When executed, this request will return a json object containing a list of all the workspaces that the user has access to like the following result:

```
{
  "value": [
    {
      "id": "f089354e-8366-4e18-aea3-4cb4a3a50b48",
      "isReadOnly": false,
      "isOnDedicatedCapacity": false,
      "name": "sample group"
    },
    {
      "id": "3d9b93c6-7b6d-4801-a491-1738910904fd",
      "isReadOnly": false,
      "isOnDedicatedCapacity": false,
      "name": "marketing group"
    },
    {
      "id": "a2f89923-421a-464e-bf4c-25eab39bb09f",
      "isReadOnly": false,
      "isOnDedicatedCapacity": false,
      "name": "contoso",
      "dataflowStorageId": "d692ae06-708c-485e-9987-06ff0fbdbb1f"
    }
  ]
}
```

A full list of endpoint can be found at https://docs.microsoft.com/en-us/rest/api/power-bi/. To make it easier to experiment with the API calls, the API documentation includes a "Try it" function.

Figure 15-6. *Executing the API function within the Power BI documentation site*

When using this site, you are asked to first log in using your user account. This will generate the required authentication token. There are several ways to generate this token depending on the account type used. This is beyond the scope of a book on Power BI administration, but Microsoft provides many references on how this can be accomplished.

Once logged in, the site provides **try it** function where the user can capture the required parameter values into the interface. In Figure 15-7 the interface for the **Get Reports in Group** function is being called. This function requires the GroupId to be provided. In this case the GroupId can be found in the json result set returned from the groups function or in the URL when you are browsing a workspace using the Power BI portal.

Figure 15-7. *Getting the GroupId from the Power BI portal*

In addition to providing the GroupId, there are also several optional parameters that can be supplied to some functions.

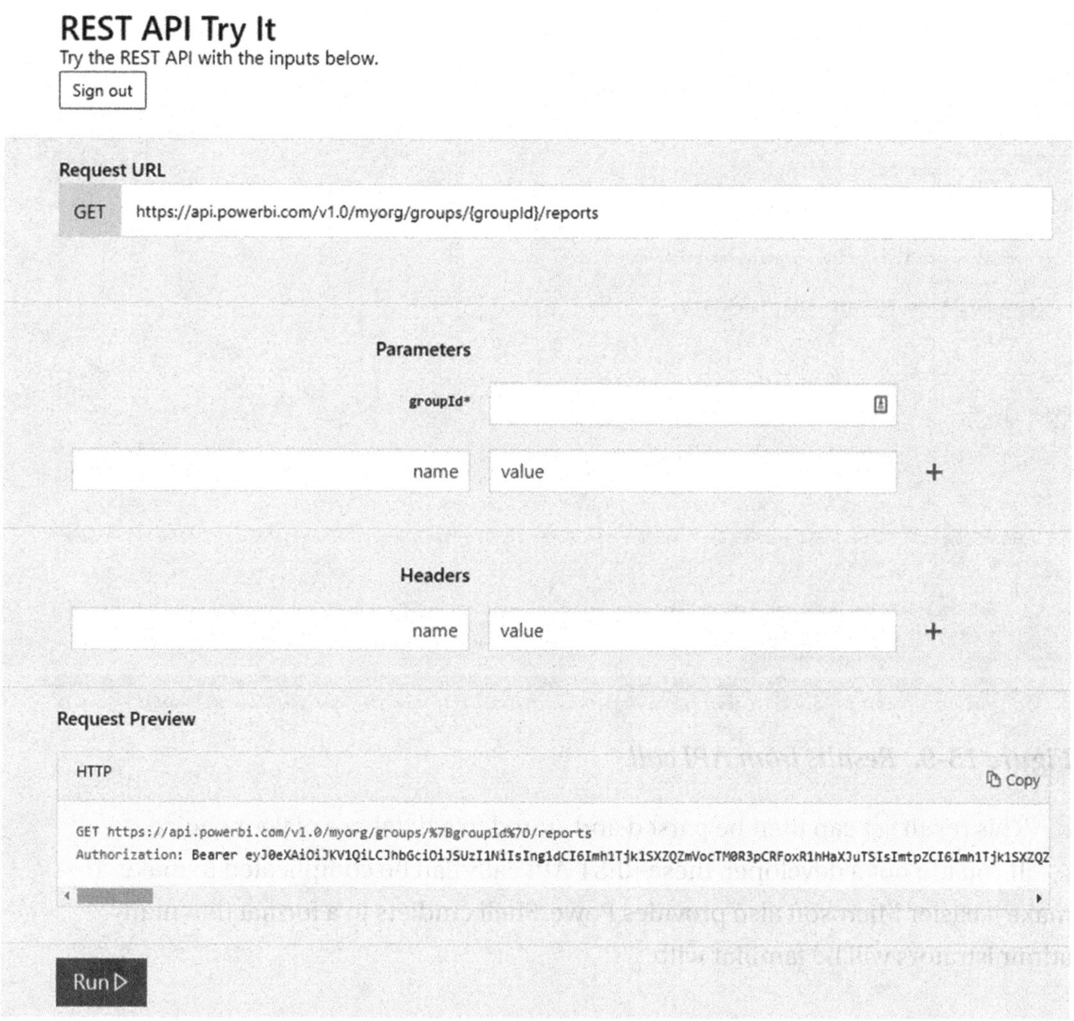

REST API Try It

Try the REST API with the inputs below.

Sign out

Request URL

GET   https://api.powerbi.com/v1.0/myorg/groups/{groupId}/reports

Parameters

groupId*   [   ] ▣

[name]   [value   ] +

Headers

[name]   [value   ] +

Request Preview

HTTP   ⧉ Copy

```
GET https://api.powerbi.com/v1.0/myorg/groups/%7BgroupId%7D/reports
Authorization: Bearer eyJ0eXAiOiJKV1QiLCJhbGciOiJSUzI1NiIsIng1dCI6Imh1Tjk1SXZQZmVocTM0R3pCRFoxR1hHaXJuTSIsImtpZCI6Imh1Tjk1SXZZQZ
```

Run ▷

Figure 15-8. *Testing API functionality using the site*

The following results are returned.

Response Code: 200

Headers

```
HTTP                                                                    Copy

cache-control: no-store, must-revalidate, no-cache
content-length: 686
content-type: application/json; odata.metadata=minimal
pragma: no-cache
requestid: c9fcb9da-064f-4529-a790-371de0bb7917
```

Body

```
JSON                                                                    Copy

{
    "@odata.context": "http://wabi-west-europe-b-primary-redirect.analysis.windows.net/v1.0/myorg/groups/021332f4-2a82-4f02-b9
    "value": [
      {
        "id": "2ca14903-cb8d-41e8-b806-cd67cc6e264c",
        "reportType": "PowerBIReport",
        "name": "Human Resources Sample",
        "webUrl": "https://app.powerbi.com/groups/021332f4-2a82-4f02-b97d-40213f5c2940/reports/2ca14903-cb8d-41e8-b806-cd67cc6
        "embedUrl": "https://app.powerbi.com/reportEmbed?reportId=2ca14903-cb8d-41e8-b806-cd67cc6e264c&groupId=021332f4-2a82-4
```

Figure 15-9. *Results from API call*

This result set can then be parsed and stored in a database of your choice.

If you are not a developer, these REST API calls can be complicated to make. To make it easier Microsoft also provides PowerShell cmdlets in a format that many administrators will be familiar with.

PowerShell

The Power BI APIs can be difficult to consume for users who are not familiar with modern development languages. However, many system administrators are used to working with console scripts such as Bash and PowerShell that allow tasks to be performed by executing commands against the system. Microsoft's shell scripting language is PowerShell and is available on all modern versions of windows. PowerShell uses custom modules called cmdlets (pronounced Command lets) to implement different functionalities. In the case of the Power BI cmdlets, PowerShell simply provides an easy to use wrapper over the REST APIs. This wrapper removes a lot of the complexity of using the Power BI APIs. Like the REST APIs the PowerShell cmdlets are not only for administrators and can be used by developers and users alike.

To use the PowerShell cmdlets, you require at least PowerShell v3.0 with .Net 4.7.1 or you can use PowerShell Core v6 and above. Installing the PowerShell module can be done from an elevated PowerShell session. This can be done by running the PowerShell as an Administrator.

PowerShell
Install-Module -Name MicrosoftPowerBIMgmt

Figure 15-10. *Installing PowerShell modules*

Once PowerShell has been installed, a full list of available cmdlets can be returned by running the line of code in Figure 15-11.

PowerShell
Get-Command -Module MicrosoftPowerBIMgmt.*

Figure 15-11. *Get available Cmdlets*

There are six modules. Each module consists of multiple cmdlets. We will look at each module and some of the cmdlets that we believe are most useful.

- **Admin Module**: This module can be used to manage encryption keys in the service as well as return events from the activity log.

  - **Get-PowerBIActivityEvent**: Returns the Power BI activities from the event log.

  - **Add-PowerBIEncryptionKey**: Add a new encryption key to a workspace in a capacity.

- **Capacities module**: This module is used for the management of capacities.

  - **Get-PowerBICapacity**: Returns a list of capacities in the tenant.

- **Data module**: This module is used to manage datasets and data sources.

    - **Get-PowerBIDataset**: Returns a list of datasets in a workspace.

    - **Get-PowerBIDataflow**: Returns a list of all dataflows in a workspace.

- **Profile Module**: This module contains cmdlets to connect to the Power BI Service.

    - **Connect-PowerBIServiceAccount:** This cmdlet is used to log into the Power BI Service. Users can log in either by providing their own user credentials or using a service principal and certificate.

    - **Invoke-PowerBIRestMethod**: This Cmdlet can be used to invoke API calls for which there are not cmdlets for.

    - **Resolve-PowerBIError**: This cmdlet provides details about the last error that occurred in the PowerShell session.

- **Report Module:**

    - **Get-PowerBIReport**: Returns a list of reports in a workspace.

    - **Remove-PowerBIReport**: Deletes a report from the workspace.

- **Workspace module:**

    - **Get-PowerBIWorkspace**: Returns a list of workspaces.

    - **New-PowerBIWorkspace**: Creates a new workspace.

    - **Add-PowerBIWorkspaceUser**: Adds an existing user to a workspace.

Before using many of these cmdlets, you will first need to log into the Power BI Service and authenticate yourself and obtain an authentication token. This can be done by executing the following command.

```
PowerShell

Connect-PowerBIServiceAccount
```

Figure 15-12. *Login to Power BI Service*

This invokes an authentication panel where you log into using your Azure Active Directory credentials.

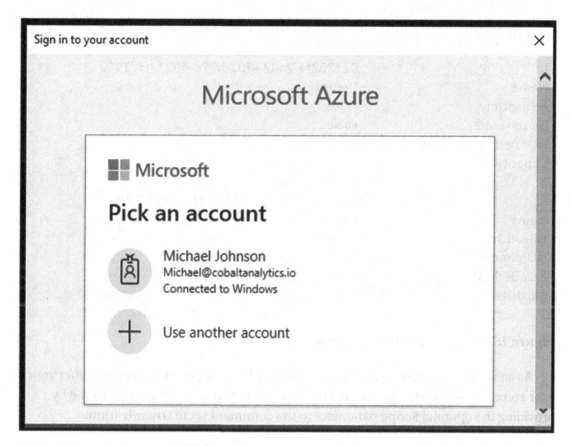

Figure 15-13. *Authenticating user login*

Note   It is also possible to setup a service principal so that these scripts can be run without requiring an administrator to log in allowing for full automation of the solution; you can find more information on setting up a service principal here `https://docs.microsoft.com/power-bi/developer/embedded/embed-service-principal`.

Once authenticated it is possible to execute the other cmdlets. Some cmdlets require parameters while other do not; in the following example, the `Get-PowerBIWorkspace` command will return a list of all workspaces that the user has access to.

PowerShell	
Get-PowerBIWorkspace	
Result	
Id	: 021332f4-2a82-4f02-b97d-40213f5c2940
Name	: Demo
IsReadOnly	: False
IsOrphaned	: False
IsOnDedicatedCapacity	: False
CapacityId	:
Id	: c9d5a74c-9e01-4306-b2b6-4f258319601a
Name	: test
IsReadOnly	: False
IsOrphaned	: False
IsOnDedicatedCapacity	: False
CapacityId	:

Figure 15-14. *View all workspaces as user*

As an administrator you often need to see all workspaces regardless of whether your user account has been granted access directly to the workspace; this can be done by providing the optional **Scope** parameter to the command set to **Organization**.

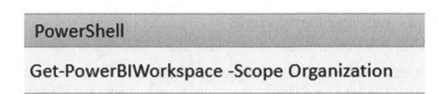

Figure 15-15. *View all workspaces as admin*

This returns all workspaces as well as additional attributes of the workspace.

Not all of the API methods are available using the Power BI cmdlets; if there is a method that you need to call and it is unavailable, the Power BI cmdlets also provide a generic cmdlet that can be used to interact with the API service. All the internal workings such as authenticating are taken care of within the PowerShell module. An example of this is calling the **Get Reports in Group** method; this method takes no parameters, but the workspace id is required in the URL.

PowerShell

Invoke-PowerBIRestMethod -Url '/groups/2f7d499d-6b72-49c9-86da-db09dc9136d6/reports' -Method Get

Figure 15-16. *Returning reports in a workspace using the invoke method cmdlet*

When methods are invoked in this way, a json result set is returned and not the PowerShell object that you get when using a native cmdlet.

Json

```
{
  "@odata.context":"http://api.powerbi.com/v1.0/myorg/groups/2f7d499d-6b72-49c9-86da-db09dc9136d6/$metadata#reports","value":[
  {
    "id":"80ddf26b-d7d7-497d-9eae-e1da0a55b997"
    ,"reportType":"PowerBIReport"
    ,"name":"POC3"
    ,"webUrl":"https://app.powerbi.com/groups/2f7d499d-6b72-49c9-86da-db09dc9136d6/reports/80ddf26b-d7d7-497d-9eae-e1da0a55b
    ,"embedUrl":"https://app.powerbi.com/reportEmbed?reportId=80ddf26b-d7d7-497d-9eae-e1da0a55b997&groupId=
    ,"isOwnedByMe":true
    ,"datasetId":"092ee1ca-02df-41d6-9504-70035d8505f3"
  }
  ]
}
```

Figure 15-17. *Json result set returned from Invoke method*

Finally debugging errors in the cmdlet calls can be difficult as the error messages returned are often not helpful. A detailed error message can be obtained by running the following cmdlet, which will return a detailed error message for the last error during that session.

Figure 15-18. *Returning error details*

PowerShell is not the only way to automate the Power BI API. If you are more familiar with .Net, then you can also look at the Power BI .Net Client Library.

Power BI .Net Client library SDK

Like the Power BI PowerShell modules, the Power BI SDK can also be used to automate many administration tasks, and like the Power BI PowerShell Module, the Power BI SDK is simply a wrapper over the REST APIs that make working with the API much easier. Currently on version three the .Net Client library can be used with any .net compatible language. The .Net client library is intended primarily from developers, but if you or your organization is more comfortable using it, then that is what you should use.

More info   For more info on how to use the Power BI SDK, you can look at `https://docs.microsoft.com/power-bi/developer/`.

Third-party tools

In addition to the tools that Microsoft provides, there are a few over-the-counter solutions provided by third parties that your organization may use to manage your Power BI environment.

Power BI Sentinel

Power BI Sentinel is a third-party SaaS application that provides a solution to many of the governance and administration tasks that are required of an enterprise solution. Power BI Sentinel is a paid product, meaning that its use will include additional costs. You can find the signup page for Power BI Sentinel at `https://www.powerbisentinel.com/`.

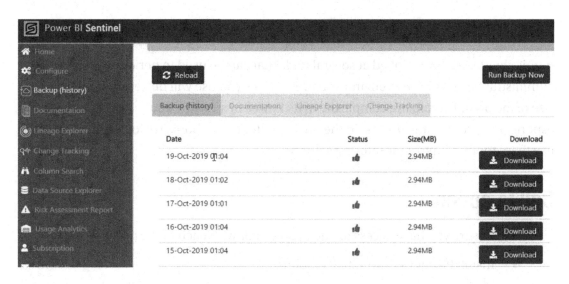

Like the tools mentioned previously, Power BI Sentinel focuses on more than just administration and governance. It also looks to fill some of the gaps that Microsoft has not yet filled. Power BI Sentinel focuses on the following three core areas:

- Disaster recovery

- Governance

- Auditing

And provides many features such as

- Linage view of data in reports

- Automated daily backups of PIBX files

- Change tracking

- Automated documentation

While all of these features can be accomplished using the APIs yourself, such a product provides a quick and easy way to create a quality administration and governance monitoring center, and it would be a good idea to evaluate if such a tool would add value to your Power BI implementation.

Summary

In this chapter we have looked at several tools that can be used to perform administrative tasks in your environment. The tools you use will be determined by the size of the organization, the complexity of its Power BI strategy, and the knowledge and experience of its administrators. In the final chapter of this book, we look at how you can use these tools to build a monitoring solution.

Call to action

- Ensure you have access to and are familiar with each of the portals.

- Install Power BI PowerShell cmdlets.

- Evaluate third-party tools.

CHAPTER 16

Monitoring

What we cover in this chapter

- Monitoring Power BI activities

- Monitoring Power BI inventory

- Monitoring Power BI capacities

Monitoring is a big part of governance. Without it you will have a hard time telling if users are following your governance strategy, including if you are compliant to the rules and regulations your organization needs to adhere to. The Power BI administrator might also want to monitor progress of the implementation of Power BI or create an inventory of Power BI artifacts for users to browse. This chapter will describe what to monitor from a governance perspective and what to monitor to build an inventory of Power BI artifacts. If your organization has Power BI Premium, you will need to monitor your capacities to make sure there are enough resources and that they are being used correctly. Monitoring capacities is also covered in this chapter. This chapter will not cover monitoring the gateway as that was covered in Chapter 14.

Monitoring activities

One of the main reasons to monitor any application is to see if it is being used correctly and its usage is in compliance with the rules and regulations the organization needs to adhere to. Power BI offers an audit log that administrators can use to see if Power BI is being used correctly and compliantly.

© Ásgeir Gunnarsson and Michael Johnson 2020
Á. Gunnarsson and M. Johnson, *Pro Microsoft Power BI Administration*,
https://doi.org/10.1007/978-1-4842-6567-3_16

Note   In the Power BI documentation, the logs are sometimes called audit logs and sometimes activity logs. In this chapter, we will refer to it as an audit log to prevent misunderstanding. Just be aware that when you read the words activity log in the Power BI documentation, it's the same thing as audit log in this chapter.

The Power BI activity/audit log can tell you who accessed what and who changed or deleted what. The audit log is part of the Microsoft 365 Security and Compliance Center. The Power BI audit log is turned off by default unless recording user and admin activity has been enabled in Microsoft 365. The audit log can be turned on in the Power BI admin portal. Figure 16-1 shows how to turn on the Power BI audit log.

Audit and usage settings

▲ Create audit logs for internal activity auditing and compliance
  Enabled for the entire organization

  Users in the organization can use auditing to monitor actions taken in Power BI by other users in the organization. Power BI audit logs are now always available for tenants that have enabled recording user and admin activity in the Office 365 Admin Portal.

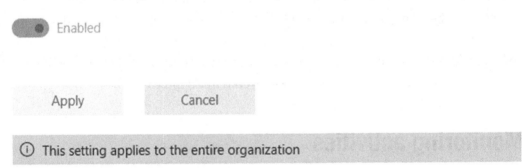

Figure 16-1.   *Turn on Power BI audit log*

   To get access to the audit log in the Office 365 Security and Compliance Center, you need to have the View-Only Audit Logs or Audit Logs role in Exchange Online or be a Microsoft 365 Global administrator. As these roles are very wide reaching and often unobtainable for Power BI administrators, Microsoft has also made the part of the audit log available through the Power BI Rest API. Extracting the data from each source is described in the following sections, as well as the pros and cons of each.

Microsoft 365

As mentioned above, the Power BI administrator needs to have the View-Only Audit Logs or Audit Logs role in Exchange Online or be a Microsoft 365 Global administrator to access the Power BI audit log in the Microsoft 365 Security and Compliance Center. The reason why Power BI administrators are not often granted those roles is that they not only give access to the Power BI audit logs but to all the Microsoft 365 logs that are stored in the Unified Audit log in Microsoft 365 Security and Compliance Center. There is potentially sensitive data in those other logs that the Power BI administrator is not allowed to see. If you are a member of one of those roles and can access the Microsoft 365 Security and Compliance Center, you can fetch data from the audit log in two ways. One is to log into the Microsoft 365 Security and Compliance Center, run the log query, and either view the results on the screen or download the results as a CSV file. Another way is to use the Office 365 Management Activity API, which is the preferred way if you want to automate the collection of the log information. To make it easier to extract the audit log using the API, Microsoft has created a cmdlet for PowerShell called Search-UnifiedAuditLog.

Note that the log is only stored in the Microsoft 365 Security and Compliance Center for 90 days, after which time it will be deleted. If you want to keep it for a longer time, you will need to collect it and store it in a different place such as data warehouse.

Tip   Your organization can increase the retention time of the audit log to 6 or 12 months if your organization has Microsoft 365 E5 or Microsoft 365 E5 Compliance add-on license. See `https://docs.microsoft.com/en-us/` `microsoft-365/compliance/audit-log-retention-policies`.

The following code shows how you can use the Search-UnifiedAuditLog PowerShell cmdlet to extract the Power BI audit log for a certain period and export it to a CSV file. Note that the -RecordType Power BI determines that you get the Power BI audit log. If you omit the RecordType parameter, you will get the audit log for all the Microsoft 365 services that are recorded in the Microsoft 365 Security and Compliance Center.

```
$UserCredential = Get-Credential

$Session = New-PSSession -ConfigurationName Microsoft.Exchange -ConnectionUri
https://outlook.office365.com/powershell-liveid/ -Credential
$UserCredential -Authentication Basic -AllowRedirection
```

```
Import-PSSession $Session -AllowClobber
Search-UnifiedAuditLog -StartDate 5/1/2020 -EndDate 7/31/2020 -RecordType
PowerBI -ResultSize 5000 |
Export-Csv -Path "c:\PowerBI\AuditLog\AuditLog.csv" -NoTypeInformation

Remove-PSSession $Session
```

Power BI REST API

If you cannot get assigned the View-Only Audit Logs role, Audit Logs role in Exchange
Online, or Microsoft 365 Global Administrator role, you can still get to the audit logs
using the Power BI REST API. As a part of the Amin part of the Power BI REST API,
there is an endpoint called Get Activity Events. To use the endpoint, you need to be a
Microsoft 365 Global administrator or a Power BI administrator. The endpoint has some
limitations as it can only be called 200 times an hour and you have to give a start and
an end time or a continuation token. The endpoint is fetching data from the Microsoft
365 Security and Compliance Center, but it will only provide you with access to the last
30 days of activities no matter what retention policy your organization is using for the
Microsoft 365 audit logs.

To call the API endpoint, you can either call it directly or use the PowerShell
cmdlet Get-PowerBIActivityEvent which Microsoft has created. The cmdlet simplifies
the authentication and parsing of the results, but can contain less information. The
reason why the cmdlet can contain less information than calling the endpoint directly
is that it is not necessarily updated every time there is a new event added to the audit
log. The following code snippet shows how you can query the audit log using the Get-
PowerBIActivityEvent PowerShell cmdlet.

```
Get-PowerBIActivityEvent -StartDateTime '2020-08-11T00:00:00' -EndDateTime
'2020-08-11T23:59:59' | ConvertFrom-Json
```

The following code snippet shows how you can query the Get Activity Events REST
API endpoint directly using the Invoke-PowerBIRestMethod PowerShell cmdlet.

```
Invoke-PowerBIRestMethod -Url "https://api.powerbi.com/v1.0/myorg/admin/act
ivityevents?startDateTime='2020-08-11T00:00:00.000Z'&endDateTime='2020-08-
11T23:59:59.000Z'" -Method Get
```

Tip   If you call the Get Activity Events directly, you have to have a single quotation mark (') around the supplied datetime. This is not shown in the documentation.

When calling the Get Activity Events REST API endpoint, the start time and end time must be within the same UTC day. This is also the case when you call it using the Get-PowerBIActivityEvent PowerShell cmdlet.

Strategy for monitoring activities

There are several considerations when deciding how to monitor Power BI activities.

- Where to export the activities data from

- How to export the audit log data

- How to store the exported data

- Enrichment of the exported data

- Reporting on the exported data

This section will try to answer these questions to help you build a successful strategy for monitoring Power BI activities.

Where to export the activities data from

As discussed above you have two options for accessing the Power BI audit log. You can either access it through the Office 365 Management Activity API (excluding the option to manually download the data from the Microsoft 365 Security and Compliance Center) or through the Power BI REST API. The only difference between the two places is how many days of data you can get. The Office 365 Management Activity API exposes the full unified audit log, which is stored by default for 90 days but can be stored up to 12 months. The Power BI REST API exposes only the last 30 days of the unified audit log. If you are starting from scratch, then using the Office 365 Management Activity API will give you more historical data and thereby a bigger chance to answer governance questions that come up. After you have harvested the historical data, we recommend you run a daily query to get the previous days' activities as well. By doing this you don't have to worry about which place you get the data from, or how to handle duplicate data (which you might have if you export partial days). To support the scenario mentioned, we recommend that you initially get data straight from the unified audit log either via the Office 365 Management Activity API or manual download from the Microsoft Security and Compliance Center. We realize that getting access to the audit log in the Security and Compliance Center can be difficult, which is why a manual download of the Power BI audit log by someone who has enough access might be the best option. If you cannot get access to the audit logs in the Security and Compliance Center, or have someone with enough access to download the last 90 days of data for you, you should use the Power BI REST API to get the last 30 days. After the initial load, you can use the Power BI REST API to get the previous days' activities each day.

Tip   Make sure you monitor the export of the audit log, since if it fails for some reason, you need to fetch the data again. Missing days in your audit log can have harmful consequences if you need the data for compliance purposes.

How to export the audit log data

As mentioned earlier, using the Power BI REST API endpoint Get Activity Events is the easiest when you have made the initial load of historical data. If we assume that you are using the Get Activity Events endpoint to export the data, the question is do you want to build your own application to query the REST APIs or do you want to use PowerShell? Building your own application can be done in many ways and with different programming languages. For this reason, we are not covering that scenario, although that can be your best option if you have the expertise and budget. If you decide on the PowerShell route, you can use the Microsoft-provided cmdlets to interact with the REST API, or use the Invoke-PowerBIRestMethod cmdlet. If you decide to use the Get-PowerBIActivityEvent PowerShell cmdlet, you should make sure it returns all the events that interest you. You should also periodically check if there are new events that are monitored in the audit log and if the cmdlet returns them.

We recommend that you query the Get Activity Events endpoint using the Invoke-PowerBIRestMethod cmdlet daily. The process is straightforward, and by querying the endpoint directly you don't have to worry about if it's returning all the events. By querying it daily, you can extract the previous days' data, so you avoid extracting partial days with possible data duplication risk. You can use many different tools to execute and automate the daily of run the PowerShell cmdlet. Most integration tools offer the ability to run PowerShell scripts either directly or as a command line. If the integration tools your organization is using do not have the ability to run PowerShell scripts, you could consider Microsoft Azure Functions or Microsoft Azure Data Factory depending on your expertise and budget.

Tip   More information about the audit log and how to collect the data can be found here: `https://docs.microsoft.com/en-us/power-bi/service-admin-auditing`.

How to store the data

We recommend that you store the audit data in your preferred data storage for analysis. This might be a database or a data lake or something entirely different. The important part is that you store the data where you can easily access it for analysis. We recommend that the data is stored in your data warehouse or equivalent to make it available for analysis. If the data is hard to reach or hard to parse, you will most likely only have it available when a governance breach happens, or an audit is being performed. Having the data available means you can use the data for other purposes, such as for preventive actions and maintenance or to document implementation progress.

Depending on how you decided to export the audit data, there might be a need to transform the raw data during export into the data warehouse/lake. When you export the data using PowerShell, the data will be either in tabular or JSON format depending on if you use the purpose-built cmdlets or the Invoke-PowerBIRestMethod cmdlet. You can decide to parse the data inside the PowerShell script or export the data in a raw format. Which way you go depends on the skillset at your disposal and if you want to keep raw originals. If you export raw JSON or CSV files, you need to make sure to have an archiving strategy in place as you don't want to parse all the files each time, especially if you are using cloud resources as it will not only take longer but also cost more money.

Note   Most integration tools can parse JSON or CSV files, but the authors have experienced that Azure Data Factory had issues with the @ sign in the JSON format outputted by the Power BI REST API.

Enrichment of the exported data

At the time of this writing, the audit log data is reasonably complete except in one area. The users are just GUID IDs. To be able to analyze the data down to the user level, you need to enrich it with user information from Azure Active Directory. In Azure Active Directory, the GUID ID can be matched to a name and possible host of other information such as department, function, etc. Not all organizations use all the possible fields in Azure Active Directory, so what is available varies from organization to organization. All organizations will have the user's name, and many will have other fields filled out. Having user information in your dataset allows for much richer reporting and is required if you need to trace a governance breach to a person.

Reporting on the exported data

If you decide that you want to use the audit log data for more than just lookups when there is a governance issue, you can create many different reports from it. An example of topics to report on are

- Most popular reports/dashboards/workspaces

- No. active users/reports/dashboards over time

- Days of inactivity by users

- Users signed up for trial licenses

- Creators vs. viewers

- Updated admin settings

- Analyzed by an external application

- Download report form the Power BI Service

- Imports (publishes from Power BI Desktop)

If you have reporting down to named users, you might want to make sure you are not violating privacy rules and regulations. Some reports are well suited to be available to all the organization, while others should be restricted to persons who are authorized to view them. Determining if a report falls into one or another category is up to the individual organization as their requirements differ so greatly.

Conclusion

The audit log data should be exported and stored where it can be stored beyond the retention policy of the unified audit log in the Microsoft 365 Security and Compliance Center (typically 90 days). It can be exported directly from Microsoft 365 via the Office 365 Management Activity API or via the Power BI REST API. Microsoft has developed PowerShell cmdlets to make the API endpoints easier to use, and it's a good idea to make use of them instead of creating a custom solution. Figure 16-2 shows the high-level architecture for gathering and enriching the Power BI audit log data.

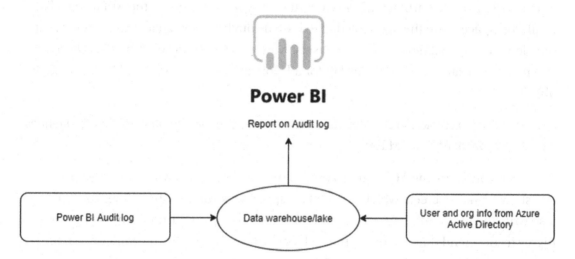

Figure 16-2. *Audit log capture architecture*

Monitoring artifact inventory

One of the key things in many governance strategies is to know what artifacts you have. Knowing what reports, datasets, etc. that exist in your tenant will help you understand the scope of your governance effort. It could also be important to know how the inventory has developed over time to aid in your implementation effort or to secure more funding for future Power BI projects. Whatever your motivation, you can build up a Power BI artifact inventory by using the Power BI REST API to query your tenant for artifacts. These artifacts are dashboards, reports, datasets, workspaces, dataflows, and capacities as well as information about the owners of these artifacts and access to workspaces. Besides creating the artifact inventory, the Power BI REST API allows you to do many tasks such as create and alter objects, as well as manage your environment. More information about the Power BI REST API can be found in Chapter 16 which covers Administration tools. This chapter will only focus on the information collection part of the API.

The Power BI REST API has many endpoints that allow you to gather information on your artifacts. Some of them will enable you to get information on artifacts in your own workspaces while others enable admins to get information on all workspaces. A recent addition to some of the endpoints of the API enables the user to query the API to get information about the object and also related objects. Getting related objects makes it much easier to gather artifact information. Before, you had to query the API to get a list of all workspaces, and then you needed to loop through all workspaces to get reports and then loop through all reports to get datasets. Now, this can be done using a single call. The following example queries the API for all workspaces in a tenant and its associated objects.

```
GET https://api.powerbi.com/v1.0/myorg/admin/groups?$expand={report,dashboa
rds,users,datasets,dataflows}
```

When you query the API, you can output the information in two main ways. You can show it on the screen, which is useful for spot checks or error handling. You can also write the information to a file or a database for storage or further processing. We highly recommend that you query the API regularly and store the information in a file or database and then put it in a managed data storage such as a data warehouse so that you can report on the data.

One of the main benefits of collecting the data is to be able to report on it. Showing the status, development over time, or just allow users to browse the inventory, all of these are good reasons to report on the data. Even though you are not ready to report on the data, you should still start collecting it as later on, you will benefit having data for a more extended period. In Figure 16-3 you see an example of a report showing the development of Power BI reports over time.

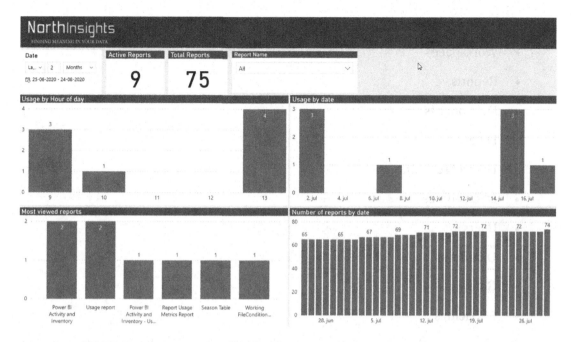

Figure 16-3. *Report inventory development*

Challenges

The main challenges when building such an inventory are

- What data to gather
- How to gather the data
- How to process the data
- How to report on the data

What data to gather

We suggest that you gather data about all the artifacts you can. You might decide to leave out artifacts that you are not using, but that might be a mistake. An example of this is dataflows. You might leave them out as you are not using dataflows. The problem is that unless you have turned off the ability to create dataflows, you cannot know if anyone is creating them if you don't collect the information. So, our advice is to collect it, and if there is no information, it will be empty. You might then decide to create an alert to notify you if anyone creates a dataflow so you can make sure they are following best practices.

We recommend that you gather information about the following:

- Workspaces

- Reports

- Dashboards

- Datasets

- Dataset refreshes

- Datasources

- Users

- Dataflows

- Gateways

- Capacities

Note that information about users are restricted to usernames. If you want more information about users, you can use the Azure Active Directory REST API or the directory service you use.

How to gather the data

There are several ways you can gather the data. Some of the methods you can use are to build a custom application, write a script in your favorite integration tool, such as SSIS or Azure Data Factory, or you can use PowerShell. If you decide to use PowerShell, Microsoft has wrapped a lot of the REST API endpoints in cmdlets. The cmdlets make it a lot easier to query the API. Microsoft has also created a cmdlet called Invoke-RestMethod that allows you to call REST API endpoints directly from PowerShell without them being wrapped in a cmdlet. The Invoke-RestMethod cmdlet allows you to use the whole of the REST API from PowerShell.

You might need to loop through one object list to get its corresponding values. An example of this is dataset refreshes. To get the refreshes you need to know which datasets belong to which workspace and then get the refreshes for them. To do that, you would typically first query all the workspaces and their datasets and then loop through each dataset to get the refreshes for them. You can see a snippet of this kind of loop below.

#4. Export out Apps and Reports to JSON file

```
$FolderAndCsvFilesLocation = "D:\home\site\rtifacts"
#FileName
$FileName = "Refresh" + $(get-date -Format FileDateTimeUniversal)
# Export location of CSV FIles
$FilePath = "$FolderAndCsvFilesLocation\$FileName.json"

$GroupsAsAdminURL = '/admin/Groups?$top=5000'
$allGroups = Invoke-PowerBIRestMethod -Url $GroupsAsAdminURL -Method Get |
ConvertFrom-Json

#Loop through each workspace to get datasets
 foreach($group in $allGroups.value)
        {
            $groupsPath = "myorg/groups/$($group.id)"
$DatasetUri = "https://api.powerbi.com/v1.0/myorg/admin/groups/" + $group.
id + "/datasets?%24top=5000"
$datasets = Invoke-PowerBIRestMethod -Url $DatasetUri -Method GET |
ConvertFrom-Json
#Loop through each dataset to get refreshes
            foreach($dataset in $datasets.value)
                {
                    if($dataset.isRefreshable -eq $true)
#We can only return refresh info on datasets that can be refreshed
                    {
$RefreshUri = "https://api.powerbi.com/v1.0/myorg/groups/$($group.id)/
datasets/$($dataset.id)/refreshes?%24top=5000"
$Refresh = Invoke-PowerBIRestMethod -Url $RefreshUri -Method GET
                    $Refresh | Out-File $FilePath
                    }
                }
        }
}
```

No matter what method you use, you will need to output the data into a place where you can further process it. This location can be a file, database, or other storage option. If you use the cmdlets, you will get the data in a tabular format, but if you use the REST API directly or via the Invoke-RestMethod in PowerShell, the output will be a JSON file. That file will need to be processed to get the content into a format suitable for reporting.

How to process the data

As with most other things related to the Power BI REST API, there are several methods for processing the data. The simplest one is to use Power BI to process the data and report on it. Power BI knows how to handle databases, csv, and JSON files, which are the most common outputs. The drawback in using Power BI is that the data cannot be exported or accessed outside of the Power BI ecosystem, and therefore is not available for any other tool. Another drawback is that if you output to files, you will need to keep all the files, as Power BI does not store data. We recommend that you process the data into a tabular format in a data warehouse or a data mart. Storing data this way will make the data management easier, and separate the tool from the data.

As a lot of the data will be in a JSON format, you need to find a way to parse the JSON into a tabular format. There are several ways to do this. If we exclude Power BI due to the limitation described above, the choice comes down to what your data integration strategy is. Are you on-premises, or in the cloud? Are you using BI professional tools or self-service tools? The answer to these questions will influence your decision.

If you are using cloud tools, then Azure Data Factory, Azure Functions, or Microsoft Power Automate might be your best choice. If you are using on-premise, you might use SQL Server Integration Services. No matter what tool you use, it needs to be able to parse the files, write the output to a database, and archive the files already processed.

Tip   When parsing the JSON file in Azure Data Factory, you need to remove or escape the @ from the @odata.context tag in the files as Azure Data Factory will not parse them otherwise.

As said before, no matter what your tool of choice is, we recommend that you store your data in a data warehouse or a data mart so that you can report on it in whatever tool you choose to use.

Depending on the tool you choose for gathering and parsing the data, your choice of automation might differ. Most of the tools mentioned before have an orchestration included, but if your tool of choice doesn't, you need to find one that will. Whatever tool you choose, your orchestration method should automate as much of it as you can. Just make sure you don't create duplicate information. In that respect it's always a good idea to try to query one day at a time, and always a whole day at a time. Of course, there might be a situation where more frequent queries are needed, and if they are, you need to handle the possible duplication.

How to report on the data

Maybe the right question here is what to report on. The issue with that is that it's unique to each organization, depending a bit on what you are trying to achieve. Do you want to allow people to browse your inventory? Do you want to tell people about the development of your Power BI implementation? Or is your main goal to govern your Power BI tenant(s)? Depending on your goals, the "what and how" you report on it might change. Our main advice here is to report on it. Don't just collect the data; make it available to your users.

Tip   You are implementing Power BI, and you need ammunition to convince management to keep funding it. Show them a report showing the development over time of your artifacts as well as usage.

Your users don't know what reports or datasets exist and don't have access to the right workspaces or apps to figure it out. Allow them to browse your inventory of reports and datasets and show them how to request access to them.

Conclusion

The main reason to collect the information about your artifacts is often to create a repository of artifacts in a tenant. This information can then be used to document what exists from a governance perspective, or to collect the information over time to see the development and thus document the implementation of Power BI. This information collecting can be useful to secure resources and to make success visible. Since users only see Power BI artifacts such as reports after they have been given access to them, you can also use the artifact inventory to allow users to find what exists, and thereby giving them chances of discovering something useful for their work. To make that work efficiently, you need to show them a description, the owner, as well as how to then ask for access to an artifact.

Figure 16-3 shows the capture architecture when you are both collecting the audit log and the artifact inventory information.

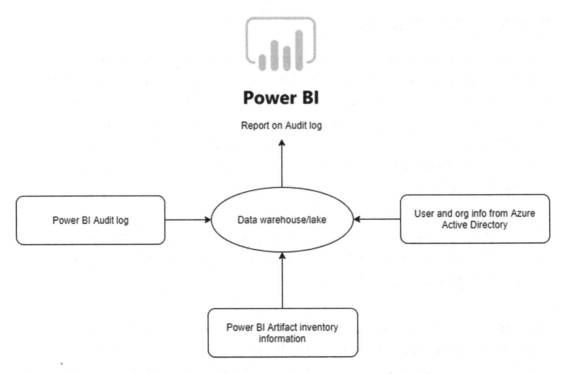

Figure 16-4.   *Audit log and artifact inventory capture architecture*

Monitoring capacities

If your organization has Power BI Premium or Power BI Embedded capacities, that provides access to dedicated hardware. This dedicated hardware is a finite resource, and the administrator needs to make sure that the hardware is being used correctly and that you have resources available. If there are not enough resources available, datasets get evicted from memory and need to be loaded back in when used. Reloading models takes time, and depending on the type of dataset, it could be mean unacceptable wait times for end users. Monitoring capacities will allow you to keep an eye out for potential issues and debug issues that have already happened.

How to monitor capacities

Power BI does not offer a REST API access to the capacities; instead there is a Power BI Template App available in AppSource. You install the app by navigating to Appsource in the Power BI Service, choosing Template apps, and finding the Power BI Premium Capacity Metrics App. When you install the app, it will add a dashboard, a report, and a dataset into a new workspace you can name. Since it's installed into a new workspace, you have access to the dashboard, report, and dataset. You can customize the dashboard and the report, and you can connect to the dataset from Power BI Desktop or in the Power BI Service to create your own reports and dashboards.

Tip   Make sure you add a refresh schedule to the dataset to keep it up-to-date.

What to monitor

The Power BI Premium Capacity Metrics App has a premium capacity health center that gives you a quick overview of the health of your capacity. It has three KPIs, Active memory, query waits, and refresh waits, which can give you an indication about if there is something you need to take a closer look at.

The active memory KPI shows how often the active memory has gone above 70% threshold in the last 7 days. It's normal that the active memory goes above 70% threshold as you want to utilize the resources you have. But if it's happening very frequently, it might indicate that you need to manage memory better. The KPI, therefore, helps you plan for when to increase your capacity or reduce the number or size of datasets.

The query waits KPI shows how many queries waited more than 100 milliseconds in the last 7 days. If many queries are waiting more than 100 milliseconds, it could indicate that there are not enough CPU resources available. A lack of sufficient CPU resources can be caused by long running queries taking a lot of resources, or too many queries for the resources available. The KPI, therefore, helps you plan for when to increase your capacity or reduce the number or size of datasets.

The refresh waits KPI shows how many refreshes waited more than 10 minutes from when they were triggered, or scheduled to start until it started execution in the last 7 days. When the refresh has to wait, it can indicate that either there is not enough memory, or there are not enough CPU resources available. The KPI, therefore, helps you plan for when to increase your capacity or reduce the number or size of datasets. Figure 16-4 shows the capacity health center in the Power BI Premium Capacity Metrics App.

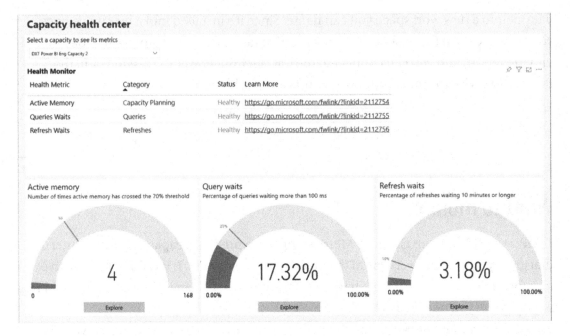

Figure 16-5. *Power BI Premium Capacity Metrics App Health Center*

Besides the health center, the Power BI Premium Capacity Metrics App has five main segments:

- Datasets

- Paginated reports

- Dataflows

- AI

- Resource consumption

- IDs and info

Each segment gives you more detailed insights into a particular area of interest when monitoring capacities.

The datasets section contains detailed information about the health of the datasets that are stored in your capacities. It includes information on refreshes, query durations, query waits, and general information about the dataset resource consumption.

The Paginated reports section contains aggregated information about the usage of paginated reports as well as some aggregated performance metrics.

The dataflow section contains information about dataflow refreshes and some aggregated performance metrics for the dataflows in your capacities.

The AI section gives you information about memory consumptions, execution, and wait times, as well as overall usage for the AI workloads in your capacities.

The resource consumption section shows the consumption of CPU and memory for the last 7 days.

The IDs and Info section shows metadata information for capacities, workspaces, datasets, paginated reports, and dataflows. It also shows who the administrators for the capacity are.

Conclusion

To monitor Power BI Premium capacities, you need to use the Power BI Premium Capacity Metrics App. The app is a template app you can find in AppSource in the Power BI Service app section. When you have installed it, you will get a dashboard, report, and dataset with information about your capacities. You can customize the dashboard and report and create new reports and dashboards from the dataset.

It's very important to monitor your capacities, as they are finite resources. If you are running out of resources, your users will have to wait for reports to load, and your developers might see failure in publishing reports and refreshing datasets.

Monitoring gateways

The gateway is the only component of the Power BI ecosystem which is not a SaaS or PaaS. You need to install it on your hardware and monitor it using your tools. Chapter 14 describes the gateway in detail, including how to monitor it. You can refer to Chapter 14 for more information.

Summary

There are several types of monitoring you can do for your Power BI environment. From a governance perspective, monitoring activities is the most important one. From an administration perspective, monitoring your capacities (if you have Power BI Premium), the On-premises data gateway (if you are using it), and the development of your inventory of Power BI artifacts is vital.

Make sure you turn on the Power BI audit log if it's not been done through Microsoft 365 and start collecting the data early. The audit log is only stored for a certain amount of days, depending on your retention policy in Microsoft 365 Security and Compliance Center.

Call to action

- Turn on audit logging for Power BI.

- Start collecting the data outside of Power BI as it's only stored within the Microsoft 365 Security and Compliance Center for 90 days by default.

- Collect your Power BI artifact inventory daily using the Power BI REST API to be able to document the development, and allow users to browse the inventory.

- Install the Power BI Premium Capacity Metrics App to monitor Power BI Premium capacities.

- Remember to add a refresh schedule to the dataset from the Power BI Premium Capacity Metrics App.

- Make sure you read Chapter 14 for how to monitor the On-Premise Data Gateway.

Index

A

Admin role, 163
Application Lifecycle Management (ALM), Power BI
  building reports and datasets, 64
  deployment (*see* Deployment model)
  design, 64
  development tools, 66, 67
  gather requirements, 64
  PBIX files, 68
  source/version control, 68–70
  testing, 64, 70, 71
App-Owns-Data Embedding, 139
Artificial Intelligence (AI), 141, 142
Automated refresh, 186
Automating monitoring, 24
Azure, 139, 140
Azure Active Directory (AAD), 111, 167, 168
Azure Data Lake Storage (ADLS), 195
Azure Information Protection (AIP), 124
Azure portal, 250, 251
Azure Power BI Embedded, 139
Azure Service Bus, 209, 216

B

Bring Your Own Key (BYOK), 60, 145, 146
Business Dictionary, 3
Business intelligence governance, 4

C

Cashed datasets, 211
Classic workspace, 154–156
Collaboration
  advantages, 35
  contributors, 46
  definition, 35
  end-user collaboration, 45
  monitoring collaboration compliance, 48, 49
  naming standards, 48
  preferred sharing method, 47
  security process, 48
  sharing options, 47
  training material, 48
Consumer training, 19, 80
Contributor collaboration, 46
Contributor role, 163
Controlling access, 192–194
Custom connectors, 230

D

Data security, 16, 17
Dataset developer, 20
Datasets/dataflows
  certification, 201–203
  power BI dataflows, 194 (*see also* Power Bi dataflows)

E, F

G

P, Q

Printed in the United States
By Bookmasters